D0729211

Emotional Intelligence for Project Managers

Second Edition

Emotional Intelligence for Project Managers

The People Skills You Need to Achieve Outstanding Results

Second Edition

ANTHONY C. MERSINO, PMP, PMI-ACP, MBA

AMACOM

American Management Association

New York • Atlanta • Brussels • Chicago • Mexico City
San Francisco • Shanghai • Tokyo • Washington, D.C.

Bulk discounts available. For details visit:
www.amacombooks.org/go/specialsales
Or contact special sales:
Phone: 800-250-5308
E-mail: specials@amanet.org
View all of the AMACOM titles at: www.amacombooks.org
American Management Association: www.amanet.org

This publication is designed to provide accurate and authoritative information in regard to the subject matter covered. It is sold with the understanding that the publisher is not engaged in rendering legal, accounting, or other professional service. If legal advice or other expert assistance is required, the services of a competent professional person should be sought.

Library of Congress Cataloging-in-Publication Data

Mersino, Anthony.
    Emotional intelligence for project managers : the people skills you need to achieve outstanding results / Anthony Mersino. — Second edition.
       pages cm
    Includes bibliographical references and index.
    ISBN 978-0-8144-3277-8 (alk. paper) — ISBN 0-8144-3277-8 (alk. paper) 1. Project management—Psychological aspects. 2. Emotional intelligence. 3. Teams in the workplace—Management. I. Title.
    HD69.P75M475   2013
    658.4′04019—dc23   2012051364

© 2013 Anthony C. Mersino.
All rights reserved.
Printed in the United States of America.

This publication may not be reproduced, stored in a retrieval system, or transmitted in whole or in part, in any form or by any means, electronic, mechanical, photocopying, recording, or otherwise, without the prior written permission of AMACOM, a division of American Management Association, 1601 Broadway, New York, NY 10019.

The scanning, uploading, or distribution of this book via the Internet or any other means without the express permission of the publisher is illegal and punishable by law. Please purchase only authorized electronic editions of this work and do not participate in or encourage piracy of copyrighted materials, electronically or otherwise. Your support of the author's rights is appreciated.

About AMA
American Management Association (www.amanet.org) is a world leader in talent development, advancing the skills of individuals to drive business success. Our mission is to support the goals of individuals and organizations through a complete range of products and services, including classroom and virtual seminars, webcasts, webinars, podcasts, conferences, corporate and government solutions, business books and research. AMA's approach to improving performance combines experiential learning—learning through doing—with opportunities for ongoing professional growth at every step of one's career journey.

Printing number

10 9 8 7 6 5 4 3 2

Contents

Acknowledgments   ix

■ PART 1
An Introduction to Emotional Intelligence   1

1   **My Growth in Emotional Intelligence   3**
    A Dangerous Situation   3
    Emotional Mastery for Project Managers   5
    Project Management Is Competitive   6
    The Rules for Project Managers Have Changed   7
    What Is Emotional Intelligence?   8
    Measuring Your Emotional Intelligence   9
    The Good News About Emotional Intelligence   12
    Applying Emotional Intelligence to Project Mangement   12
    Emotional Intelligence Is Vital to Project Managers   18

2   **A Brief Primer on Emotional Intelligence   21**
    The Popularity of Emotional Intelligence   21
    Some Useful Definitions   22
    How to Improve Your Understanding of Emotional
        Intelligence Concepts   29
    Learning About Emotional Intelligence Is Only the First Step   30

■ PART 2
Project Management Begins with Self-Management 33

3 **Self-Awareness   35**
   An Introduction to Self-Awareness   35
   Emotional Self-Awareness   36
   Accurate Self-Assessment   50
   Self-Confidence   52
   Techniques to Improve Your Self-Awareness   53
   Personal Action Plan: Self-Awareness   60

4 **Self-Management   61**
   The Emotional Intelligence Model for Project Management   62
   Self-Control   63
   Prethinking or Foreshadowing   72
   Techniques to Improve Our Self-Control   87
   Personal Action Plan: Self-Management   93

■ PART 3
Building Project Stakeholder Relationships 95

5 **Social Awareness   97**
   An Introduction to Social Awareness   97
   Empathy   100
   Seeing Others Clearly   106
   Organizational Awareness   112
   Emotional Boundaries   117
   Techniques for Improving Our Social Awareness   122
   Personal Action Plan: Social Awareness   125

6 **Relationship Management   126**
   An Introduction to Relationship Management   126
   Stakeholder Relationships   129
   Developing Others   144
   Telling the Truth   149
   Additional Principles of Relationship Building   158
   Techniques for Managing Relationships on Projects   167
   Personal Action Plan: Relationship Management   172

■ PART 4
Using EQ to Lead Project Teams   173

7 Project Team Leadership   175
An Introduction to Project Team Leadership   175
Communications   177
Methods of Project Communications   181
Conflict Management   185
Inspirational Leadership   191
Additional Considerations for Team Leaders   194
Techniques for Improving Project Team Leadership   199
Personal Action Plan: Project Team Leadership   202

8 Creating a Positive Team Environment   203
What Makes a Great Project Team?   203
How PMs Set the Tone and Direction for the Project   205
The Team Within the Team   216
Techniques for Creating a Positive Team Environment   218
Personal Action Plan: Creating a Positive Team Environment   221

**9 Leveraging Emotional Intelligence on Large and
Complex Projects   222**
Are You Ready to Lead Large and Complex Projects?   222
Characteristics of Large and Complex Projects   223
Concerns for Large-Scale Project Managers   224
Applying Different Leadership Styles   226
Applying Emotional Intelligence to Virtual Project Teams   233
Emotional Intelligence Techniques for Large and
    Complex Projects   238
Personal Action Plan: Leveraging Emotional Intelligence
    on Large and Complex Projects   241

10 Success with Agile Projects   242
Agile Project Managers, Scrum Masters, Coaches,
    and Team Leaders   242
Servant Leadership Is an Alternative to Command and Control   248
Agile Leaders Need to Be Emotionally Intelligent   249
Social Awareness and Relationship Management   249
Positive Regard   250
Techniques for Improving Our Success with Agile Projects   251
Personal Action Plan: Success with Agile Projects   253

Epilogue   255

Appendixes
A   Emotional Tally Sheet   257
B   Assessment for Emotional Self-Awareness and Self-Control   260
C   Stakeholder Management Tool   262
D   Emotional Intelligence Movies and Scenes   265
E   Books on Emotional Intelligence   267
F   Emotional Intelligence Assessment Instruments   269

Index   271

Acknowledgments

Writing a book was a lot more work than I imagined, and it is not something that I could have done on my own. I am extremely grateful to all those people who graciously invested their time and energy to help me with my emotional growth and with this book.

The support of two published authors eventually convinced me to start writing. Jim Taylor gave me the idea to write on emotional intelligence and project management. Rajesh Setty was instrumental in pointing out that I was better off to begin writing than to continue planning to write.

Rich Blue and Nancy Rollins of the Center for Life Enrichment taught me about emotions and how to recognize what I was feeling. I am particularly grateful to Rich for his continued unwavering belief and constant encouragement during my personal growth work. He has been behind me 100% since I first met him in 2001. I have been part of several powerful support groups at the Center for Christian Life Enrichment (CLE). Group participants taught me about relationships and leadership, and they pushed me to do my very best. My coed group included Meredith, Laura, Beth, Tom, Jo, Mike, Kim, Jane, and Barry. Ramp it up, guys! My men's group included Tim, Barry, Rick, Bill, Cortney, Stephen, Tim, Neale, Dennis, and Jim. My brother Ted also helped me to define how to apply emotional intelligence to project management.

For the first edition, my editor Christina Parisi, was a tremendous help in writing something that made sense to others. Steve Cohn was also a great coach and an inspiration during the writing process. Jim Friel, Chris Samp,

Don Knapp, Barbara Brown, and various others read early chapters and provided valuable feedback and encouragement.

I would be remiss not to recognize the tremendous support of my family. Both my daughter Krista and my son Jack are creative inspirations to me and a source of positive energy. They have a higher EQ now than I had just 10 years ago! They have been terrific about giving me the space to write this book at home and have not complained (much) when I wasn't able to attend some school or sporting event.

I have to thank God. I am grateful to Him for surviving my childhood and for the ability to write despite getting a D in English in High School. God also planted in me a hunger to learn and to grow and become a better person. It is only through His grace that this book has come to fruition.

Finally, and most important, I want to thank my wife Norma. She has been my partner for nearly 20 years, and I know that she has my back in all that I do. She has given me the space to write, the encouragement to excel, and has taken care of our kids and house so that I had few distractions and obstacles. She partnered with me in my personal growth and therapy work and didn't ask me to do what she wasn't doing herself. She has also pushed me to be a better husband and man, and I am grateful that she continues to challenge me and expect great things from me. I love you Norma!

PART 1

An Introduction to Emotional Intelligence

My Growth in Emotional Intelligence

■ A Dangerous Situation

"Do you have any idea how dangerous it is not to be in touch with your feelings?" This question was posed to me in the summer of 2001 by Rich, a therapist who has since become my career coach and mentor. His words stopped me in my tracks. Dangerous? That was a curious word choice. What could be dangerous about not being in touch with my feelings? I was thirty-nine years old and had been a successful project manager (PM) for over seventeen years. I had a record of slow but steady career progression. I had been certified as a Project Management Professional (PMP) since 1995. I owned my own project management consulting business and lived, taught, and even breathed project management. No one had ever asked me about feelings before. No one had ever mentioned that there might be danger involved. What could be dangerous? What was so important about feelings?

Rich's question resonated with me, but I wasn't sure why. It didn't feel dangerous to be out of touch with my emotions. However, I had a nagging sense that he saw or knew things that I didn't. On some level I recognized that the way I approached work wasn't always effective. Hard work did not always make the difference in the outcomes of the projects I managed. I wondered how others seemed to succeed with less effort. I also felt insecure about the lack of personal and professional relationships I had built, and I suspected that it was hurting me. As much as I wanted to deny that my career and relationship challenges might be related to my emotions, I began to suspect that Rich might be right.

The truth was that I wasn't aware of my feelings or emotions. I was about as emotionally aware as a small green soap dish. If I could have taken an emotional intelligence test at that time, I would have been considered the village idiot.

With Rich's help, I began to see a connection between my lack of emotional awareness and my limited success in project management. Up to that point, my project management career had been a bumpy road. While not quite a dead end street, my career path hadn't exactly taken a superhighway either. Lately that road didn't seem to be taking me anywhere. I had recently been passed over for a key promotion at Unisys. My career ladder had literally run out of rungs. Perhaps I had been promoted to my level of incompetence and was therefore living proof of the Peter Principle.

Eventually I found I could no longer ignore Rich's question about the danger, and I decided to do something about it. I knew I needed to make some changes. I was ready to make more of an investment in my emotions and relationships. Initially, it wasn't for personal reasons. It was all about ROI, my return on investment for improving my emotional intelligence. I believed that my career would benefit from it. And after spending most of the last five years working on my emotional intelligence, I am happy to report that my career has benefited significantly.

As I grew, I learned how my work relationships reflected my world view. Until then, my relationships with my project teams and other stakeholders were weak or nonexistent. That was largely the result of my project management style as a taskmaster. I was all business. Unfortunately, I placed a higher value on tasks, productivity, and outcomes than on relationships. I lacked empathy. I had a way of driving the people on my project teams that was hostile and irresponsible. My coworkers may have called me driven, but they would never have characterized me as a warm and fuzzy relationship person. At best people warmed up to me over time.

My big shift came when I began to recognize the value of emotions and relationships in the workplace. I became aware of feelings and learned to trust them as a source of information. I learned to recognize and acknowledge when I felt angry, scared, or happy. I also began to pay attention to what those around me were feeling and to consider that information when making decisions. By doing this, I was able to better manage my projects and to be a better leader of people.

I learned the importance of stakeholder relationships and invested in relationships with friends, coworkers, and other leaders. I learned how critical relationships and support were to achieving success on large projects. My relationships began to grow, along with my ability to lead others.

The results were nothing short of impressive. The investment and changes I made began to improve my effectiveness as a PM. Within a year of beginning my work on emotions and relationships, I was asked to lead a fast-moving project of twelve people. As I demonstrated success with this team, my responsibilities grew until I was managing seventy-five people across the United States and internationally. As I continued to learn and apply my skills in this area, I was able effectively to lead large teams, build strong relationships with project stakeholders, and achieve the goals of the projects I was managing.

■ Emotional Mastery for Project Managers

I am quite sure that many of you are thinking "of course, you idiot" when I talk about mastery of emotions leading to success as a PM. You were probably among the five million people who bought one of Daniel Goleman's books on emotional intelligence—and then actually read it. Yes, of course emotions play a role at work, no matter what your position. They are of special concern to those of us in project management and leadership. Emotions play a direct role in our success as PMs and leaders.

I was not one of the five million people who bought Goleman's first book, *Emotional Intelligence: Why It Can Matter More Than IQ,* when it came out in 1997. In fact, I wasn't even sure what emotional intelligence was when I first began working on my emotional awareness. It wasn't until I decided to include emotional intelligence as part of the curriculum for the project management course I taught at Northwestern University that I began to read the published materials on the topic. By then I had accepted the fact that I lacked emotional intelligence, proving, I suppose, that admitting I had a problem was the first step toward resolution. More than that, I had begun to grow, make changes, and experience greater success as a PM.

After my own powerful experience with emotional intelligence, I conducted research to see what experience other PMs had with emotional intelligence. In late 2005, I conducted a brief survey of over 100 PMs to determine their beliefs and attitudes about emotional intelligence. The results were interesting. Most of the PMs I surveyed thought that emotional intelligence was important to success as a PM and were interested in learning more. However, the survey also indicated that most PMs didn't know very much about emotional intelligence.

Since 2005, I've presented this topic at over forty different events attended by thousands of PMs. Most people identify readily with the topic. While there are some who are "naturals" at emotional intelligence, most of the people I spoke with wanted to know how they could learn more about emotions and emotional mastery.

Is this surprising? Not really. Sure, PMs understand basic project management techniques and the contents of the *Guide to the Project Management*

Body of Knowledge (PMBOK® Guide). They have also pursued PMP certification and become black-belt masters of project scheduling tools, such as MS Project, Artemis, or NIKU. In fact, those are prerequisites for success even as a junior PM; consider them entry criteria. But to advance your career, you will need strong interpersonal skills or soft skills—and emotional intelligence provides the framework for those skills. Do you see a connection between emotional intelligence and your own success as a PM? Are you trying to advance your career? Do you ever feel frustrated by lack of opportunity even though you have done all you can to improve your technical project management skills? Perhaps you are doing things the hard way as I did, working harder to make up for soft skills.

> You cannot make up for soft skills with hard work.

To advance as a PM requires understanding and mastery of emotional intelligence concepts. Yes, mastery of emotional intelligence. PMs who master emotional intelligence can develop their careers by delivering more consistently and by taking on larger and more important projects. In fact, success with large and complex projects depends largely on the level of emotional intelligence of the PM.

PMs who master emotional intelligence will set themselves apart from other PMs. They will be able to achieve more with the same team. They will excel in their careers. And they will feel more satisfied with themselves and their relationships with others.

> PMs who master emotional intelligence will set themselves apart from other PMs.

■ Project Management Is Competitive

Most PMs feel the need to set themselves apart from other PMs. If you feel under pressure to compete, you are not alone. Project management is a very competitive field. As an example, consider the growth in PMP certification as shown in Figure 1-1. PMs increasingly seek certification as a way to differentiate themselves from other PMs. PMP certification has skyrocketed as a result. When I achieved my PMP certification in 1995, I was number 4,410. By the end of 2006, shortly before the first edition of this book was published, the total number of certified PMs had exploded to 221,144. By the end of

Annual Growth in Certified Project Managers (PMPs)

Figure 1-1: Growth in Certified Project Managers (PMPs).

2011, that number had more than doubled to 467,390, and it continues to grow steadily. In addition, the PMI has introduced five other project management certifications that allow PMs to further differentiate themselves.[1]

PMP certification does not in itself make a PM more capable; it simply proves that you have the requisite project management experience and can pass the multiple-choice certification exam. To be truly effective, you need to be able to implement projects and work well with your team. Emotional intelligence will help you do that.

Emotional intelligence and certification are two very different things. However, the pursuit of PMP certification demonstrates that PMs are seeking every advantage they can get. Emotional intelligence can be just one more way of setting themselves apart. I believe that this will lead to an increased interest in developing and applying emotional intelligence to project management.

■ The Rules for Project Managers Have Changed

When I started in project management back in the late 1980s, the project triple constraints ruled. On time, on budget, and within scope was the PM's mantra.

---

[1]Project Management Institute (PMI). *PMI Today*. Project Management Institute, Inc. 1993, 1994, 1995, 1996, 1997, 1998, 1999, 2000, 2001, 2002, 2003, 2004, 2005, 2006, 2007, 2008, 2009, 2010, 2011.

That may still be true, but I think that things have gotten a whole lot more complicated, and I think there are a lot more expectations of PMs today.

Have you heard the phrase "do more with less?" You are not alone. Not only do PMs need to manage the triple constraint, they need to do it with fewer resources. This could include project administrators or support people who directly aid the PM, but it might also include key resources needed for the team.

In addition to doing more with less, PMs are expected to be domain experts. The days of being a good PM who could lead any team are over; PMs today need to be SAP savvy, or have a Lean 6 Sigma black belt, or have CRM, CPA, or MSCE certification. I've seen ads for project management positions that require ITAR—and I don't even know what that is!

Finally, I believe there is more pressure on PMs to lead the way through change. All organizations are under pressure to change and innovate. One has only to look at what happened to Kodak or Sears as prime examples of what happens when you don't change fast enough. Both Kodak and Sears were once leaders in their industries. Now they are mere shells of their former selves because they didn't change as fast as their competitors. Organizations often use projects or programs to introduce or drive change. So PMs are usually the ones who come face to face with resistance and inertia and must be good at implementing change for their projects to be successful.

■ What Is Emotional Intelligence?

The term emotional intelligence was actually coined by two psychologists, Peter Salovey and John D. Mayer, in 1990. I am a little surprised they didn't call it the Salomayer Principle or something similar. I bet if they had known that Daniel Goleman would come along in 1995 and use the term for the title of his best-selling book, they would certainly have used their own names. In any case, they simply called it emotional intelligence and gave it the following definition:

> Emotional Intelligence: "the ability to monitor one's own and others' feelings and emotions, to discriminate among them and to use this information to guide one's thinking and action."
> —Peter Salovey and John D. Mayer[2]

[2] Peter Salovey and John D. Mayer. *Emotional Intelligence, Imagination Cognition, and Personality*, Volume 9, No. 3. Amityville, NY: Baywood Publishing Co., 1990.

While Salovey and Mayer continued their research work, in 1995 Goleman wrote *Emotional Intelligence: Why It Can Matter More Than IQ.* This was the right message at the right time, and soon Goleman was a best-selling author whose name became synonymous with emotional intelligence. Goleman has since gone on to write several more books on the topic. In a recent book, Goleman and coauthor Cary Cherniss state that emotional intelligence, at the most general level, refers to:

> "the abilities to recognize and regulate emotions
> in ourselves and in others"
> Daniel Goleman and Gary Cherniss[3]

As a PM, I hold a pragmatic view of emotional intelligence, thinking of it as "knowing and managing our own emotions and those of others for improved performance." I am interested in the application of emotional intelligence to life in general, as well as specifically to the field of project management. In a project setting, the understanding and use of emotions helps us to have more enjoyable, predictable, and successful projects. That is what the remainder of this book is about.

■ Measuring Your Emotional Intelligence

Each of us has some level of emotional intelligence. The question is, how do we know what that level is? It would certainly be convenient if emotional intelligence were as easy to measure as height or weight. Unfortunately, that is not the case. Numerous different assessments of emotional intelligence are available. The instruments tend to differ in three areas: the person providing the assessment, the mechanism for measurement, and the underlying framework.

In terms of who provides the assessment, most of the available emotional intelligence assessments are self-reported. In other words, the individual being assessed completes the instrument himself or herself. For a more objective and complete view, there are also multirater instruments that can provide 360-degree reviews.

Emotional intelligence assessments also vary in how emotional intelligence is measured. Some are based on traits, and others on abilities. Examples

---

[3]Cary Cherniss and David Goleman. *The Emotionally Intelligent Workplace.* Hoboken, NJ: John Wiley & Sons, Inc., 2001.

Table 1-1: Emotional Intelligence Mini-Assessment

	YES	NO
1. Do you feel like you should be more excited about a special event than you are?	☐	☐
2. Do you find yourself not crying under circumstances when you believe others would cry?	☐	☐
3. Do you pride yourself on never getting angry?	☐	☐
4. Have you ever been told you are abrasive, unfeeling, or uncaring?	☐	☐
5. Are you frequently surprised that your expectations of others differ from what actually happens?	☐	☐
6. Do you feel that the problems others have are largely their own fault?	☐	☐
7. Do you find it difficult to work with people on your team whose background differs from your own?	☐	☐
8. Do you find yourself upset or unable to focus when your spouse or a team member is upset?	☐	☐
9. Do you blow up with your spouse, children, or project team over seemingly innocuous remarks or circumstances?	☐	☐
10. Would your closest friends or spouse say that you had problems managing your emotions?	☐	☐
11. Do you frequently make jokes or use sarcasm?	☐	☐
12. Do you storm out of meetings, send flaming emails, or slam doors?	☐	☐
13. Are your relationships with your project team, managers, or sponsors superficial and limited to the task at hand?	☐	☐
14. Do you find that you have minor skirmishes with specific individuals on an ongoing basis?	☐	☐
15. Do you feel like the victim of others or that you say yes when you really want to say no?	☐	☐
16. Do people leave your project teams because of you?	☐	☐
17. Do you find it difficult to communicate?	☐	☐
18. Are you ever surprised that your team doesn't understand your project objectives?	☐	☐
19. Do you experience conflict on projects that never seems to get resolved?	☐	☐
20. Do you want to do a better job of establishing charisma or presence as a leader?	☐	☐
TOTAL	___	___

of assessments that measure traits include answering questions about how individuals respond in various situations. The instruments that measure abilities might follow a photo or a short video with a series of related questions.

Finally, assessments vary in terms of the underlying framework of emotional intelligence competencies. As shown in Chapter 2, many researchers have developed their own frameworks for emotional intelligence. Some of the best known are Daniel Goleman, Peter Salovey, John Mayer, and Rueven Bar-On.

All of the assessments suffer from a question of validity. By validity, I mean the ability to consistently and reliably measure emotional intelligence in individuals. While the authors of each assessment instrument will tout the validity of what they are measuring, there are no validated instruments for measuring emotional intelligence. See Appendix F for a review of the more popular instruments available and their claims to validity.

Before we entirely give up the idea of measuring emotional intelligence, we should take a look at what some of the existing tools can tell us about ourselves. It is possible to get an idea of your level of emotional intelligence using a simple set of questions, such as those shown in Table 1-1. Though the outcome will be subjective, it will provide some information about your level of EQ. Take the mini self-assessment by reviewing each item and checking "Yes" or "No" as it applies to you.

To score the mini-assessment, count the total number of no responses and use Table 1-2 to interpret your results.

Table 1-2: Scoring the Emotional Intelligence Mini-Assessment

Score	What it means
17–20	You are doing great; you are in the minority of PMs who understand emotional intelligence. This book may help you to fine tune your approach.
13–16	You are doing well, but could use some improvement in a few key areas.
7–12	You have some strong areas but also have opportunities to improve in others. Some work on emotional intelligence will help you to deliver more consistently.
1–6	You have significant opportunities to improve your emotional intelligence. An investment in this area will provide a great pay-off for you in terms of project outcomes and career success.

■ The Good News About Emotional Intelligence

The good news about emotional intelligence is that no matter where you are now, most experts agree that you can improve your level of emotional intelligence. In fact, experts agree that you can continue to improve your level over the course of your life. I know this to be true because I have done it. Over the last five years I have gone from "village idiot" to being aware of and managing emotions. Maybe "emotional genius" is in reach for me!

Here is more good news. Improvements in your emotional intelligence will help your career as a PM. No matter what your emotional starting point is, if you improve your level of emotional intelligence, you will do a better job of managing projects. The remainder of this book is going to tell you how to do just that. We are going to discuss in detail the various aspects of emotional intelligence; how they apply in the project management environment, and the specific activities and exercises you can use to help you improve your emotional intelligence. This will undoubtedly also help you to succeed as a PM.

■ Applying Emotional Intelligence to Project Management

My own experience has shown that emotional intelligence makes a big difference in terms of performance as a PM. Apparently, I wasn't the only one who thought there was a likely correlation between emotional intelligence and performance in project management. The PMI has commissioned at least two research studies to dig into this topic.

The first PMI study was conducted in 2005 and documented in the 2006 book, *Choosing Appropriate Project Managers*, by J. Rodney Turner and Ralf Mueller. It details research that Turner and Mueller conducted on four hundred projects around the world. They wanted to test the relationship between the success of a particular project and the PM's competency. They broke that competency down into IQ, emotional intelligence or EQ, and the PM's competency in managerial terms (MQ).[4]

It wasn't a big surprise that their research showed a strong correlation between emotional intelligence and project success. It was a little surprising that little or no relationship existed between project success and IQ. In other words, emotional intelligence was more important than pure intelligence.

---

[4]Project Management Institute *(Choosing Appropriate Project Managers)*, Project Management Institute, Inc. (2006). Copyright and all rights reserved. Material from this publication has been reproduced with the permission of PMI.

Specifically, the competencies of self-awareness, conscientiousness, sensitivity, and communication were found to be significant for all types of projects. In Turner and Mueller's words, "Consistently with the general management literature we found that the emotional group of competencies, EQ, was the most significant for successful project outcomes." Turner and Mueller concluded that "project managers must be emotionally intelligent."

> "Project managers must be emotionally intelligent."
> —J. Rodney Turner, PhD, and Ralf Mueller, DBA

This was exciting, not just because it confirms what many of us already believed, but because it is one of the first studies to officially link the PM's emotional intelligence to the success of the project.

Turner and Mueller used their data from the 400 projects to further analyze what success looked like. They found that a core set of emotional competencies were required for all projects. Those core competencies include:

- Self-awareness
- Motivation
- Conscientiousness
- Interpersonal sensitivity
- Emotional resilience
- Influence

In case you are wondering about the title, *Choosing Appropriate Project Managers*, the point that Turner and Mueller were making is that certain emotional competencies are shown to be important to the success of various types of projects. Organizations should consider that information and *choose* their PMs based on those competencies.

The second PMI sponsored research was presented in the 2009 book, *Emotional Intelligence and Projects,* by Nicholas Clarke and Ranse Howell, which documents a research project carried out on 67 project managers. The project sought to identify relationships in the following areas:

1. Relationships between emotional intelligence abilities and specific project manager competencies identified as critical within project contexts.
2. Relationships between emotional intelligence and transformational leadership behaviors.

The research by Clarke and Howell built on the previous research by Ralph Mueller and J. Rodney Turner. Clarke and Howell studied the relationship of those emotional intelligence measures to competencies that previous research has shown to be important to success as a project manager: communications, teamwork, attentiveness, and managing conflict.

Another interesting aspect of this study was that the researchers attempted to control for personality, general intelligence level, and PM certification. I was a little puzzled at first by the control for personality. If my personality turns out to be ineffective, does this mean I cannot be a project manager? Not to worry—the control for personality is to try to isolate any characteristics that may be inherent and unchangeable from those characteristics, like EQ, that can be trained.

The bottom line from the Clarke and Howell research? Project managers interested in growing in their project management and leadership abilities should invest in emotional intelligence. Specifically they should develop their ability to use emotions to facilitate thinking, understand emotional meanings, in empathy, and in their overall level of emotional intelligence. These were shown to be linked to the PM competencies of teamwork, managing conflict, and attentiveness. These were also impacted by the personality traits of emotional stability and openness.[5]

Based on my own discussions with PMs and surveys of PMs, I have come to believe that most PMs understand emotional intelligence at a conceptual level. The challenge is that they lack the tools to apply it to projects. After all, how do you apply emotional intelligence to project management? It wasn't immediately apparent to me. My research showed that it wasn't all that apparent to others either. The research says that it is important, but what has been missing is a practical guide to how to actually do it. This book is the first book of its kind to spell out in detail how to apply emotional intelligence to projects.

The starting point for applying emotional intelligence is when we acknowledge that project management is getting work done through others. As PMs, we are dependent on others for our success. To achieve anything significant, we need a team. Big, important projects generally require large, effective project teams as well as an effective PM. As a PM, I personally want to take on larger and more complex projects since I believe that is going to advance my career. That is where the application of emotional intelligence pays off big.

---

[5] Project Management Institute *(Emotional Intelligence and Projects)*, Project Management Institute, Inc. (2009). Copyright and all rights reserved. Material from this publication has been reproduced with the permission of PMI.

"Project management is getting work done through others."

Emotional intelligence can help PMs to:

1. Develop stakeholder relationships that support the project's success
2. Anticipate and avoid emotional breakdowns
3. Deal with difficult team members and manage conflict
4. Leverage emotional information to make better decisions
5. Communicate more effectively
6. Create a positive work environment and high team morale
7. Cast a vision for shared project objectives that will attract, inspire, and motivate the project team

Let's look at each of these benefits in more detail.

1. Develop Stakeholder Relationships That Support the Project's Success

Relationships are the key to success as a PM. This includes the relationships with our team members as well as with the other project stakeholders. Strong relationships with all project stakeholders will buffer us during difficult times, help us gather more complete information, support us when we need it, and enable us to make better decisions. We will address stakeholder relationships in detail in Chapter 6, Relationship Management.

2. Anticipate and Avoid Emotional Breakdowns

Emotional breakdowns happen when we lose it. They are the office equivalent of road rage. Over the life of a project, we can experience significant stress. For some of us, this stress will push us over the edge and cause us to do something undesirable. In Chapter 4, Self-Management, we will discuss underlying causes and triggering events for emotional breakdowns, ways we can recognize when we are at risk of a breakdown, and techniques for avoiding breakdowns.

3. Deal with Difficult Team Members and Manage Conflict

In an ideal project, there are no difficult team members and conflict is manageable. Unfortunately, that is rarely the case in practice. When we seek out high-performing individuals for our teams, we often encounter difficult team members. Emotional intelligence can provide us the tools to work with difficult individuals, help us identify ways in which we contribute to the problem, and help us to work through issues with those parties. It helps us in a similar way to address the inevitable project conflict. Emotional intelligence can help us to recognize or even anticipate conflict and deal with it before it derails the project. After the groundwork for recognizing and anticipating conflict is laid in Chapter 5, Social Awareness, we will address stakeholder relationships in Chapter 6, Relationship Management.

4. Leverage Emotional Information to Make Better Decisions

In their 2004 book titled *The Emotionally Intelligent Manager,*[6] David R. Caruso and Peter Salovey identified six principles of emotional intelligence. The number one principle cited in their book was Emotion Is Information.

> "Emotion Is Information"
> —David R. Caruso and Peter Salovey

Our emotions are like our own personal radar. They provide us with a steady stream of information about ourselves, our team members, and our environment. When we are in touch with and able to access our emotions, we can leverage that information to make better decisions. If we are not in touch with our emotions, we are missing out on vital information about our environment (see Figure 1-2).

Emotions provide us with the extra data points that we need to make better decisions. They give us an intuitive or gut sense of what we need to do next. In a world where being right 51 percent of the time is often enough to make the difference, those extra data points may be just what it takes for us to be successful. We will discuss emotional data throughout the remainder of this book. We will examine decision making in Chapter 7, Project Team Leadership.

5. Communicate More Effectively

Emotional intelligence helps us to understand ourselves as well as those around us. By understanding the emotions and motivations of our team members

---

[6]David R. Caruso and Peter Salovey. *The Emotionally Intelligent Manager; How to Develop and Use the Four Key Emotional Skills of Leadership.* Hoboken, NJ: John Wiley & Sons, Inc., 2004.

Figure 1-2: Personal Radar Warning.

and other stakeholders, we can choose the words and messages that will make our point and resonate with the audience. We can anticipate difficult moments and take extra care to send just the right message with the correct emotions, whether we are speaking one-on-one with a stakeholder or addressing a group. We will address communications using emotional intelligence in Chapter 7, Project Team Leadership, as well as in Chapter 8, Creating a Positive Team Environment, and Chapter 9, Leveraging Emotional Intelligence on Large and Complex Projects.

6. Create a Positive Work Environment and High Team Morale

As PMs, we are responsible for the emotional tone of the project. We can approach this in a number of ways. We can leave the emotional tone of the project to chance or to the various members of our team. The results we get will be unpredictable. Alternatively, we can systematically and proactively manage that project environment to create the positive outcomes we are seeking. The strategic application of emotional intelligence will allow us to create a productive and successful environment with high morale and esprit de corps. We will address this in Chapter 7, Project Team Leadership, as well as in Chapter 8, Creating a Positive Team Environment.

7. Cast a Vision for Shared Project Objectives That Will Attract, Inspire, and Motivate the Project Team

Shared project objectives are important for getting buy-in and commitment from our project team. Unfortunately, this is not always as easy as it sounds. Establishing shared objectives requires understanding the emotions and objectives of those on our project teams and then casting a vision for the project that enables those individuals to fulfill their objectives within the project. One of my first project management mentors always told me that as a PM you are dependent on your resources for success. He used to say:

> "As a PM, you live or die by your resources."

As my career has progressed, I have come to fully appreciate what he meant. The ability to attract and inspire the best project resources is going to make our projects succeed; without this ability, our chances of success are greatly diminished. We will address resources in Chapter 8, Creating a Positive Team Environment.

■ Emotional Intelligence Is Vital to Project Managers

While emotional intelligence is important to managers and leaders of all types, the unique environment of projects makes the application of emotional intelligence critical to PMs for three reasons. First, each project is unique. As PMs move from project to project, we constantly experience a change of teams, sponsors, and other stakeholders. Only rarely do we have the benefit of the same stakeholders and project team. This puts pressure on us to assess, understand, and manage the emotions of our team and stakeholders to build relationships. We need to do this each time we start a new project.

The second reason is that projects are temporary. Unlike general management, projects have a beginning and an end. This puts pressure on PMs to move quickly. We don't have the luxury of time to develop strong relationships and create a positive team environment. If we don't work on relationships early in the project lifecycle, our projects can get derailed and never have a chance for success. We cannot afford to get our projects off on the wrong foot.

The third reason is the limited power and authority of the PM. In most cases, PMs do not have direct authority or power over the project team members. They cannot simply direct others to do what is needed. PMs need to use more sophisticated strategies to get their team members to achieve the desired outcomes. Without an understanding of the application of emotional intelligence, PMs may struggle to get the work of the project completed.

Given the importance to PMs, it may surprise you to find that emotional intelligence is not directly addressed in the *Guide to the Project Management Body of Knowledge* (PMBOK® Guide), which addresses the technical aspects of Project Management in detail. The closest the PMBOK® Guide comes is in the area of interpersonal skills, which has been relegated to an Appendix. Interpersonal skills are broken down in the Fourth Edition of the PMBOK® Guide as follows:

- Leadership
- Team building
- Motivation
- Communication
- Influencing
- Decision making
- Political and cultural awareness
- Negotiation[7]

You can see that there is quite a bit of overlap between the PMBOK® Guide and the emotional intelligence topics. I firmly believe that our ability to leverage these interpersonal skills is directly related to our level of emotional intelligence. Unfortunately, the PMBOK® Guide falls short of providing steps on how to develop and apply the interpersonal skills listed above. This book will provide the detailed guide to developing and applying those interpersonal skills.

If this emotional intelligence business seems a little daunting, take heart. Improving your awareness of emotional intelligence and applying it to projects is not difficult. It has the potential to provide rich rewards for you.

---

[7] Project Management Institute (*A Guide to the Project Management Body of Knowledge*), Project Management Institute (2004). Copyright and all rights reserved. Material from this publication has been reproduced with the permission of PMI.

Even small steps can make a large difference in your life and in your projects. All it takes is the desire to learn and grow and the courage to step out of your comfort zone. It may even require change.

Change is difficult for all of us. In fact, we resist change because it is easier to let inertia keep us on our current course. Staying the course was familiar to me, yet on some level I knew that it wasn't giving me the results I wanted. Once I realized how much danger was involved in staying on my previous course, I became very motivated to try something new. One definition of insanity is trying the same thing and expecting different results. If you want to get different results or different project outcomes, consider trying something different by learning about and applying emotional intelligence techniques.

A Brief Primer on Emotional Intelligence

Before we discuss the details of applying emotional intelligence to projects, it will be helpful to explore the background of emotional intelligence. This chapter provides more detail on the concept of emotional intelligence and how the writings of Daniel Goleman and other emotional intelligence researchers have contributed to the field. Using Goleman's generic model of emotional intelligence as a starting point, we will discuss an adaptation of that framework which is applicable to projects and PMs. We also provide some useful definitions for emotions, families of emotions, and emotional intelligence. Finally, we will conclude this chapter with some resources on where to go for additional information on emotional intelligence.

■ The Popularity of Emotional Intelligence

Emotional intelligence is a popular though often misunderstood term. It would be hard to have missed the buzz about it since Daniel Goleman's 1995 book *Emotional Intelligence: Why It Can Matter More Than IQ* became a national bestseller. What made Goleman's book so popular were two claims: (1) that emotional intelligence may be more important than intelligence quotient (IQ) and (2) that you can improve your emotional intelligence. Those claims are what made headlines and got emotional intelligence noticed. And while I believe those claims are true, it is not as simple as that to be successful with emotional intelligence.

I suspect that the PMs who bought Goleman's first book hoping to improve their performance and project success rates were sadly disappointed. The book was interesting and even entertaining in some places, but it fell short of providing the practical means of applying emotional intelligence to project management or to life in general. The PMs I know are interested in learning things that will help them become better PMs and leaders. They want to understand how to apply techniques to improve their projects.

This chapter will help you to understand the basic concepts of emotions and emotional intelligence and how important these concepts are to PMs.

■ Some Useful Definitions

Emotions

> *Emotion:* "A mental state that arises spontaneously
> rather than through conscious effort and is often accompanied
> by physiological changes; a feeling: the emotions of joy,
> sorrow, reverence, hate, and love."
> — *The American Heritage Dictionary*

There is a little bit of controversy among researchers over exactly what are emotions. While most researchers agree on a core set of emotions, they differ on including less well-known emotions, such as ecstasy, vigilance, adoration, and disgust.

I have learned to use a simple approach to understand a wide range of emotions. This approach uses six primary feeling words to represent groups of emotions as described by David E. Carlson in his book, *Counseling and Self-Esteem.* The primary feeling words can be summed up in the acronym SASHET: sad, angry, scared, happy, excited, and tender.[1]

Figure 2-1 shows these six primary feeling words, as well as the range of emotions each of these words represents. Notice that the figure shows an increasing intensity of each emotion as you move from the center of the wheel to the outside.

As you can see, the SASHET framework includes three "negative" families of emotions: sad, angry, and scared. These emotions are negative only

---

[1] David E. Carlson. *Counseling and Self-Esteem.* Nashville, TN: Thomas Nelson, Inc., 1995.

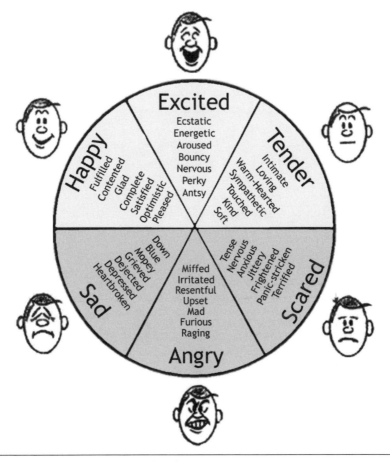

Figure 2-1: The SASHET Families of Emotions.

in the sense that they are perceived as negative. As we will see, all emotions provide us with data about ourselves and our environment. Just because we experience negative emotions doesn't mean that we feel negative.

The SASHET framework also includes the three "positive" families of emotions, which are happy, excited, and tender, and all the subtle variations of those emotions.

Using the SASHET framework, we learn to distinguish among the various groups of emotions. It is not critical that we pinpoint the exact emotions we are feeling. However, it is important to know which of the feeling families we are experiencing.

Emotional Intelligence

We briefly introduced emotional intelligence in Chapter 1 and provided some of the definitions used by various researchers. Emotional intelligence is sometimes called emotional quotient, or EQ, to show the relationship to IQ, or intelligence quotient. Some researchers use emotional intelligence, EI, and EQ interchangeably. For the remainder of this book, we will use the term EQ to mean emotional intelligence.

As previously noted, Daniel Goleman is the most recognized emotional intelligence researcher and journalist. He gets credit for the popularity of emotional intelligence. However, he wasn't the first to study EQ. As indicated in Chapter 1, the first emotional intelligence researchers included Peter Salovey and John D. Mayer. Some would also credit Harvard education professor Howard Gardner as the initiator of the original research work on emotional intelligence.

While some of the research work on emotional intelligence is common, each researcher uses a slightly different approach. This is not unexpected for a field that is relatively young, but other factors are also at work. There is a great deal of prestige and financial reward at stake and that has led to controversy among the researchers. For example, there is disagreement over something as simple as exactly how to define an emotion. There is even disagreement over some of the claims made in the popular press about the value of emotional intelligence.

We briefly mentioned emotional intelligence assessments in Chapter 1; this is another area of disagreement in the research community. Can we objectively measure emotional intelligence? If objective and accurate emotional intelligence tests were available, they would be at least as valuable as IQ testing—perhaps even more valuable. Unfortunately, this has led to a proliferation of various emotional intelligence instruments (as evidence, my brother and I developed the simple tool found in Chapter 1). It has also fostered a great deal of criticism among the various authors of emotional intelligence instruments. At this stage, my recommendation is to use the assessment that provides the information you need. Information about some of the most popular emotional intelligence assessments can be found in Appendix F.

The good news is that some level of agreement has been reached about the framework to be used for applying emotional intelligence. This has not always been the case. Mayer and Salovey published one of the earliest frameworks for applying emotional intelligence in their article "Emotional Intelligence" (1990). Daniel Goleman first published a framework for emotional intelligence in his 1998 book, *Working with Emotional Intelligence*. Figure 2-2[2]

---

[2]Peter Salovey and John D. Mayer. Emotional Intelligence, *Imagination Cognition, and Personality*, 1990, 9(3).

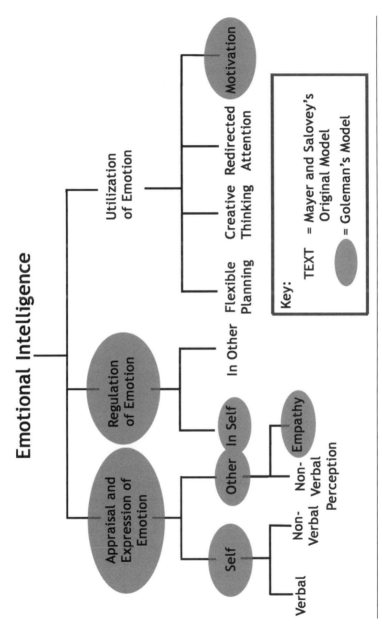

Figure 2-2: Comparison of Early Emotional Intelligence Frameworks.

Figure 2-3: Goleman's Framework of Emotional Competencies.

shows the Mayer and Salovey framework and highlights the areas where Goleman's work overlaps it.

The various frameworks have evolved and converged a little in the years since they were first introduced. In particular, the Goleman framework has become better organized and easier to understand and apply. Perhaps because of this—or because of the popularity of his books—Goleman's framework has become the de facto standard for applying emotional intelligence. This framework is shown in Figure 2-3.[3]

This framework is made up of four quadrants. Two of the quadrants represent personal competence or a focus on self. The other two quadrants represent social competence or a focus on others.

Goleman's framework is very helpful and easy to understand and apply. However, I found it necessary to adapt his generic framework to better meet the needs of PMs. Starting with the Goleman framework, I drew out the most relevant aspects of the model as they apply to projects and PMs. I then added other competencies and factors that were important for PMs. The resulting framework is shown in Figure 2-4. This framework was modified specifically to focus on the most relevant concepts of emotional intelligence for PMs and to show the application of those concepts. Here is a summary of the differences between the generic model and the PM-focused model:

[3] Daniel Goleman, Richard Boyatzis, and Annie McKee. *Primal Leadership*. Boston: Harvard Business School Press, 2002, p. 39.

Figure 2-4: Emotional Intelligence Framework for Project Management.

1. The structure has been changed. I put the first competencies to be mastered at the bottom to show upward progression. I also added a fifth category called Team Leadership as an overarching group of competencies to be mastered after the first four emotional intelligence domains.
2. Some competencies were deemphasized, including self-confidence and self-assessment.
3. Some competencies have been dropped altogether to allow a focus on the most important competencies for PMs. They include trustworthiness, conscientiousness, adaptability, achievement drive, initiative, service orientation, influence, change catalyst, building bonds, and teamwork and collaboration.
4. I added the social awareness competency of emotional boundaries, and the relationship management competency of truth telling.

This is the framework we will use throughout this book. Let's take a brief look at this framework and the five domains.

Self-Awareness

The first domain of the framework is self-awareness, which means understanding ourselves and our emotions. It involves the competencies of emotional self-awareness, accurate self-assessment, and self-confidence. Self-awareness is the first building block of emotional intelligence. Until we understand how we feel and can accurately assess our emotional state, we will understand emotions from only an intellectual point of view. We need to be able to understand emotions at a gut level—what is going on with us.

Accurate self-assessment includes understanding our own strengths and weaknesses and being willing to explore them both on our own and with others. Self-confidence is the ability to be grounded, secure, and self-assured in whatever situation we find ourselves.

Self-Management

Building on the emotional understanding we gain with self-awareness, we use self-management to manage and guide our emotional state. Self-management is the ability to control our emotions so they don't control us. In fact, the domain of self-management includes just one competency—self-control.

Self-control is a critical competency important for everyone. We have all experienced people and situations that have pushed our buttons and tried our patience. Self-control is what helps us to maintain our cool and not "lose it."

Social Awareness

Social awareness occurs when we expand our awareness to include the emotions of those around us. The domain of social awareness includes empathy, organizational awareness, seeing others clearly, and emotional boundaries.

Empathy is a critical skill for PMs and leaders of all types. Empathy is the ability to understand and relate to the feelings of others; to put ourselves in their shoes. Organizational awareness is the ability to interpret the context for emotions in an organization. It includes the spoken and unspoken rules and values that guide each organization.

Seeing others clearly is the ability to accurately assess and understand others. As PMs, it is important that we are able to understand and interpret the emotions of our team members and other stakeholders. We all have this skill in varying degrees.

Emotional boundaries help us to understand where we end and where others begin. If we have a solid command of emotional boundaries, we are more likely to speak up and say no when we should, we will have more realistic expectations of others, and we will take responsibility for our own emotions and actions and let others be responsible for theirs.

Relationship Management

Relationship management means using the awareness of our own emotions and those of others to build strong relationships. Those strong relationships will serve us on our projects. After all, projects are nearly always team efforts. The domain of relationship management includes the competencies of stakeholder relationships, developing others, and truth telling.

Stakeholder relationship includes the systematic identification, analysis, and management of the relationships with our project stakeholders. Developing others is making an investment in the growth and development of those we work with through feedback and coaching. Finally, truth telling looks at responsible ways in which we can be direct and honest.

Team Leadership

Team leadership is focused on the emotional skills needed to effectively lead project teams. This includes communications, conflict management, and inspirational leadership.

PMs need to be great communicators. There is no way around that fact. The larger the team, the more important communications become. The communications competency includes the ability to understand and manage the emotional tone of the project team through communications, as well as the ability to be congruent between actions, one-on-one communications, and communications in groups.

An important part of project management is conflict management. The conflict management competency is not new, rather, the focus is on ways to resolve project conflict using emotional intelligence.

Inspirational leadership looks at how project team leaders need to cast a vision that will engage, motivate, and inspire the team.

■ How to Improve Your Understanding of Emotional Intelligence Concepts

The good news is that after reading these first two chapters, you probably already know more about applying emotional intelligence than most of your fellow PMs. I highly encourage you to continue reading and learning more about emotional intelligence through a variety of sources.

In my November 2005 survey, I asked PMs how they learned about emotional intelligence. The sources most frequently cited were discussions, magazines/journals, books, classes, and blogs or web sites. Let's look at each of these sources in detail.

Magazines and Journals on Emotional Intelligence

Magazines were cited most often as the source of information about emotional intelligence. Emotional intelligence is frequently referenced in *PM Network Magazine* and other popular magazines. Visit your local library or search the Internet for articles.

Books on Emotional Intelligence

Appendix E contains a list of books on emotional intelligence, with a quick summary of each. For those interested in just one or two books, you will find my favorites listed here.

Coaches and Mentors

I highly recommend working with a mentor or coach. Working with my personal coach, Rich Blue, was essential for me in learning emotional intelligence techniques and improving my effectiveness. A staggering number of emotional intelligence coaches can be found on the Internet using Google or other search engines.

Assessments

Emotional intelligence assessments can also provide some information for us. Despite the limitations already mentioned, any information is better than no information. More information on available assessments can be found in Appendix F.

■ Learning About Emotional Intelligence Is Only the First Step

While it is important to learn about emotional intelligence, that is only the first step. I learned about emotional intelligence through a combination of coaching, studying, and ongoing application. I won't downplay the importance of coaching and study but I truly believe that people learn best by doing. There is a big difference between studying a concept and applying it. Thus, this book focuses on the application of the topics and concepts.

To make the most of what we learn about emotional intelligence, we need to apply it to our lives and projects. This book is heavy on application. Each chapter provides a series of techniques that are summarized at the end of the unit. Choose some or all of the techniques and put them to use after reading each chapter. This will help you to get the most out of this book.

PART 2

Project Management Begins with Self-Management

As leaders, we must focus on ourselves before we can try to manage or lead others. Without mastery of our own emotions, we will never be in a position to lead others.

Self-awareness and self-management are the two key aspects of self-leadership. With self-awareness, we identify our own emotional states and the sources of our emotions. Self-management means handling or directing our emotions with skill. This is not possible without awareness.

Self-Awareness

■ An Introduction to Self-Awareness

Self-awareness, which is the first building block of emotional intelligence, is our ability to recognize our own emotions and their effects on us and others. Without being aware of and understanding our own emotions, it will be difficult to move into the other emotional competencies, such as self-management, social awareness, and team leadership.

You've probably heard the phrase "you must be present to win" in reference to a raffle or drawing. This concept has great relevance to self-awareness. As used here, present means "in the moment." Self-awareness is about the here and now. With self-awareness, we strive to get in touch with exactly what we are feeling right now. It is about knowing ourselves in this moment.

Self-awareness is not about what happened yesterday or what will happen tomorrow. Yesterday's events are only relevant if they affect how we are feeling right now. Otherwise, leave the past in the past. The key to self-awareness is to focus on what we are feeling now.

Self-Awareness Is the Starting Point for Emotional Intelligence

Understanding what we feel and what is going on with us is the basic skill we need for self-awareness and for all emotional intelligence. Recall from Chapter 2 the SASHET families of emotions as shown again in Figure 3-1. To be self-aware means that we need to know which of these feelings we have, right

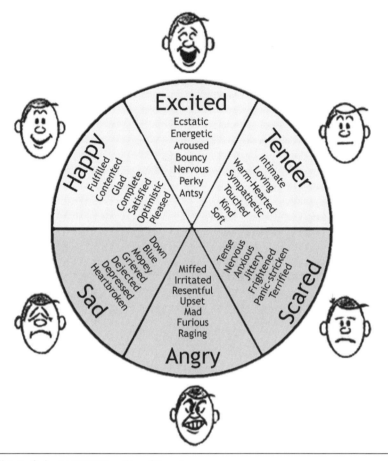

Figure 3-1: SASHET Families of Emotions.

now, in the moment. Are we feeling sad, happy, excited, or some combination of all of these?

As shown in Figure 3-2, the Emotional Intelligence Model for Project Management includes the following competencies under the domain of self-awareness: emotional self-awareness, accurate self-assessment, and self-confidence. We are going to talk about each of these in the following sections.

■ Emotional Self-Awareness

Self-awareness is the ability to understand our own emotions. It is about being conscious or mindful of our own emotional state. Self-awareness may

Figure 3-2: Emotional Intelligence Model Showing Self-Awareness.

be challenging for us for a number of reasons. First, our emotions can be as volatile as the weather. Feelings mix, morph, and evolve, often in a short span of time. One minute we might feel excited and happy about a friend's plan to visit us. A moment later, we might be scared or angry about the same event.

Second, we may actually experience a mix of emotions at any one time. We can be excited, happy, scared, and angry all at once. More commonly, we have one emotion at the surface that masks or dominates other emotions. Those underlying emotions are often more informative to us. Consider a parent who waits up for a teenager with a curfew of 10:00 PM. If the teenager shows up at home at 1:00 AM, the parent will often express anger. The parent is likely feeling scared, which is the more important secondary emotion.

A third reason that self-awareness may be difficult is due to childhood wounds that inhibit our ability to access our feelings or simply to poor modeling of emotions by our parents. For most of my life, I suppressed many of my emotions. This was partly a result of growing up in an alcoholic family where everyone (except my dad) was denied the opportunity to show or express emotions. My siblings and I quickly learned that it was safer to mute, ignore, or hide what we were really feeling.

Some of the things our parents modeled or taught us about emotions were just plain wrong or unhealthy. While I think my own case was perhaps extreme, I have talked to enough people to believe that MOST of our parents unwittingly taught us things that were worthless or unhealthy. Like the rule about waiting an hour after you eat before swimming, our parents simply taught us what they thought was right. Or they modeled what they had learned from their parents.

Figure 3-3 is a list of common sayings about emotions that you may have heard. Check off the ones that were common in your house when you were growing up.

Learning about emotional intelligence often includes unlearning what we were taught and breaking unhealthy bad habits. It is not easy work—you might argue that it would be easier to learn something completely new rather than overcome what has become second nature by the time we are adults.

As an adult, I found that all my emotions were dampened. In particular, though, I found it difficult to feel happy, angry, or sad. What I lacked in happiness, anger, and sadness, I made up for in fear. I was afraid most or all of the time. I was scared about how I was performing at work, scared about money, scared about how I was being perceived, and scared about nearly everything. I still deal with a lot of fear in my life, but not nearly as much as I did when I was younger.

It took a lot of hard work over the course of nearly five years before I was able to access my emotions directly. This included working with a coach, as well as with two support groups. I learned various techniques for getting in touch with my emotions. I learned to recognize the physical sensations that lead to emotions. I learned to journal. Eventually I was able to feel angry and sad and to deal with the fear I felt all the time.

We are all different when it comes to being aware of our emotions. For most people, the kind of work that I went through is unnecessary. However, each person may find that some emotions are easier to recognize than others. Some people may be in denial about how they really feel about a situation. Most of us want to believe we are strong and unaffected by various circumstances. It's rare that you can work on a project without experiencing at least one emotion, and this emotional awareness directly affects how successful we are in our work. We actually become stronger when we recognize the under-

Sadness

I'll give you something to cry about

There is no crying in baseball

Don't cry, everything is going to be OK

Big boys don't cry

Don't be sad, everything is going to be OK

Stop it you big crybaby

Self-Confidence

Don't brag

Don't be too cocky

Who died and put you in charge?

Fear

You better be scared!

I'll give you something to be scared about

I am going to send you to a juvenile home / call the police

If you don't do this, I am going to beat you!

Come on, don't be a scaredy cat.

Happy / Excited

Why are you all happy?

Calm down / pipe down / quiet down right now or else

Take it easy

Anger

Don't get angry

Don't let anyone get to you / get your goat

Expressing Emotions

Don't say that or you will upset your father/mother

If you can't say something nice, don't say anything at all

Children should be seen and not heard.

Figure 3-3: Common Parental Messages About Emotions.

lying feelings we're experiencing. Self-awareness is about developing this capacity. It is similar to building a physical muscle in our bodies. Let's look at specific ways that we can begin to train ourselves to recognize our emotions.

Getting Physical with Our Feelings

You may recall the famous line from the TV series *The Incredible Hulk*, "You won't like me when I am angry." In the 2008 movie of that name, David Banner tracked his pulse rate by always wearing a special heart rate monitor watch. It alerted him when his pulse was above a specific threshold level that would lead to his transformation into the Incredible Hulk.

These heart rate watches are not a big deal—I have one. You can get one for a couple of hundred bucks. Like the Hulk, you can set a threshold on your watch to set off the alarm. Wouldn't it be nice if we had a device like that watch to tell us what emotions we are feeling at any one time? For many of us, that device is our body.

Emotions manifest themselves physically in our bodies, and we can use these sensations to recognize our emotions. What we feel emotionally is reflected in what we feel physically. If you are having trouble feeling an emotion or cannot name what you are feeling, you might be able to use your body as a clue. You can train yourself to recognize what it feels like to be happy or sad.

How do we know which sensations go with each feeling? Figure 3-4 provides a quick guide to the sensations that go with each of the feeling families. We need to consider things like heart rate, feelings of heat or cold, muscle tightness, and our own eyes. It is important to note that these physical sensations can vary from person to person. As you begin to pay attention to your own body, you may note minor variations from the list provided.

Using Our Faces to Determine Our Feelings

While our physical sensations provide one clue about what we are feeling, our bodies help us assess our feelings in other ways. For example, our faces also provide information about our emotional state. The eyes have been called the window to the soul.

In the 1960s, Silvan Tomkins and Paul Ekman were psychologists who first conducted extensive experiments that documented the strong link between facial expression and emotions. They found that across all societies, underlying emotions resulted in a common set of facial expressions. Tomkins and Ekman decoded the facial expressions and catalogued 3,000 unique expressions having emotional meaning. That is, they determined 3,000 different ways for our faces to express emotions. Just as important, Tomkins and Ekman noted that these facial expressions are difficult to fake and that makes them an accurate predictor of underlying emotions.

Am I advocating that you learn the 3,000 different facial expressions and the corresponding emotions? No. The face just provides us with additional data to aid in emotional self-awareness. By understanding what emotions look like, you can use your own face to better understand what you are feeling. If other methods fail to tell us how we are feeling, the face is a reliable indicator.

By studying our own faces, we can learn about the emotions we are feeling. We can use our own faces as a guide. We don't have to know 3,000

Figure 3-4: Physical Sensations for SASHET Feelings.

expressions. We have to learn only the various ways in which the six families of feelings will show on our faces.

The chart shown in Figure 3-5 contains a quick taxonomy of the faces representing the SASHET families of feelings, including a picture and a brief description of each feeling family. In Chapter 5, we will use our understanding of how emotions appear on our faces to understand the faces and emotions of those around us.

If you are skeptical that faces reveal emotions, consider people who make large financial decisions based on emotions. Yes, I am talking about professional poker players. Poker players have long been aware of the fact that

Figure 3-5: Facial Expressions for the SASHET Feelings.

faces reveal emotions. The term "poker face" has come to mean a face that reveals no hint of a person's thoughts or emotions.

I like to watch the World Poker Tour on television. In fact, for a short time I was a junkie and could not stop watching it. I was fascinated by the various ways in which the different players would hide or camouflage their faces so as not to reveal their emotions to their opponents. Each player would try to mislead the other players about what he or she felt. At the same time, the players tried to read the emotions of the other players by observing their faces and body language.

Most players use sunglasses and hats to hide much of their faces. One player named Phil Laak has been dubbed the "Unibomber" for his tendency to wear dark glasses and a hooded sweatshirt to cover much of his head. When he is in a stressful situation (or if he wants others to think he is under stress), Phil will take in the drawstrings on his hood until none of his face is visible to the other players!

Write It Out

Another way to determine what we are feeling is to journal. We can use journaling to explore our feelings in the moment. We may also reflect on something that occurred in the past and experience again the feelings we felt previously (or should have felt). We can also use journaling to look to the future and explore how we may feel about something we have not yet experienced.

There are many different ways to journal, and you may have to experiment to find one that works for you. I have kept a daily journal for the last ten years, and I simply use it to jot down what is going on with me emotionally. I sometimes write as if I am praying. You might write as if you are writing to someone else or to yourself.

Emotional Red Flags

Yet another tool that can help us be more self-aware is emotional red flags. As I learned about emotional intelligence and about myself, I became aware of ways in which I acted that were less than helpful. I learned to recognize behaviors that were early symptoms of my own emotional problems. I called these emotional red flags.

These emotional red flags helped me increase my self-awareness and enabled me to to identify and deal with the underlying emotional problems. As I began to recognize the symptoms of these red flags, I was empowered to make better choices and change the outcomes. Here are six emotional red flags that you can use to gain insights into your emotions.

1. Inappropriate Humor

We would all probably agree that humor is good, especially on projects. I used to consider myself very funny and believed it to be one of my strengths. In reality, I was using humor in indirect and inappropriate ways because of my fear. I was afraid to tell the truth and make my point directly, so I would make a joke instead. As an example, consider when someone showed up late to a project team meeting. Instead of confronting the issue directly, I would make a joke like "looks like the trains didn't wait for you today." I was angry that they did not show up on time. Unfortunately, I wasn't aware of my anger, so

I did not voice it directly. Or, I was not comfortable expressing my anger, so I hid it. In either case, my use of humor was indirect and not effective at addressing the behavior of my team member.

My automatic joking was a way of masking my true feelings of anger or fear. That was a clue that I was not aware of my emotions. Now before I make a joke, I ask myself "Why do I feel the need to make a joke right now? What emotion am I feeling?" Most likely I feel angry, sad, or scared. When angry, I may choose to single someone out and try to make fun of them. Or if I feel sad, I may try to draw attention to myself or get affirmed by others with a cheap laugh. When scared, I may make a joke about someone to shift the attention from me. In each of these cases, I need to look beyond the humor to determine the underlying emotion.

2. Use of Sarcasm

The use of sarcasm is closely related to inappropriate humor. Perhaps sarcasm is just humor taken to an extreme. We use sarcasm for the same reasons as inappropriate humor—we don't want to say something directly. As an example of sarcasm, consider when you say to your boss "everyone thinks the new expense approval policy is a GREAT idea" and then you tack on "just kidding." The "just kidding" is the exclamation point that makes sarcasm and inappropriate humor easy to spot. When you say "just kidding," you are saying "don't get mad at me for saying what I really feel."

For some excellent examples of sarcasm in modern culture, you can check out *The Family Guy, Thirty Rock,* or *The Big Bang Theory.*

3. Passive–Aggressive Behavior

Another red flag is passive–aggressive behavior, which can be very subtle and is often confused with simply being a jerk. One description of passive aggressive behavior is:

> Passive–aggressive behavior means obstructionist resistance to
> authoritative instructions in interpersonal or occupational situations.
> It can be used to deal with stress or frustration by attack a person
> in subtle, indirect, and seemingly calm ways. It can reveal itself as
> resentment, stubbornness, procrastination, sullenness, or
> intentional failure to perform assigned tasks.

Passive–aggressive behavior can manifest itself in the project environment in various ways, including showing up late for meetings, failing to follow instructions, failing to meet deliverable deadlines, or failing to ask for approval in advance. Let's look at a couple of these in detail.

Being on time for meetings can be challenging. There are a lot of meetings on a project, and it may be difficult to be on time for all of them. If individuals are late, it doesn't necessarily indicate passive–aggressive behavior. As PMs, we need to learn to discern between occasional tardiness and passive–aggressive behavior.

When individuals intentionally show up late for meetings, they are sending a passive message to the other people attending that meeting. That message may be something like "I don't like this project," "I really didn't want to come," or "I have better things to do."

Of course sometimes people are late for reasons other than passive aggressiveness, and this is what makes it a bit tricky. We are all late sometimes. It happens to everyone. If an individual is late only once in a great while, that is no big deal. It is also not a big deal if we recognize that we are going to be late and call to let others know or provide advance notice. However, when we have a pattern of showing up late, something else may be going on.

I once worked for a project director who would lock the conference room doors at the time that the meeting was supposed to start. Anyone who came late would be forced to knock at the door and then would be subjected to ridicule upon entering the conference room. It was his way of trying to force people to be on time. I think this is a bit heavy handed. I try to communicate directly and privately with the individual to let that person know why I feel it is important to be on time to meetings and to understand any issues he or she may have.

Another category of passive–aggressive behavior is overstepping authority, such as failing to ask for approval in advance. There is a fine line between a go-getter and someone who breaks the rules or rebels against authority figures. All PMs have heard the old adage, "It is better to ask for forgiveness than approval." That saying likely came from a passive–aggressive person. It might very well be true. But that adage can also be construed to mean "Do whatever you want." Certainly as PMs we need to show initiative. This means that sometimes we have to act in the absence of clear authority. However, we also need to be aware of what is really going on. Is there some underlying reason for acting this way? For example, is it unclear what we are responsible for? If so, we should get clarification from our manager so that our lines of responsibility and authority are clear. If we show a pattern of not getting approval from our leaders, or acting as if it is not required, we may be acting passive aggressively.

The emotion that underlies all passive–aggressive behavior is anger. It sounds ugly, but it is true. When we act in passive–aggressive ways, we are angry. Perhaps we resent the authority figure in the situation. What ends up happening is that we act in ways that look like we are complying but we really aren't. We show up late. We "misunderstand" instructions from the boss. We turn in deliverables late. We act in the absence of authority. We may do all these things without being aware of our anger or our passive–aggressive behavior.

4. Playing the Victim

Another common red flag is playing the victim. This was something I did frequently. I used to complain about why I was unable to change jobs, why I lived in a certain part of the country, how I was stuck in the wrong line at the supermarket, and a host of other situations. I was playing the victim by not going for what it was that I wanted.

Now that I recognize this behavior in myself, I am more sensitive to it in others. Playing the victim instead of completing an activity, changing jobs, staying in a lousy marriage, working for bad bosses, not going for a better position or being a leader, and numerous other outcomes are possible scenarios. The rationalization for victimhood includes all the reasons or the people who "prevented" them from doing what they should have done. It all smacks of victimhood.

I know a woman who, after divorcing her husband, continues to work at the same company and in the same department as her ex-husband and his new girlfriend. As uncomfortable as that sounds, she claims she can't find a better job and, so, she is resolved to stay in that position.

Behind the victim-like behavior is a lack of honesty about why we don't go for what we say we want. We pile up all the reasons we cannot pursue our goals or all the people who prevented us from getting what we want. We do this instead of going flat out for what we say we want. The truth is that we aren't motivated sufficiently to really go for it. So, we blame other people or circumstances instead of just admitting that we don't want it enough.

Living life as a victim is not very satisfying. It is also irresponsible and dishonest. We have all been given one life to live, and we need to take full responsibility for that life. Being a victim is dishonest because it doesn't address the real reasons for our inaction. A more truthful approach would be to admit we just didn't want it enough or we were too damned scared to go for it 100 percent.

We will talk more about playing the victim in Chapter 6 when we discuss the principle of co-creation.

A Bad Day at the Lake Is Better Than a Good Day at Work

I was recently out for an early morning run and noticed some guys out fishing in the lagoons near my house. Out of nowhere, I remembered a phrase that I used to love about 20 years ago. It was "A bad day at the lake is better than a good day at work."

I guess you could say that things have changed for me in the last 20 years. I used to believe in that type of thinking—that work wasn't fun or rewarding. Rather, it was something you did to pay for the things that you really enjoyed. What a waste of our talents and valuable life energy!

My current philosophy is that work should be fun. Your work should be something you are passionate about, something that brings you energy and a feeling of being alive. I feel lucky in my role as a consultant because it plays to my strengths, and I enjoy it. I am working with people I like and respect and the work is both challenging and rewarding. I am happy and excited to head into work each day.

Thinking that we have to work or that we would be better off somewhere else is a good example of being a victim. After all, we can choose where to work, and we have chosen our current job. It is a choice; we are not forced to be there. Complaining about our situation or fantasizing about other jobs is indulging in victimhood. Here are some questions we can use to shift the focus from victimhood to responsibility:

- How am I contributing to the current situation at work?
- What can I do differently to make a positive impact?
- How can I manage my emotions to stay positive in a negative or toxic environment?
- How can I change the tone or mood at work?

The key to moving away from victimhood is to focus on the positive steps we can take. These may include personal stress management, cutting back on work hours, and avoiding or confronting negative and verbally abusive people. We can also seek help from our manager, the HR department, or even reach out to coworkers who want to stay positive and healthy.

If your work isn't fun and energizing, or if you are just hanging in for the weekend, you may be in the wrong job or at the wrong company. You are likely broadcasting this loud and clear through your emotions and body language, even if you don't say it. You may as well have a sign on your desk that says "I'd rather be anywhere else but here!" Worse, you are creating an image or brand for yourself that is negative, and almost certainly you are attracting other like-minded individuals to be on your teams.

It may be appropriate to change jobs. If you have done what you can to stay positive, manage yourself, and change your work environment, then you should seriously consider changing companies or jobs. Perhaps you need to be on the lake—as the captain or hired hand of a charter boat. Perhaps you need to be teaching children, painting pictures, or growing organic tomatoes. Figure out what makes you feel alive and energized, so you hop out of bed in the morning. And then go do it with passion.

5. Hostility

Hostility is the least subtle of all the red flags. Hostility is in your face. Examples of hostility would include blowing up in a meeting, storming out, using your physical presence to intimidate others, muttering under your breath, and making threats. Hostility is about anger and acting out.

While some may view hostility as a healthy expression of anger, this is not the case. Hostility is not responsible. In Chapter 4, we will explore more constructive and responsible ways of dealing with anger.

6. Reactivity

Another clue to our own feelings and emotions is how we react to others. Do you see any red flags in others? Do people in general bug you? By that I mean do you find yourself feeling ticked off or angry? When people bug us, it is a clue about how we feel. "If you spot it, you got it" is a phrase that captures this idea very well. Typically, what bothers us the most about others is an issue that we need to deal with ourselves. So if you have issues with someone else's behavior, ask what that tells you about yourself.

An example of reactivity for me is when someone tells me to do something, or I feel like they are trying to control me. I was recently asked to send a reminder about a meeting that occurs every two weeks. My first reaction was annoyance—I don't like to be told what to do. And, if I think about it, these are the types of things that happen to me all the time. I probably would not even notice this particular annoyance if I hadn't been looking for it.

When I reflected on it, I realized that I was annoyed by this request for two reasons. First, I don't like to be controlled. I also realized that in this case, I was already feeling angry with the particular individual who asked me to send the reminder. There was a previous issue between us. They had not done something else that I had expected. and I was feeling hurt about it. So the question about the meeting bugged me, because it was a painful reminder of the state of our relationship.

What else can our reactivity tell us? Our awareness of our reactivity can move us to action, help us to get clear, and show us ways to improve our relationships. Or, our reactivity may reveal a desire, a need, or a hunger in us that is not being met. An area that I am very reactive around is when people act entitled or when they ask to have things their way. I was recently in a meeting of approximately 30 people—some I knew and some I did not. A man I did not know entered the conference room and walked over to the thermostat and set it on 70 degrees. He did not consult anyone, poll the room, or make any sort of announcement. He just decided to set the thermometer at 70 because HE wanted it at 70. I was outraged about him, but after reflecting on it I realized that the incident told me more about myself than about him. My reactivity to this individual revealed a hunger in me to be more entitled.

Do you recognize any of these red flags in your behavior? Are you sufficiently aware and objective about your own behavior to know if you behave in these ways? If so, what is really going on with you? Are you scared, angry, or sad? Awareness of the red flag behavior and the underlying emotion is the first step toward breaking the cycle. By watching for these red flags, and then exploring the emotional causes, we can begin to act more responsibly. Our teams and stakeholders will definitely appreciate that, and we will be better PMs because of it.

Intensity of Feelings

Once we understand what feeling or feelings we are having, we can also describe the intensity of the feeling. This is partly represented by the words we use that represent the intensity of the feeling, as shown in Figure 3-1. And it is child's play.

I was impressed when my son was taught emotional self-awareness at his elementary school. The school was using a curriculum called PATHs (Promoting Alternative Thinking Strategies). The materials that my son brought home from school were terrific; simple and easy to understand. As an example, Figure 3-6 is representative of one of the ones he had as a take home exercise. It is a simple metaphor that anyone, including kids, can easily use to explain the intensity of their feelings.

Emotional Self-Awareness Is Important

No doubt you are beginning to wonder why we have spent so much time talking about getting in touch with our feelings. Being aware of our feelings is critical for a couple of reasons. First, the reality is that most of us are not good at getting in touch with our feelings. We go through most of our days either too busy to feel or finding ways to shield ourselves from feeling. As

Feeling Intensity Chart

Figure 3-6: Feelings Scale.

humans, we have learned to use food, TV, shopping, work, drugs, sex, alcohol, more work, hobbies, and anything else we can find so that we don't have to feel. Feelings are often too scary or painful, so we have learned to become numb.

Second, being aware of our feelings is the single most important trait and first building block of emotional intelligence. If we don't know how to interpret our feelings, we will not be good at the other aspects of emotional intelligence. It is our own personal radar, feeding us information about our environment. If you only have time to learn one thing about emotional intelligence, learn about self-awareness.

■ Accurate Self-Assessment

The second competency of self-awareness is accurate self-assessment. This is a lower priority than emotional self-awareness, yet it is still critical for PMs.

Self-assessment is about viewing ourselves accurately and seeking feedback from others to improve our performance. In *Working with Emotional Intelligence*, Daniel Goleman describes accurate self-assessment in terms of people who are:

- Aware of their strengths and weaknesses
- Reflective, learning from experience
- Open to candid feedback, new perspectives, continuous learning, and self-development
- Able to show a sense of humor and perspective about themselves[1]

Learning about our strengths and weaknesses should be an ongoing effort throughout our lifetimes. In Chapter 6, we are going to look at some specific assessment instruments that can help us get to know ourselves better and identify strengths and weaknesses. We can (and should) also leverage those around us to learn more.

As noted earlier, I have been blessed to have several different mentors, coaches, and managers who have invested in me over the course of my career. They have provided me with valuable feedback, as well as guidance that I use to improve my performance.

Let's look at an example that demonstrated one of my particular vulnerabilities. A client dropped a book off at my desk. By the way, you should know it is not a good sign when anyone gives you a book and says "This may come in handy." They may as well give you a deodorant stick or a bottle of mouthwash! Therefore, imagine my embarrassment when my client did exactly that and handed me the book, *Angry All the Time*. Ouch!

I don't know if I was angry before he gave me the book, but I was definitely angry afterward! More accurately, I felt disappointed and sad. Emotions were supposed to be my strength, right? Why didn't he recognize my expertise in this area?

What my client accurately perceived was that I was angry. I had snapped at one of the team leads on the program in a team meeting. So, why was I angry? In this particular case I was angry on the surface, but deep down I was scared about failure. It was not a capital offense, and I wasn't angry all the time, but it was something worth keeping an eye on nonetheless. Later I was grateful that my client thought enough about me to bring it to my attention.

One of the people I am learning to benefit from is my wife, Norma. She knows me better than anyone and is one of my best sources of feedback. Learning to view my spouse as my coach has been a positive shift for me. Look for someone in your life who is close to you and feels comfortable giving you feedback. Once you've asked for feedback, make sure you are receptive to it.

---

[1] Daniel Goleman. *Working with Emotional Intelligence*. New York: Random House/Bantam Books. 1998.

■ Self-Confidence

The third competency under self-awareness is self-confidence. Like accurate self-assessment, we would agree that all PMs need self-confidence. No one wants to follow a leader who lacks self-confidence.

In *Working with Emotional Intelligence*, Daniel Goleman describes self-confidence as:

> *Self-Confidence:* "A Strong Sense of
> One's Self-Worth and Capabilities."
> —Daniel Goleman

He goes on to say that individuals with self-confidence:

- Present themselves with self-assurance; have "presence"
- Can voice views that are unpopular and go out on a limb for what is right
- Are decisive, able to make sound decisions despite uncertainties and pressures[2]

An unlikely champion of self-confidence was Bill Gates. When he retired from Microsoft in July 2008, he and his team made a video about his last day and what he would do after retirement. In the video, Bill is hamming up the fact that he is a geek, that he drives a cheapo car and is apparently forgetful, that he is a wannabee rock star, and even that he could have been a running mate for one of the presidential candidates at that time. He engaged the help of numerous celebrities, rock stars, and politicians to participate in the video. The video came across as entertaining and wonderfully self-effacing.

It is telling that Bill Gates has the self-confidence to poke fun at himself. Why would anyone with a strong sense of his or her own self-worth and capabilities need to poke fun at himself or herself? They don't, of course. But only those who have a strong sense of their own worth and capabilities are able to joke about their shortcomings.

Similarly, Al Gore was seen as robotic, stiff, and boring as both vice president for eight years and as a presidential candidate in 2000. Then, after losing the 2000 presidential election, he started doing speaking engagements. When he hosted *Saturday Night Live* in December 2002, he poked fun at

---

[2] Ibid.

himself and his situation. As a result, he became more human and more likable. He also seemed more confident.

Individuals who lack self-confidence don't give themselves the freedom to laugh at themselves. It is as if they are on the defensive all the time, trying to make sure no one sees through their façade. The reality is, however, that other people usually see us just as we are, confident or not.

Ask yourself the following questions:

1. Are you aware of your weaknesses, or the areas where others might get a chuckle about you?
2. Are you willing to let others have a laugh at you about those areas? Would you even make a joke out of it and let others laugh at you?
3. Do you ever feel as if you wouldn't dare let others know about mistakes you've made?

If you are too serious about yourself or feel threatened by the idea that others might see your weaknesses or flaws, consider loosening up a bit. Those around you probably know about your weaknesses, foibles, and blind spots even if you don't talk about them or bring attention to them. They may even see your weaknesses more clearly than you do!

Self-confidence is an area where I feel that I have improved over the years. It has helped that I have improved my overall level of emotional intelligence over the last ten years. I now feel more comfortable with myself, with my project teams, and with the other project stakeholders. I am confident when expressing my views and making tough decisions. And I am more comfortable letting others see the real me.

■ Techniques to Improve Your Self-Awareness

Now that we understand the first emotional intelligence domain of self-awareness, what can we do to improve our competency in this area? There are many ways we can increase our emotional self-awareness. The following are my favorite techniques:

1. Keep a Feelings Journal

As discussed earlier, journaling can help us to get in touch with our feelings. For best results, we should make notes in our feelings journal throughout the day on what we are experiencing and what feelings result from our experiences. Our notes don't have to be extensive; a journal entry may look like this:

"Talked with Jim this morning and congratulated him on getting his deliverable completed ahead of schedule. I left feeling happy."

The journal can help us track our feelings over the course of the day or week. Once we have journaled for a few days or weeks, we can look for patterns like:

- Balance of negative feelings versus positive feelings
- Same feelings every day at the same time, for example, sad every morning
- Predominant feelings, for example, always scared
- Feelings tied to relationships, for example, angry whenever I talk to my brother
- Dead spots where you are not able to feel anything, for example, numb over a significant loss
- Blind spots, for example, never feeling angry or never feeling happy

I recommend that you keep a feelings journal for a full thirty days. It can be a helpful way to become more aware of what you are feeling and what is triggering those feelings. It may feel awkward at first, but keep doing it. This is an extremely powerful way to gain insight into what's going on with you emotionally.

2. Track Emotions with a Tally Sheet

Another simple way to track our emotions over time is to use an emotional tally sheet. A couple of examples of emotional tally sheets are shown in Appendix A. The first example could be used by an individual to track emotions over the course of the week. At the simplest level, just knowing how often you experience each emotion will aid you in becoming more self-aware.

You can also be more intentional by setting a timer or other reminder so that you record your emotions every thirty minutes or hour. This will give you a more complete view of the range of emotions you experience throughout your day and week. Do this when at work and at play to get the best view of your emotional range and what triggers specific emotions.

3. Conduct a Physical Inventory

Another self-awareness technique is to conduct a physical inventory using the sensations in your body to help determine what you are feeling. Remember the physical signs that we introduced in Figure 3-4. As you go through the course of a normal day, stop periodically and take a physical inventory to help you understand what you are feeling. Check your heartbeat and see if it is fast or slow. Check to see if you feel hot or cold. Look for areas where your muscles are tight. Use these physical indicators to help you determine what is going on with you emotionally.

It is important to remember that we may feel a combination of two or more emotions at any one point in time. While one feeling may dominate, it may be the emotions that are further below the surface that we need to understand and address. For example, if someone does not complete a deliverable on time and does not let us know, we may feel a combination of anger and fear. We might be angry because they did not let us know. We might be scared because we are going to have to slip the schedule or miss other commitment dates. The feeling of anger may dominate in this case. However, it could be the fear underneath that anger that is more important to understand and manage.

4. Checking Your Face in the Mirror

Like the physical inventory in the previous item, you can use the face in the mirror technique to help you become more aware of your emotions. Use the pictures and descriptions of faces that we described in Figure 3-5. Check your face periodically to see what is being shown to others.

You can also train yourself to get better at this by reversing the exercise. As you feel an emotion, check your face in a mirror to see what your expression looks like. With practice, you will be able to recognize what you are feeling without having to rely on your face.

5. Use Paired Sharing

Paired sharing is a simple but powerful technique you can use to better understand what you are feeling at any point in time. It is similar to having a conversation with ourselves except that we have the help of another person. It is almost like thinking out loud, except the focus is on our feelings more than our thoughts.

The way it works is to get together with another person. The two of you will take turns speaking and listening. The first person will talk for a set period of time; two or three minutes work very well. There is no script. That speaker talks about what he or she is feeling in that moment, even if that feeling is elusive. The speaker just keeps talking about whatever comes to mind without editing or censoring. The key is to keep it about emotions and about the here and now. It is okay if there are pauses or periods of silence.

The person listening has a critical and somewhat difficult task and that is simply to listen. This involves maintaining eye contact throughout and not providing any type of feedback to the other person. This means no verbal clues (e.g., uh-huh) and no nonverbal clues, such as nodding or smiling. This may require a little practice for both speaker and listener since giving feedback is such an ingrained part of listening for many of us. To use the paired sharing technique, it is important to simply listen and to let the person doing the talking determine where to go next.

When the allotted time is up, the pair will switch roles; the speaker becomes the listener. The same rules apply for speaker and listener. The second speaker can comment on what the first speaker said earlier; however, the listener should not respond. Their job is to listen with no feedback.

The pair-sharing technique can be used with people we know well or even those we don't know at all. It works great for couples. The technique is intended to provide space for the speaker to say what is in their heart. The listener is simply there to provide the space for the speaker. They don't need to know any history or any context; they simply listen to the speaker.

The process continues until the two are able to get down to what they are feeling. Most people will get in touch with their feelings within two or three rounds at most. It is especially helpful for those emotions lying under the surface.

This technique is quite simple and the description probably sounds more difficult than it is in practice. However, don't let the simplicity fool you; it is a powerful way to get in touch with what is going on with you. Try it a couple of times and see if it helps you to get in touch with your feelings.

6. Backtrack

Backtracking is when we retrace our steps to determine why we are feeling a certain way. I find it most helpful to understand when I am feeling negative emotions, such as sadness, anger, or fear. I will sometimes feel a vague sense of unease, as if a dark cloud is hanging over my head. By using the backtracking technique, I can often connect the dots on what I am feeling and why.

This is similar to the process you follow when you lose something. What would you do if you lost your keys? You would stop and retrace your steps leading up to the point where you lost them. Usually, you find that there is a logical place for the keys based on the steps you took.

The process of backtracking works the same for our feelings, as shown in Figure 3-7. In a recent case where I used this technique, I was at the end of my work day. I was on my way home, and I felt disturbed. I had a sense of unease that I could not attribute to anything specific. I then reflected back on the day and the exchanges I had with various people on my project. I

Figure 3-7: Backtracking Process.

thought about all the meetings and the conversations. And then it struck me very clearly. In my meeting with my manager, he was critical of one of my team members. That criticism hurt.

The criticism hurt on several levels. First, it hurt because I knew it was true. My manager was right in his assessment of my team member, and I knew it. I felt personally criticized, as if I should have done a better job. I felt as if I should have acted sooner to address this performance issue. I even felt scared that I was perceived as not performing at my highest level. Second, it hurt because I liked this particular team member. I felt defensive because he was doing so many positive things. Third, it hurt because I knew I needed to act on the situation, and I was reluctant to do that. I knew that it would mean taking this person off the team. That made me feel sad.

When I backtracked over the day and identified this exchange, it was easy to understand how I felt. There was a mix of negative feelings at that moment. After the meeting with my manager that day, I had moved on with other meetings and discussions and those negative feelings moved to the background. It was as if my subconscious didn't want me to dwell on those thoughts. That worked to insulate me from my feelings until I slowed down at the end of the day. At that point, I was unable to keep the negative feelings at bay any longer.

My wife sometimes helps me to backtrack. If I come home from work in a less than positive state, she may say something like "so what is going on with you?" She will force me to think back over the day to determine why I am sad, angry, or scared. It works. By backtracking through my day, I can identify what happened to cause me to feel the way I do.

Whether you do it alone or with the help of another, the backtracking technique can be helpful to understand what you are feeling in the moment. When you feel some discomfort or unease and are unable to pinpoint the cause, review your day and the interactions you had with others. This will often help you to identify the source and the specific feeling you are experiencing. That will put you in a position to do something about it.

7. Use Quiet Time

The seventh technique is using quiet time. It could also be called reflection or meditation time. You could use prayer, meditation, reflection, yoga, breathing exercises, or any other technique that helps you to relax and tune in to yourself. It is all about ways of getting in touch with what you are feeling right now. As with all the awareness techniques, it is about focusing on the here and now.

It can be difficult to find quiet time in the course of our full and busy lives. The fullness and busyness can be used to avoid getting in touch with ourselves. The antidote to this busyness is to slow down, be quiet, and get in touch with our emotions.

If you already have a practice of using prayer, meditation, or breathing exercises, then continue that technique that works best for you. If you don't have experience with a particular technique, experiment to see what works best for you. There are plenty of resources available to you on the Web and in your community. But you really don't need anything other than yourself for this. You can simply sit quietly and breathe deeply. Try to put the noise of the day out of your mind and get in touch with what you are feeling.

It may sound simple, but please give it a try before you dismiss it. When I take the time to do this, I am often surprised by the results. It has helped me to recognize a pattern of feelings that I experience around travel. Every month I make one or two trips to teach courses out of town. It is typical for me to fly out on Sunday afternoon for a class that starts on Monday morning. Invariably, I get scared and anxious as the weekend approaches until I peak sometime Sunday afternoon when I am frantically packing the materials I need for my class while the taxi waits in the driveway to take me to the airport. By then, I have myself in a complete tizzy running around frazzled instead of taking a quiet moment to say goodbye to my wife and children.

I don't mind traveling and I enjoy teaching classes. But both require a certain level of effort and attention. Travel often includes delays and disappointments. Classes can bring surprises and a level of performance anxiety because of the importance of doing a good job. As a result, I feel anxious about going out of town for these classes.

It wasn't until I took the time to get quiet with myself that I recognized this pattern. I prayed about the weekend and realized how scared I was about traveling. Then I recognized that I always feel scared leading up to these trips. That gave me the power to do something about my feelings. I began to prepare earlier and spend quality time with my family prior to my trips.

Whether you pray, meditate, use breathing techniques, or simply reflect quietly, use quiet time to get more in touch with yourself. Focus on what you are feeling now, in the moment.

8. Track your Reactivity

As we discussed, reactivity to others provides meaningful information about ourselves. I recommend that you create a reactivity journal and begin to track your reactivity to others. Make a note every time that someone does something that bugs you, or you find yourself getting angry about something. It is really simple to do—just record the person and event that made you reactive.

I challenge you to do this for a week and see what you learn about yourself. It may sound easy or dumb but I want to encourage you to simply try it. I practiced this for a week recently and easily captured 28 items. It is easy when you are as reactive as I am! Those 28 items provided information about my thoughts and emotions that revealed things I was not fully aware of, or able to access directly.

■ Personal Action Plan: Self-Awareness

The first building block of emotional intelligence is self-awareness. Self-awareness is our ability to recognize our own emotions and their effects on us and others. Review and complete the Emotional Intelligence Assessment Checklist in Appendix B, if you have not already done so.

Key Takeaways

1.
2.
3.

My Strengths and Weaknesses in the Area of Self-Awareness

Strengths	Weaknesses
1.	1.
2.	2.

My Actions or Goals Based on What I Learned

1.
2.
3.

4

Self-Management

Self-management happens when we begin to use our awareness of our feelings to manage ourselves. Building on the base of self-awareness, we use that information to control and manage our emotions. Self-management is the ability to control our emotions so that they don't control us. That is the simple but powerful truth about self-management. We need to use what we know about our emotions to control and manage those emotions and our behavior. This includes techniques that help us to regulate our emotions, to identify and prevent emotional triggers, and to identify and prevent thinking that can lead to emotional breakdowns.

Why is it important to manage our emotions? The alternative is not very attractive. Individuals who don't manage their emotions in the business world are called rage-aholics and drama queens. They cause others to sigh, roll their eyes, even leave the room in fright, and respond themselves with anger. It should go without saying that if you cannot manage yourself you cannot manage others. No one wants to follow someone who is not in control of himself or herself. The stereotypical boss who is valued because he or she uses whatever means necessary to get the results from a team is a relic of the past.

I had a caveman manager like that for several years. He was a loose cannon; a rage-aholic who survived only because he achieved results. I worked for him on a couple of large projects and he had the same *modus operandi*—to berate people, run roughshod over them, and intimidate them into performing as he wanted. And it didn't matter if you were on his team or somehow in the way of his success. He treated everyone the same.

61

In fairness to this manager, the stakes were high, and it was a high pressure job. We were involved in recovering red projects, that is, projects that were failing. The environment was very stressful. That said, the end did not justify the means. There were better ways of achieving the results. The manager simply was not able to use any other means because he did not have control over his emotions.

When I worked for this manager years ago, he was valued by the organization for the results he was able to achieve. These days, I don't think that organizations tolerate or want that kind of behavior. They want positive results, of course, but are unwilling to sanction caveman-like methods that reflect a lack of emotional self-control. PMs and leaders today are expected to be in control of themselves and their emotions.

That is not to say that anger doesn't have a place in business or in project management. Channeled productively, anger can move us and our project team members better than any other emotion. The key is to have control over anger, just as we need to control all of our emotions. That is all part of self-management.

PMs and leaders of all types need to control themselves and manage their emotions. They cannot afford to let their emotions overtake them and dictate their behavior or they will find they aren't leading anyone for very long.

■ The Emotional Intelligence Model for Project Management

In Figure 4-1, we show the emotional intelligence model for project management and the domain of self-management. As shown in the diagram, self-management includes the single competency of self-control. Self-control is the ability to be in control of our emotions so that they do not control us.

Self-Awareness Precedes Self-Management

Self-awareness is a necessary predecessor to self-management and self-control. After all, if we don't know what we are feeling it can be difficult to do anything about it. Awareness can be a big help when it comes to managing negative emotions. When we are feeling a negative emotion, we can often disarm or control the impact of that feeling just by being aware of what it is and why we are feeling it.

For example, if I feel scared before a meeting with an important client, I can often calm myself simply by naming the feeling and acknowledging the reasons for it. Once I realize that I am scared, I can do something about it.

Figure 4-1: Emotional Intelligence Framework Showing Self-Management.

Almost anytime I am doing something important, I am going to feel scared. So when I feel scared, I simply remind myself that this means it is important. Meetings scare me because they are important. Recognizing that I am scared because the meeting is important to me is usually enough to calm me and remind me that my feelings (fear in this case) are serving me.

■ Self-Control

What Is Self-Control?

Self-control is the ability to remain composed in spite of our emotional state. This does not mean forcing a smile when we are sad or angry. It does mean registering sad and angry feelings, as well as controlling our reaction to those feelings. For most PMs, managing the negative feelings is going to be the biggest priority.

Negative Feelings Can Cripple a Team

In a team environment, negative emotions can be crippling, especially when they stem from the leader. This environment provides plenty of opportunities to practice self-management. Emotions can run rampant on projects where the stakes are high for both individuals and organizations.

Projects can be stressful due to the constraints placed on them. Deadlines are usually aggressive if not downright unrealistic. Budgets are often set without regard to the work required. The scope of work can be unrealistic or subject to interpretation or negotiation. They often involve doing things for the first time. Many PMs take the success or failure of the project personally. These factors can place a lot of pressure on the them. PMs need to learn to manage their own stress and calm others by their example.

All of this can cause negative emotions in the project team and the PM. Negative emotions can poison the project environment, especially those emanating from the leader. Anger, disappointment, rage, sadness, and fear all need to be monitored and managed so that they don't impact the rest of the team. That doesn't mean stuffing these emotions, dismissing them, or pretending they don't exist. It does mean managing those emotions.

There is nothing like the pressure of an intense project to bring out the best and the worst in us. Any tiny crack in our emotional foundation is brought to light and often, when exposed to heat and pressure, it will result in unpleasant side effects. Tough times tend to reveal our true emotional nature.

If we don't manage our emotions in the project environment, very bad things can happen. In addition to poisoning the atmosphere of the team, we can get a reputation for being out of control. Others may avoid working with us and our team. We may have a difficult time retaining the best resources, and we will tend to attract team members who are comfortable working in negative environments. Our team members might quietly try to sabotage the project. Our relationships with stakeholders will suffer.

I have been there myself. Sadly, I have lost control of my emotions on a project more than once. Sometimes the consequences were no big deal, and the project moved on. Other times, my lack of emotional control hurt me and my team.

In one particularly painful example, I was managing a large international project. I had a poor relationship with one of the team leads working for me. The relationship had deteriorated to the point where it was adversarial. There was an ongoing battle of wills about this team lead's travel to the client site. It culminated one day when my team lead sent me another travel request via e-mail. I was incensed and had reached my breaking point. I was also feeling under pressure due to some criticism from the client about the project team's performance. Without thinking about my reaction or waiting to calm down, I replied to the e-mail in a terse and critical way. The team member was angry about my response and escalated it to my manager, who called me to ask "What gives?" It was embarrassing. Worse, it led to a painful, formal investigation that dragged on for two months.

Of the many mistakes that I made in this situation, the main one was that I responded inappropriately out of anger. I should have calmed down, evaluated alternative courses of action, and then chosen an appropriate response. I also should have been addressing the underlying relationship breakdown that was the undercurrent for the issue. As it was, I responded too quickly and emotionally, without thinking. I was not managing myself. The e-mail response was the single event that I wish I could have taken back.

In this particular situation, the e-mail and the formal investigation showed that I needed to manage myself better. When the investigation had run its course, the individual felt he could no longer work for me and left the project. That turned out to be very helpful to me and to the overall project. It was something I wish I had addressed sooner and directly.

Self-Control Is for All Emotions

As noted, self-control is critical for negative emotions because they can poison the atmosphere in a team. But we also need to exercise control over our expression of positive emotions.

Consider a situation in which you are happy and excited over the achievement of a significant milestone just prior to a meeting with a team member who is upset about a conflict. Exhibiting your positive emotions would be inappropriate in this discussion, just as they would be in a situation when someone has just received bad news, such as a death in the family. As the PM, you may need to dampen your excitement or happiness in such situations.

There are lots of opportunities for emotional self-control on a long project. In fact, being on a prolonged project can be like riding an emotional roller coaster. The longest project I ever managed was three years. During that time, the team went through a lot of emotions. We reached six major client milestones and numerous minor milestones. We kicked off new years, new phases of the engagement, and new initiatives. As a team of nearly 100 people, we experienced promotions, demotions, firings, resignations, the births of babies, marriages, and deaths in our families.

Over the course of that project, it was important that I managed my emotions. I shared the excitement of reaching important milestones with one part of the team while sharing sadness over the loss of a key resource in another part of the team. I also had a team lead who lost his father and father-in-law within six months. It was critical that I managed both the highs and the lows during this time.

The larger the team and the longer the project, the more likely it is that you will have a wide range of emotions at any one time. As the PM and leader of the team, you have to be balanced and not go to extremes. This requires a high degree of emotional self-control.

Self-Control Helps Us Avoid Emotional Breakdowns

An emotional breakdown is an involuntary response to an emotional situation. We are "losing it" when we have an emotional breakdown. Road rage is an extreme form of emotional breakdown. Individuals who experience road rage become unpredictable and out of control. Unfortunately, we don't see a physical sign like the one in Figure 4-2 warning us of impending emotional breakdowns.

While road rage may be unheard of in a project environment, emotional breakdowns are not. The stress and strain of everyday life can cause emotional breakdowns. Add to that a challenging project environment and the likelihood of emotional breakdowns is very high.

In *Emotional Intelligence*, Daniel Goleman uses the term "emotional hijacking" for these breakdowns. He contends that our emotions are hijacked by our primitive neurological systems. These systems were designed for our protection and survival. They also set us up for emotional hijacking, which is an extreme form of the fight or flight response mechanism.[1] Let's take a closer look at what is involved in an emotional hijacking.

Emotional Hijacking

If we were to diagram it, an emotional hijacking might look like the picture in Figure 4-3 below. When we get a stimulus, which is generally either people or events, it will either lead us to a swift emotional reaction or to a thoughtful response.

---

[1] Daniel Goleman. *Emotional Intelligence: Why It Can Matter More Than IQ.* NY: Random House/Bantam Books, 1995.

Figure 4-2: Warning of Emotional Breakdown Ahead.

Respond Don't React

Ironically, the same stimulus can cause us to have either a reaction or a response, depending on our emotional state and our interpretation of the events. Consider the case where you are driving on a highway. If someone were to cut you off, you may have either a reaction or a response. If I am in a good mood and not in a hurry to get somewhere, I might just give a wave to someone who cut in front of me on the highway. This would be a response, something that I chose. If I were having a bad day, fighting with my wife, or

Figure 4-3: Respond, Don't React.

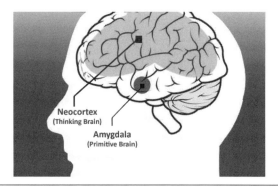

Figure 4-4: Thinking Brain and the Amygdala.

had just received a critical performance review, the same exact scenario might lead me to an automatic reaction.

The difference between these two alternatives is what happens in our brain. We actually have two brain systems—our primitive brain, made up of the amygdala and the limbic system, and our thinking brain, made up of the neocortex (see Figure 4-4). Our primitive brain is hardwired to react to specific threats. This is the fight-or-flight fight response which is there for survival. When the amygdala is under a heightened state of alert, it can go off with little provocation. Properly stimulated, the primitive brain causes us to react without engaging our neocortex or thinking brain. The primitive brain is faster, and it can actually prevent the thinking brain from engaging. Literally, we act without thinking.

Thinking Brain and Amygdala
Whether we call that an emotional hijacking or emotional breakdown, the result is the same; our emotions have taken over, and we are not in control. Emotional breakdowns are involuntary. We are reacting to an event without control of our behavior.

The alternative approach is to choose a thoughtful response, which needs to come from the neocortex. How can we think about a response if the neocortex is slower than the primitive brain? The key is to calm the amygdala and slow things down long enough to allow ourselves to think. We need to stay cool.

The best PMs tend to stay positive and unflappable no matter what comes their way. I am jealous of those men and women. For my part, I have to continually strive to do better and better in this area.

I once hired a project leader based on his stated ability not to lose it. I knew that I felt under pressure on this particular project and that I needed someone who would remain cool. In the interview, he said that he prided himself on "staying one degree cooler than everyone else in the room." That was critical for us on this particular project and his statement got him the job. We worked well together for two years and during that time, true to his word, he was usually one degree cooler than everyone else.

What is this ability to stay one degree cooler than everyone else? This is what some experts refer to as emotional resilience. Emotional resilience helps us to maintain calm when others are losing it.

Not everyone is able to stay cooler than everyone else. In fact, many people experience some sort of emotional breakdown during work. Each person may have one breakdown that is more likely to occur than any other. Here are some examples of emotional breakdowns that you might see in a project environment:

1. Angry Tirades

Whether at work, in public, or in private, we have all seen someone explode with anger and blast someone else. We may know individuals who are likely to explode. Perhaps we even avoid certain people for fear they will blow up on us.

2. Door Slamming

Not able to take any more, a person leaves the room and slams the door behind them. Our modern offices today are more likely to be open cubicles, so instead of door slamming, you might hear phone slamming or mouse slamming.

3. E-mail Letter Bomb

Our modern office tools make sending an angry e-mail easier than ever. This is a common way for people to vent anger on a project. Most of us have probably sent something we wish we hadn't, or we have seen others do it. It's not pretty, and it says a lot more about the sender than the recipient.

4. Withdrawal and Isolation

This is when people pull away, avoid meetings, and perhaps even dodge specific people on the project.

5. Holding Grudges and Getting Even

Holding grudges often comes in response to unfavorable decisions being made, criticism received, or some other perceived slight. This type of breakdown often results in a secret vow to get even. A score may even be kept of who is winning and who is losing. This breakdown is especially harmful because it may be secret and it can go on for a long time.

6. Criticizing

This breakdown results in criticism intended to hurt another. Unwarranted criticism often comes from individuals who are feeling insecure, threatened, or emotionally vulnerable. Criticism is often the response to the hurt we feel. Criticism may be buried in helpful sounding remarks or it may be out in the open. Either way, the impact is the same.

7. Sarcasm and Inappropriate Humor

Sarcasm is a red flag for emotional breakdowns as discussed in Chapter 3. Both sarcasm and inappropriate humor are learned responses to situations in which we don't want to address the truth directly.

8. Playing the Victim

Playing the victim is also one of the red flags for emotional breakdowns that we discussed in Chapter 3. When people play the victim, they act powerless and not responsible for their actions. They will blame someone (or perhaps the entire world) for their situation and their actions. This is disempowering to the individual and unacceptable to the team.

How many of these emotional breakdowns do you experience? Look at the list and reflect on last week, last month, and last year. Have you had more than one of these? Do you experience all of these or have one or two preferred breakdowns?

My own common breakdowns include e-mail letter bombs, criticizing, sarcasm, and inappropriate humor. I have become aware enough to eliminate many of these responses from my repertoire, and I have the grace and peace of mind to not go down on myself if I have a relapse. I just say "There I go again" and try to determine what caused the emotional breakdown.

If you are having trouble identifying your emotional breakdowns, try getting some input from others. Take the time to ask your peers, team members, or your spouse how they see you. They will be glad you are investing in yourself and you might be surprised to learn more about yourself from them.

Emotional Breakdowns May Be Preceded by Emotional Triggers

Specific emotional breakdowns may be traced back to emotional triggers. An emotional trigger is a situation, external stimulus, or activating event that leaves us vulnerable to emotional breakdown. Triggers are not necessarily the cause of the breakdown, but they serve as a catalyst or provide fertile ground for a breakdown.

One way we can protect ourselves against emotional breakdowns is to identify the emotional triggers that immediately precede breakdowns. By sensitizing ourselves to what leads to the breakdown, we can break the cycle.

Adele Lynn identified the following ten emotional triggers in her book *The EQ Difference: A Powerful Plan for Putting Emotional Intelligence to Work.*

- Moods and attitudes of others
- Pre-thinking or foreshadowing
- Dwelling
- Personality
- Hot words/hot buttons
- Perceived criticism
- Physical environment
- Illness or physical conditions
- Situations[2]

You may recognize many of these emotional triggers at work in the project environment.

Moods and Attitudes of Others

Most of us are vulnerable to the moods and attitudes of others. When others are feeling down or angry, it can have a negative impact on us, leaving us open to an emotional breakdown.

This has been the case for me as a result of growing up with an alcoholic father. In my childhood, I was acutely attuned to the moods of my dad. It was one of the ways I tried (unsuccessfully) to control my chaotic home environment. If my dad was in a good mood, I could let up and relax a little. If he wasn't, well, then I was on edge and always on the lookout for some kind of trouble.

Do you take your cue on how to feel from how those around you feel? Do you get bummed out when your boss is angry or sad? Do you ever say "Well, I was in a good mood until you called me" or something like that? If this applies to you, consider taking the following actions to understand and begin to protect yourself from emotional breakdown:

1. Who Is It?
Try to evaluate whose moods make you feel the most vulnerable. It could be your spouse or your parents. Perhaps, like me, you are vulnerable to your boss or other authority figures. Determine who it is that causes this trigger for you.

---

[2]Adele B. Lynn. *EQ Difference: A Powerful Plan for Putting Emotional Intelligence to Work*. New York: AMACOM Books, 2005.

2. Why Is It?

If possible, try to understand why you feel vulnerable. Is it because you grew up with a parent with addiction or boundary issues? Or is it because you want so much to please your spouse or fear the loss of their love? The cause may be easy to understand, or it could require some help from a trained therapist.

3. Cut the Cord

Try to desensitize yourself to the moods of others as much as you can. Envision yourself with this key person who is in a bad mood. Practice laughing a little and saying "Wow, you sure are in a bad mood today" or something similar.

4. Don't Take It Personally

Don't personalize or try to control how the other person feels. They are responsible for their feelings, just as you are responsible for your own. If they are reacting to something you said or did, let them have their reaction. Don't walk on eggshells when you are around them or try to cushion the blow of what you say.

For some people, just becoming aware of the connection between the breakdown and the moods of others can be enlightening. It is the first step toward choosing different, healthier responses.

■ Prethinking or Foreshadowing

Foreshadowing is when we predict negative outcomes or events in the future. For example, when we experience some critical issue that threatens to delay our project, we may predict that our client is going to be upset or, worse, that the project will be cancelled.

Some of us, myself included, have a tendency to anticipate the worst. We may even pride ourselves on being able to see the worst in every future situation. But in the project environment, this can be both a deadly poison to team morale as well as a trigger for emotional breakdown.

Chicken Little was one of those who anticipated negative future events. Chicken Little interpreted a small piece of evidence (a falling acorn, I think) to mean that the entire sky was falling. Of course, the sky was not falling and eventually Chicken Little learned a valuable lesson—learn more about emotional intelligence.

Before you e-mail me about proper risk management for a project, let me distinguish between unhealthy foreshadowing and proper risk planning.

PMs need to address risks, as well as to have a healthy skepticism about potential outcomes of tasks and projects. They need to be able to challenge overly optimistic estimates and outcomes and help the team plan for risks and the unexpected. That is all a part of being a good PM. That is not the type of negative foreshadowing I am discussing.

Behind foreshadowing is fear, which leads to irrational thoughts. For me, it became apparent as I worked with a coach that I was predicting negativity in the future. I began to see that I frequently talked as if I was about to be fired or cut from the project team. I often tied this to some negative vibes I was picking up or news that I heard. My coach helped me to see that it was irrational and unhealthy and could even become a self-fulfilling prophecy. When I lacked self-confidence and acted out of fear, I was short and critical of others. This in turn reduced productivity and caused others to question my leadership. Fortunately I was able to break the cycle and avoid being fired.

Here are some steps you can take if you find yourself foreshadowing:

1. Identify the Pattern

The first step is to identify the pattern of negative thinking. First, keep a journal of your negative predictions and track the outcomes. Second, check it out with your boss. This will only be possible to the extent you have an open relationship with your superior and trust it will not backfire. Third, develop a trust relationship with a friend or coworker and use that person as a sounding board. Check out your thoughts and negative predictions and ask what that person thinks. The more objective that other person can be, the better. Someone that works for you is less likely to be objective than a spouse or a peer.

2. Interrupt the Foreshadowing with Logic

Once you see the pattern, try to interrupt it with logic. Be patient; this can involve some level of internal strife. When my coach began to point out my negative thinking to me, I resisted. I was vested in seeing the negative, and I wanted to continue as I always had. I was mired in it, and it was comfortable. It took time to recognize that after two and a half years on a stressful project engagement, I wasn't on the verge of being fired.

It also helps sometimes to say "There I go again" when you catch yourself predicting negativity. Laugh aloud and say "Whew, glad that isn't really going to happen."

Breaking a pattern like foreshadowing can be difficult; in particular if you have done it for as long as you can remember. Remember that change is possible and with change comes a tremendous payoff.

Dwelling

Dwelling occurs when we become fixated on one particular thought, remark, event, injury, or outcome. Our minds obsess and that incident becomes the focus of all our attention. We become stuck. This dramatically impacts our performance and leaves us vulnerable to emotional breakdown.

Have you ever found yourself dwelling or obsessing over something? If you have, you know that you cannot perform well as a PM. It reminds me of the behavior of my computer when it is busy doing something else in background when I am trying to use it. Even the simplest task can be slow. The program may say it is "not responding" and will sometimes even crash. That is probably how you appear to your stakeholders when you are dwelling and obsessing and they need something from you.

I have fallen prey to dwelling and obsessing on a minor scale. My mind got stuck on something and then just churned away. It was not enough to prevent me from being effective, but it did keep me awake at night on several occasions.

I have also had people who worked for me become so obsessed and stuck on things that they were unable to perform at acceptable levels. In one particular case, it began to affect his interpretation of events. He began to misinterpret things that were said, to take every comment as a personal attack, and to become overwhelmed. No matter what was said, the team member seemed to hear "You are not good enough." This was not actually the case, and it caused him to become ineffective.

Let's hope that you do not suffer from dwelling and obsessing on that same scale. As PMs, we can easily become obsessed with our performance and that of our team, as well as on the success of the project. Here are some ideas for dealing with this behavior if you find yourself falling into that trap on your project.

Become Aware

First, be aware of the behavior and see it for what it is. Sometimes it is enough to simply acknowledge it in order to break the cycle. If you have a tendency to dwell and obsess, become alert to signs that you are getting sucked in.

Get Clear

Take action to be clear or to get over it. Whatever the hurt, it probably tracks back to some injury caused by someone else. What do you need to do or say that would help you feel okay? This might mean having a difficult conversation with someone about their behavior. It is amazing how often taking a simple but courageous step can relieve us from the obsession.

Recharge

If you find yourself dwelling or obsessing, evaluate whether you are getting enough rest and downtime away from the project. Some time away may help to keep your emotions in check. Also, invest in hobbies; in particular those that involve other people. Try also taking regular vacations that are long enough to allow full relaxation.

Break the Link

If a particular person is the root of your obsessions, try to get as far away from that person as possible. While not as effective as getting clear, it may help to eliminate the obsessive behavior.

Don't Try NOT to Think About It

Sometimes, if we are consciously trying not to think about something we find we cannot stop. Instead, dedicate a specific time to dwell, obsess, and worry about it. Limit this time to something reasonable like ten to twenty minutes at the end of the day. You might find that having a specific time set aside for dwelling allows you to get it out of your system and then put your mind back on what is important.

Relax

Try relaxation techniques, such as breathing, prayer, or meditation. These can often break the cycle.

Tease Yourself

If we take ourselves too seriously, we often set up conditions that lead to obsession. Try teasing yourself about how silly you are being. Sometimes you can acknowledge the behavior and poke a little light-hearted fun at yourself.

Seek Professional Help

If you are unable to break the cycle on your own, it might be helpful to enlist the help of a professional. Your mental health and professional performance is worth whatever it costs to eliminate dwelling and obsessing from your life.

If your mind is dwelling and obsessing, you will not be open and available to work on your project, and you won't be much of a PM or a leader. Do what you need to do to remove obsessions; this will also protect you against emotional breakdowns.

Hot Words and Hot Buttons

The focus of the following section is on triggers that affect many of us: hot words and hot buttons. A hot word or hot button is a word or issue that triggers a specific and undesirable behavior in us, leaving us open to threats.

I recently had a team member whose hot button was failure. He was acutely attuned to feelings of failure and was on the lookout for that condition. This stemmed from the fact that he perceived himself as a failure. No data supported his feelings of failure about himself. Those feelings came from an internal sense of inadequacy that no amount of striving would overcome.

Whether it was rational or true, the individual had this sense of failure about himself. He also projected on me that I was saying he was a failure. I did not feel this way about the man and valued him as part of the team. However, the words I used triggered him to feel like a failure. When I told him that I did not believe "the team would succeed" using a particular process, he heard "you are a failure." My style of challenging people to perform at a higher level backfired; all he heard was criticism. It would have been more effective to congratulate, acknowledge, and give recognition. This very capable team lead eventually had an emotional breakdown.

Give Yourself a Checkup

Think for a moment about the hot buttons or hot issues that trigger you. Are there any specific concerns that you tend to react to or that cause you to blow up? Do you think that others avoid bringing up issues to sidestep an argument with you?

Here are some things you can do if you want to understand your own hot buttons.

Get a Second Opinion

One quick way to get more input on your hot words or hot buttons is to check with someone you trust. There is no substitute for including others in your analysis and getting honest and accurate insights. More often than not, when we suffer from issues, it is because we are trying to work it out on our own. As noted before, this input could come from a spouse or significant other, a trusted coworker, or a coach or mentor. Ask them if there are issues that they feel they cannot discuss with you.

Go Beyond the Hot Button

Once you know you have a hot button, take steps to determine the underlying issue and feelings (e.g., feeling like a failure, lack of self-confidence).

What is really going on for you? If you are struggling with self-confidence or inadequacy, perhaps you need to focus on that issue rather than the actual hot button or hot word.

As with the other emotional triggers, it may help to laugh at ourselves when we find that a hot button has set us off. We may also need to seek professional help.

Criticism and Blame

Criticism and blame can often be triggers for emotional breakdown. This is particularly true when the criticism is unwarranted, particularly if we feel that we were not fairly treated or were not given a chance to explain or defend ourselves. The criticism doesn't even have to be real; perceived criticism can also trigger an undesired response from us.

Criticism and feeling blamed have been a problem for me in the past. If I thought someone else was being critical of me, I would feel deflated and depressed. The criticism hurt because it resonated with what I already felt about myself. I was my own worst critic. My discussions with others leads me to believe that this is very common and that many people are their own worst critics.

Unfortunately for me, my past response to criticism or blame was to freak out and immediately turn around and blame someone else. When problems occurred, I was often short with people, I lacked tact and empathy, and I immediately would dig in to figure out exactly who was responsible for the problem. This led to some ugly confrontations on past projects. This has been one of my most common emotional breakdowns.

The good news is that over the last few years I have learned to deal with criticism in healthier ways. Here are some of the ways I now deal with criticism and blame.

My Own Worst Enemy

With some work I have learned to recognize when I am being my own worst critic. Only rarely do I find that others are criticizing me; more often it is just me. If I can eliminate the voice in my head that criticizes my work, I can overcome the feeling of being criticized.

Look Ahead

Anticipate situations where I will feel or be criticized by others. Often, I know ahead of time when I am vulnerable to feeling criticized. If I do, I can visualize criticism coming from others and then practice healthy reactions. One healthy reaction is to calmly turn around and ask the critic what is going on with them or why they feel the need to criticize.

Check It Out
In some situations, we perceive criticism that is actually not criticism. Check it out to determine first if it is actually criticism and, second, if that criticism is meant for you. Sometimes we may be reacting to comments or feedback from others that is meant to be helpful and not critical. Instead of personalizing someone's comments as criticism or blame, check it out. Ask the other person what they meant by their remark. If you receive true criticism, evaluate what part of that criticism you can use. Discard the rest.

The New Wheaties
When I was a kid, Wheaties was called the breakfast of champions. A former coworker taught me that feedback is actually the breakfast of champions. If we want to be champions, we need to be open to feedback. We may even need to go so far as to seek it out.

Could Be Just Them
Sometimes we need to be reminded that other people have their own opinions and that doesn't make them right. Also, many people, myself included, are not that good at providing constructive feedback. So before we overreact to some comment from someone else, we need to consider the source. More often than not, criticism says more about the person who criticizes than the one receiving the criticism. Sometimes we need to ignore or discount the feedback from others.

Doesn't Change Anything
Remember that even if true, criticism and blame do not make you a bad person.

Set a Mistake Quota
Mistakes are part of being human, and we all should expect to make them if we are growing. If you are not making mistakes, you are not trying hard enough. You may want to consider setting a quota of mistakes each day or week. I used to joke with a project team that we would strive to make only new and very creative mistakes. We certainly should not make the same mistakes, of course, but our focus should be more on success than on not making mistakes. If your goal is to not make a mistake, you will be too cautious to be effective at anything.

Finally, I would like to refer to the words of Theodore Roosevelt and his view of critics. Though these words of his are often quoted, they are worth repeating.

> "It is not the critic who counts, not the man who points out how the strong man stumbled, or where the doer of deeds could have done better. The credit belongs to the man who is actually in the arena; whose face is marred by the dust and sweat and blood; who strives valiantly; who errs and comes short again and again; who knows the great enthusiasms, the great devotions and spends himself in a worthy cause; who at the best, knows in the end the triumph of high achievement, and who, at worst, if he fails, at least fails while daring greatly; so that his place shall never be with those cold and timid souls who know neither victory or defeat."
> —Theodore Roosevelt

Physical Environment

Our physical work environment and specific situations can leave us vulnerable to emotional breakdowns. This should not be surprising. Imagine how you feel when you are in environments that are hot, cold, noisy, cluttered, filthy, or isolated. If we are not physically comfortable, we may be vulnerable to an emotional breakdown.

There also may be specific situations that leave us emotionally vulnerable. For example, I feel vulnerable when I am in a large crowd of people. I also find that the winters in Chicago cause me to feel vulnerable to breakdowns. Chicago in the summer is a tremendous playground. However, in the winter it is more like Gotham City. The days often seem cold, gray, and so dreary that they suck the life out of you. It can really make you appreciate the few sunny days we experience during the winter!

Illness and Fatigue

Illness and fatigue can also leave us vulnerable to an emotional breakdown. Like our environment, they can leave us feeling less than our best. When we don't feel well or are extremely tired, we let down our guard and become vulnerable to emotional breakdowns. An extreme example of this would be individuals experiencing some type of chronic pain. It is hard to show grace and not react emotionally when you are experiencing chronic pain. In a similar way, fatigue can leave us vulnerable to a breakdown. I know that if I don't get enough sleep and let myself get run down, I risk making emotional mistakes.

The idea of the triggers is to be aware of the conditions for failure and see that as a sign of risk. I can mitigate the risk, when I recognize it, by taking immediate action to remove myself from the situation. This might include stepping out of the building for some fresh air or going home for the day. This could be getting something healthy to eat or going to the gym.

Stinking Thinking Can Cause Emotional Breakdowns

There is one more type of emotional breakdown, and it is caused by the way we think. As strange as it sounds, we can affect the way we are feeling based on our thoughts. It is through distorted thinking that we set ourselves up for an emotional breakdown.

This distorted thinking is also called stinking thinking. We can literally think ourselves into feeling bad and that can leave us vulnerable to an emotional breakdown. Just when things seem to be going well, our mind convinces us that things are falling apart. It seems that we self-sabotage. Negativity, despair, and global thinking are the keys themes that I notice. See if you can relate to any of these or if they are causing emotional breakdowns for you.

1. All or Nothing Thinking

With all or nothing thinking, we see things as a total failure if they fall short of perfect. We see no good in an imperfect situation.

As an example, consider what happened to me recently on a return trip from Washington, DC, to Chicago. My class in DC finished early, and I sprinted to the airport with the hopes of catching an earlier flight. As it turned out, I was able to leave on a flight that was one hour earlier. However, I had to give up my first class upgrade and sit in a middle seat in coach. I felt a sense of loss and was angry as I flew from Washington to Chicago in that center seat in economy class.

When I arrived at home that evening and my wife asked me about the trip, I said it was awful. Although I did get home earlier than planned, I considered it a bad trip because I did not get everything I wanted. I was unable to see beyond the fact that I gave up my first-class seat. Beware of all-or-nothing thinking. If you find yourself doing this, try to turn it around and affirm what went right. Try to recognize that things (and people) will never be perfect.

2. Always and Never

Another form of stinking thinking is when we see one negative event as a never-ending series of defeats or failures. The clue to this type of thinking is when we use words like always and never. This sounds like my daughter when she says "We never get to do anything fun."

Do you use words like always and never? When you and your project team need to work through a weekend, do you find yourself thinking "We always have to work on our weekends," or "I never get any time to myself?" If someone else gets promoted, do you think "I never get considered for better jobs?" When we use the terms all or never, we are choosing to be a victim of circumstances and viewing life as beyond our control.

The key to breaking this type of thinking is to be alert to the use of the words "always" and "never." Rarely is it true that things are always or never a certain way. Instead of using always or never, look for and acknowledge the exceptions. More important, empower yourself by thinking through the ways that you can create different outcomes for yourself. If you feel like you never have enough time for yourself or you want a better job, determine what steps you can take now to have more time or get that better job. Remind yourself that you have a say in the outcome of your life.

3. Being Negative

Being negative is when we choose to focus only on the disagreeable things that happen. If we dwell on the negative, that becomes our reality.

I did this recently after teaching a class. In this case, there were twenty-six students. As I went through the students' evaluations of the course, one was particularly harsh. The student felt there were "too many irrelevant stories" and that I should have "kept the class moving." While the other twenty-five evaluations were all very positive, I focused only on the one negative evaluation.

Another situation occurred on a large, long-term project I was managing. At the end of the first year, we solicited feedback from our clients on how we were doing. There was a mix of positive and constructive feedback. I chose to focus on one negative statement. The client stated that the delivery of "software was often late and of poor quality." To this day, that is the only piece of feedback that I remember.

In both of these cases, I vividly remember the negative comments and little, if anything, else. I chose to focus only on the negative.

We can also be negative by ignoring or discounting the positives. Instead of focusing on the negative, we choose to discount or reject examples where we did well or were successful. We find a reason for the positive not to count because it wasn't good enough or because anyone would have done the same thing if they were in our shoes. This type of thinking really strips us of the happiness and satisfaction we should experience.

I sometimes do this to myself by hiding behind my project team. When there is a success on a project, I say to myself "This was the result of having a strong team" or "any PM could have succeeded in this situation."

Negative thinking and behavior can be so ingrained that you are unable to see it without the help of others. If you are a person who focuses on the negative, you may not be aware of it. You can start by asking your friends and family if they see you as a negative person.

Breaking the habit of being negative can be tough. If you do find out that you are negative, ask others for support. Practice finding the positive in every situation, in yourself and your performance, and in every other person.

4. Filling in the Blanks

We fill in the blanks when we interpret things a certain way, usually negatively, without any facts to support our interpretation. We attribute a negative interpretation to a person or situation without any justification.

For example, consider a situation in which you've submitted a project proposal to a client. If the client does not get back to you immediately, you may jump to the conclusion that they did not like you or your proposal. You may start to think things like "that was a waste of time, I shouldn't have spent my time working on that." A more accurate interpretation is that you simply expected the client to respond faster than they actually did.

5. Should Statements

The word "should" is a red flag. It has many negative connotations and where possible I advise you to strike it from your vocabulary. When someone tells you that you should do something or should have done something, they are meddling, controlling, or shaming you. Should is a word that makes the hair on the back of my neck stand up.

You may direct should statements at yourself with the intent to motivate. You might say something like "I should have known better than to trust Jeremy" or "I shouldn't have told them they could take until Monday on the deliverable." Should statements can lead to guilt and frustration. If you use should on yourself or on others, stop. It is unhealthy.

One way to overcome use of the word should is to use "I want" statements. Instead of saying "You should turn in your status report by Friday" (or, worse, "You should have turned in your status report last Friday"), say "I want you to turn in your status report by Friday." The expression "I want" is a more direct and clean way of stating your expectations for the desired behavior.

6. Personalization and Blame

Personalization is when we take responsibility for events that are not entirely within our control. We take personally what could be simply a random event. We might combine personalization with a should statement and say something like "I should never have said that to Jonathan; he quit the team because of me."

Personalization can be tricky for PMs and leaders. Sometimes it is entirely appropriate to take responsibility for the results or outcomes of the team we are leading. Sometimes we need to step up and say "That was my fault." However, it is not always healthy to take responsibility for everything that happens.

Blame is the opposite of personalization. This is when we are quick to affix the blame for an event or incident. Blame is when we put the responsibility for ourselves and our situation on others.

A more balanced approach is to think of the principle of co-creation. We co-create everything that happens to us. We are partly responsible and others are partly responsible. We will talk more about co-creation in Chapter 6, Relationship Management.

Identifying Your Own Patterns of Stinking Thinking

The common theme with all stinking thinking is its negative connotation. We are choosing to be negative instead of positive. This thinking often represents our own fears and dark thoughts.

The first step toward overcoming stinking thinking is to recognize what you are experiencing. This type of thinking is a habit and perhaps one that we have had all our lives. We need to be able to see and recognize the habit before we can change or eliminate it. As with the other self-management concepts we have talked about, we can use some of the following techniques to overcome distorted thinking:

Journal

Keep a journal of what has occurred—your thoughts, and your feelings. You can use this to track back and understand how your negative thoughts are impacting you.

Get Help from a Friend

Get input from a trusted friend, spouse, coworker, boss, or mentor. Use their feedback to see where your thinking is distorted.

Seek Professional Help

As noted earlier, you may need to seek professional help if you get stuck and cannot get to the next level without it.

Other Reasons to Manage Our Emotions

Avoiding emotional breakdowns is pretty important, but there are other situations where managing our emotions is also important. For example, how we manage our fear directly plays into the risks that we take and the potential rewards. Anger can also be used to our advantage is we understand how to harness it.

Managing Our Fear

There is a relationship between fear and our behavior when we are scared that can lead to success or failure. Fear can keep us from doing things that we shouldn't. Fear can also cause us to procrastinate, wait until the last moment, or not act at all. Our fear of failing in a particular situation can actually become a self-fulfilling prophecy.

I have let fear cause me to fail, and it hurt. Years ago I had an important interview for a long-term consulting engagement. I was excited about the opportunity and frankly, I wanted the position. But I was scared. And unfortunately for me, I was not aware enough at the time (i.e. self-aware) to appreciate exactly how afraid I was.

My fear was not so much about the opportunity as about the interview. I was so excited about the engagement that I was afraid I would blow it or that somehow my desire for this opportunity would be apparent.

So what did I do? Well, I let my fear nearly cause me to create the exact thing I was worried about. I procrastinated; I stalled and didn't get ready on time. I left my house late. And I arrived 15 minutes late for the interview. My fear of blowing it nearly cost me the position.

What I need is to do a better job of catching myself when I am afraid. Sometimes simply naming the fear is enough to take the energy out. It also helps me to determine what my fear is telling me. In the case of the interview, it was telling me that it was important to me. Using the fear as information is the essence of emotional self-management.

Fear can also be a positive. Looking back on my career, I realize that most of my growth took place when put myself in situations that I was in over my head and afraid. I can recall going in to work and being afraid of failing, fearing that I would not know what I was doing or that others would realize that I didn't know what I was doing. These were the times when I grew the most in terms of my experience and development.

When I was in high school, my best friend Wes was the class president. He was funny, popular, and got along with everyone. I remember every year he did something that I thought was crazy—he volunteered to be a cheerleader for the (girls) powderpuff football game. The powderpuff cheerleaders would dress up with wigs and makeup and go through some pretty silly cheers. I thought it was crazy and a bit dangerous to dress up and make a fool of himself, but Wes seemed to enjoy it. He used to ask me to join him but I never dared to push through my fear and take the risk.

Fast forward to my first job out of college as a young engineer at IBM in 1985. As project assignments were offered, other young engineers jumped at the projects, even ones that they knew little about. In contrast, I almost never volunteered for new assignments. As with the cheerleading, I wasn't anxious to jump in—frankly I was afraid.

My fear cost me. I was at IBM nearly 10 years. During that time, my career progressed, but not as fast as I would have liked. My fear prevented me from taking risks and that slowed my progress. No risk meant little or no reward. Looking back, the best thing I did at IBM was when I left my comfortable job there in 1993.

I have found that I grew the most when I pushed through my fear or put myself in tough situations. Conversely, when I was comfortable in a job, such as at IBM, I was not learning and growing. And more importantly, not adding as much value to my customers.

So I have learned that for me, feelings of comfort and familiarity are not desirable; in fact, they are dangerous to my career. That is one of the reasons that I grew to love project management so much—projects have a beginning and an end. Even long projects will come to an end and I will need to seek out something new.

As an independent consultant today, I recognize that I have no choice but to push through my fear and take risks. I have also learned that most of the fear I feel is unwarranted. It is actually more dangerous for me to get comfortable and complacent in one role—that probably means I am not growing as quickly as I could as a consultant.

The choice is obvious if you want to grow as a PM and a leader and to become more valuable to your employer and customers. You need to stop seeking comfort. You may even need to push yourself out of your comfort zone even to the point where you are burning your boats behind you. How do we know when we should seek something other than comfort? We should orient to our own satisfaction level. In every situation, we should be monitoring our own level of satisfaction and using that as an internal gauge for whether we are doing the right thing.

If you were to be completely honest right now, many of you could identify at least one goal or aspiration that you are not pursuing because of fear. I want you to encourage you to make friends with fear, to understand what it is that makes you afraid, and to evaluate the cost of that fear on your life. Courage is not the absence of fear. Rather, it is when we choose to act in spite of our fear. If you want to grow, you have to push through fear and take some risks.

Consider the following questions about the role of fear in your life:

1. What is the cost in your life right now of your fear? What could you achieve by pushing through your fear?
2. Look back over the last five years of your life and identify when you took a risk. What was the result? What did you learn?
3. What is it you are most afraid of losing right now? Do you have a comfortable management position with a safe and stable company?
4. What is your level of satisfaction with your current situation? What would be more satisfying?

My mentor Rich Blue has been on a kick lately to embrace failure. He keeps encouraging me to live a big life by saying "If you aren't failing then you are not taking enough risks."

Harnessing Our Anger

Before working on emotions, I didn't recognize that I was frequently angry. I was harsh and mean spirited when it came to anger. I never hit or choked anyone but I did use my words to give a punch or a jab whenever I was provoked. What I thought at the time were funny comments or playful jabs were in reality very mean-spirited comments that were quite hurtful to people. I am surprised my career survived at all given how unpolished I was.

The reality is that anger is power, and that power can fire us up. Instead of having it leak out in comments or mean-spirited wisecracks, we can channel our anger in constructive ways. The power anger generates can cause others to stop and listen to us; it can also move us toward our goals. We just need to manage the anger.

> ### Anger is Power!

Managing anger means that we don't get physical and hit or choke people. We are also not shouting or yelling at people, slamming doors, or making sarcastic comments. If we do that, our anger is going to get us fired. In today's highly sensitive HR environment, we need to be careful we don't respond emotionally—as with an angry outburst—and wind up saying something that lands us in trouble. We can't afford to be seen as the guy or girl with a chip on their shoulder.

Even if we don't have some sort of incident that can lead to firing, we have to be careful that we don't allow anger to affect our effectiveness. We need to use our anger strategically. It may not even require raising our voices— it may be enough to say "I noticed that I am feeling more angry as this meeting goes on."

The lesson here is that we need to pay attention to our all of our emotions and be aware of ways that may help or hurt us. Fear should be monitored, along with satisfaction level. I'm more in touch with my fear than I have been over the course of my life. But I still recognize that there are situations where I go unconscious and let my fear shut me down.

■ Techniques to Improve our Self-Control

First, remember that minor emotional breakdowns are common. Even people who have a high capacity to endure pain will eventually hit a wall and break down in some way. The good news about emotional breakdowns is that they are predictable. If we can identify the triggers that set us off, we can begin to predict when we are vulnerable and are likely to experience a breakdown. That predictability can help us avoid or reduce the severity of the breakdown.

Second, breakdowns often escalate slowly. We don't normally go from a calm and peaceful state directly into a breakdown. Rather, we go through a series of steps that build until we are primed for a breakdown. That slow escalation provides time for us to interrupt the process and prevent the breakdown. Knowing that breakdowns are predictable and escalate slowly gives us motivation to interrupt the breakdown before it occurs.

The following section talks about some of the ways to improve our self-control and emotional resiliency and reduce the likelihood and severity of our emotional breakdowns.

1. Know Thyself

As previously mentioned, the key to self-control is self-awareness. Make it a point to understand your specific emotional triggers, your patterns of stinking thinking, and things that reduce or build up your emotional resiliency. Be a student of you!

There are times when you are quite resilient to what others say, while at other times you are highly sensitive and let others push your buttons. Pay attention to those times when you let other people push your buttons. What are the specific conditions where you are likely to let your guard down? Is it when you are tired, stressed, sick, feeling unappreciated or criticized, or not taking care of yourself? Try to avoid putting yourself in those situations where you aren't able to choose a graceful response.

2. *Use HALT*

HALT stands for Hungry, Angry, Lonely, and Tired. These four conditions are warning signs that we might be vulnerable to emotional breakdowns. Conversely, they can serve as a gauge of our level of emotional resilience. Whenever you are Hungry, Angry, Lonely, or Tired, your resilience is low and you are at risk of having a negative reaction or emotional breakdown. You are less likely to make good choices about your responses to stimulus.

The key thing that the HALT acronym tells me is whether or not I am putting myself at risk. The more of the four components I am experiencing at one time, the more vulnerable I am. It is a quick test, and it works well for nearly everybody.

If you wanted to elaborate on HALT or create a more personal version, you could come up with additional things that might set you up for a break-down. This is a list of some of the things my audiences have shared with me over the years:

- Always on with WIFI and my smartphone
- Working late by myself
- Long-term conflict
- Business travel
- Long commutes
- Long and contentious meetings

3. Evaluate Your Physical Environment

Are you as comfortable as you can make yourself? What needs to change to make you comfortable? If you are isolated, what can you do to feel more con-nected? If you are a work-at-home professional, try staying connected with Instant Messaging or go to work in a public space, like a Starbucks, rather than stay at home in isolation. Is your work area continually cold? Get a small space heater.

4. Take Care of Yourself and Stay Healthy

If you don't take care of yourself, it will be hard for you to care for others. Taking care of yourself includes eating healthy foods, exercising, and getting enough sleep.

Keep yourself healthy to prevent illness and fatigue. Take basic preventative care to avoid getting sick by washing your hands frequently and avoiding direct contact with those who are sick. If you do get sick, don't try to be a hero. Some people think it is important to come to work even when they are sick. They mistakenly believe that the team is better off with them there. Unfortunately, illness can spread and cripple an entire team. Set a good example for everyone else by staying home and getting better. Even if you believe you are indispensable, the team is better off without you while you recuperate.

5. Sharpen the Saw

Stephen Covey talks about the importance of sharpening the saw in *The Seven Habits of Highly Effective People*. In essence, he is talking about self-renewal. This means taking your vacations as well as investing in training and development. Are you too busy on your project for vacation or training? That is a common refrain and one that is easily debunked. First of all, no one person is that critical to a project. Second, there will never be a perfect time on your project to take vacation or go to training. The busier your project, the more you will benefit from downtime away from it.[3]

6. Avoid Long Work Weeks

We all have to stretch once in a while, and we all have a different level of stamina. However, if you are working more than forty-five, fifty, or sixty hours every week, you are likely setting yourself up for fatigue and illness.

7. Get Support

When feeling sick, tired, or worn out, you need to seek support from others. This support could be from your manager, a trusted coworker, friends, a spouse, or a mentor. Reach out to others and engage them on an emotional level. Get the help you need to stay on top of your game.

8. Reduce Your Stress Level

PMs should be familiar with the need to reduce stress and have at least one method that they employ. There are a multitude of stress reduction methods from easy things, such as exercise and self-care, all the way through more radical approaches, such as getting a new job or leaving an abusive relation-

---

[3]Stephen R. Covey. *The Seven Habits of Highly Effective People: Powerful Lessons in Personal Change*. Salt Lake City, UT: Franklin Covey, 1989.

ship. Previously discussed techniques include prayer and meditation. My coach is a big believer in breathing techniques. The point is that there are a lot of different ways to reduce stress, and I encourage you to experiment until you find one that works for you. On the other hand, if you are one of those people who thrive on stress and intentionally create it in your life, what I write here won't matter much to you anyway.

9. Talk It Out with Someone

Besides having several different mentors and coaches outside work, I have had the luxury over the last two years of having a good friend and member of my program management team who is always willing to be a sounding board for my ideas. I have found this invaluable. If you don't have someone in your professional life whom you can bounce ideas off, find someone. It is a bonus if you can also ask them to hold you accountable to make changes or follow through on your commitments.

10. Give Yourself a Time Out

If you find yourself heading toward a breakdown, give yourself a time out. Leave the building, go to lunch early, quit for the day, or just head out to the nearest coffee shop for a snack. If you are at home, you can punch a pillow or hit a bed with a tennis racquet. Some people find exercise helpful.

11. Write a Letter or E-Mail You Will Not Send

A technique that Abraham Lincoln reportedly practiced was to write letters he did not plan to send. The idea is that through expressing your emotions in writing, you are able to release any emotional charge. This worked well for Abe when he used paper and pencil but may not work as well today with our modern office tools. For example, we may type an e-mail that we don't plan to send and then actually end up sending it inadvertently. Some organizations monitor all e-mails, even unsent ones. Other organizations use keystroke logging software to record everything typed at a keyboard including documents, unsent e-mail, and instant messages.

12. Use Appropriate Humor

There is nothing like laughter to remind us to not take ourselves too seriously. You can crack a joke, watch a sitcom, read something funny, or find someone amusing to hang out with. Scott Adams is great at skewering PMs in the

Dilbert cartoon; check out his collection online. If you can afford it, add a really funny person to your project team. Of course, they would need to have an official role and work assigned to them or your project sponsors might not find it all that funny.

13. Take Great Care of Yourself

We need to take good care of ourselves to reduce stress and to help prevent emotional breakdowns. This includes taking vacations, getting enough sleep on a regular basis, resting when sick, and getting support from others. You can also reduce stress levels by laughing out loud, going for a walk, spending time with people you like, or spending time on hobbies or interests.

Sometimes taking care of ourselves means we make plans to do the things we really want or need to do or to get together with people who nourish us. Don't wait for things to happen to you or react to the invitations of others; make plans to do the things that you find nurturing. Get out the calendar now and block out the time for the activities and events that you want to do and that you find nourishing. Be prepared to say no to invitations that don't enrich you; you aren't obligated to attend any events you don't want to attend.

14. Develop a Personal Emotional Dashboard

One thing my mentor Rich has recommended is to create a personal emotional dashboard. We are all familiar with the dashboard of a car or the complexity of a dashboard in an airplane cockpit. Imagine the same thing for your emotional state. Think of it as an expanded version of the heart rate monitor used by the Incredible Hulk.

You might have gauges for specific emotions, or nourishment levels. There would certainly be a warning light for those emotional red flags that you experience. Some other useful warning lights could include building up resentments, numbing out, or criticizing or blaming.

I have created a personal emotional dashboard for myself. It included the following gauges:

- Self-Care—this would be the equivalent of the gas gauge!
- Mutuality
- Telling the truth
- Satisfaction
- Standards
- Responsibility

My dashboard had the following warning lights:

- Sarcasm
- Resentments
- Criticizing or blaming
- Gossip
- Defensiveness
- Emotional boundaries

15. Don't Strive to be Perfect

Perfectionists find that people never quite measure up to their expectations. They can be just as hard on themselves as well. Instead of going for perfection, strive for excellence, which can be defined as doing your very best in every situation. Celebrate excellence and don't get sucked into thinking that everything needs to be perfect.

16. Plan and Prepare Ahead

Some of us set ourselves up for stressful situations or negative outcomes by arriving late or unprepared for early morning meetings with team members or other project stakeholders. This can cause us to lose momentum or feel lousy for the rest of the day. Next time you have an important meeting, try getting to bed early, getting up early, and getting in to work before everyone else. Allow yourself some quiet time to review your notes and objectives for the meeting, as well as to think about the emotions of each person who will be attending. Your calmness and quiet confidence will show clearly and even be contagious.

A related idea is to prepare for the day as a pilot prepares for a flight. Pilots have a preflight checklist that they run through before every flight. Your "preflight" checklist includes all the things that you need to pay attention to or plan for before the day begins. This could include thinking through key meetings, reviewing your priorities list, crafting the key messages you want to communicate, or simply getting grounded with prayer or meditation.

■ Personal Action Plan: Self-Management

Self-management is the ability to manage our emotions so that they don't control us.

Key Takeaways

1.
2.
3.

My Strengths and Weaknesses in the Area of Self-Management

Strengths	Weaknesses
1.	1.
2.	2.

My Actions or Goals Based on What I Learned

1.
2.
3.

Building Project Stakeholder Relationships

In Part 3, we shift from focusing on ourselves to focusing on others. In particular, we will explore the emotional and social skills that support relationships.

Leading others is all about relationships. If we build solid relationships with team members and other project stakeholders, we improve our ability to lead. Without relationships, leadership is difficult or impossible.

Relationships build on the foundations of emotional self-mastery that we established in Chapters 3 and 4. Our ability to build relationships comes from our emotional self-awareness and self-management. We cannot skip over those steps. It is tough to build strong relationships with others if we are struggling with our own issues.

We will start with Chapter 5, Social Awareness. Social awareness involves our ability to read people and situations. Part 3 concludes with Chapter 6, Relationship Management, which deals with developing strong relationships with others.

Social Awareness

■ An Introduction to Social Awareness

Social awareness is the ability to understand the emotions of others. It is one of the five building blocks of our project management framework for emotional intelligence as shown in Figure 5-1. It includes the competencies of empathy, organizational awareness, seeing others clearly, and emotional boundaries.

Simply put, social awareness is the ability to accurately read situations and people and to understand and empathize with the emotions of others. I believe that most PMs have at least some level of social awareness. It is impossible to progress very far as a PM without social awareness for the following reasons.

First, as discussed in Chapter 2, project management is about getting work done through others. If you cannot understand and relate to others, it will be difficult to get work done through them.

Second, all projects are temporary (or at least they are supposed to be). As PMs, we don't usually have the luxury of gradually building long-term relationships with our teams. Rather, we need to work with new teams and new stakeholders on a regular basis, maybe as often as every six or nine months. Each new project brings with it the potential for different faces and relationships and the urgency to move quickly to develop productive relationships. Our ability to quickly and accurately read and understand others is critical to our success.

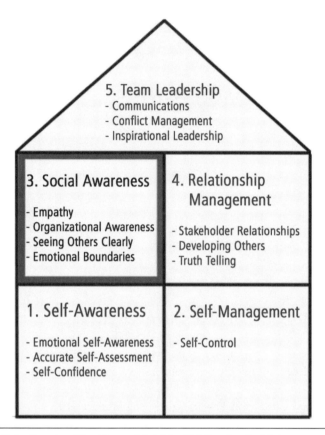

Figure 5-1: Emotional Intelligence Model for PM Showing Social Awareness.

Finally, projects are risky and successful delivery is never guaranteed. PMs need all the help they can get to succeed. Being adept at reading situations and people is one way that PMs managers can improve their chances for success.

So how do PMs use social awareness? It comes into play whenever we are working with others; that is, all the time for PMs. Here are some typical situations where social awareness is at work:

1. Understanding the verbal and nonverbal communications of different stakeholders
2. Understanding the motivations of our team members so that we can align them with the objectives of the project
3. Improving your understanding of stakeholders and politics
4. Providing feedback and constructive criticism to team members

5. Recognizing and addressing hostility, conflict, and other negative behaviors

Social awareness is part of our own personal radar, which provides us with a rich source of information about our environment. Recall how David Caruso and Peter Salovey made the point in their book *The Emotionally Intelligent Manager* that emotion is information.[1] Now think about that for a moment. Emotions provide us with information about our environment. Social awareness is specific information about the people we are interacting with on our teams, as well as about the organization and political climate.

Unfortunately, not everyone is able to leverage this radar or the information it provides. Self-awareness is the precursor to social awareness. We understand others through awareness of our own emotions. Individuals who have a difficult time recognizing their own emotions will struggle to recognize emotions in others. In the next section, we are going to dive into the topic of social awareness and provide some tools and examples on how to improve your skills in this area.

What the Experts Say About Social Awareness

Mayer and Salovey were the first emotional intelligence researchers to address the concept of Social Awareness in their 1990 paper titled "Emotional Intelligence." That article contained one of the first Emotional Intelligence Frameworks. Although they did not call it social awareness, that is essentially what Mayer and Salovey described in the section of their framework called "Appraisal and Expression of Emotion" in others, as shown in Figure 5-2.

Mayer and Salovey introduced two subcomponents of that domain of appraisal and expression of emotion in others: nonverbal perception and empathy. Nonverbal perception is the ability to recognize the unspoken emotions of others. Nonverbal cues include facial expressions and body language.

The second subcomponent, empathy, is the ability to comprehend and experience someone else's feelings. Mayer and Salovey were the first to link empathy to self-awareness. That is, to feel what others feel you must first be aware of what you feel. As discussed, Daniel Goleman's research built on the work of Mayer and Salovey. Goleman first called this domain "social competence"; later, in the framework included in *Primal Leadership,* he changed it to "social awareness." That framework included the three social awareness competencies of empathy, service orientation, and organizational awareness.

---

[1] David R. Caruso and Peter Salovey. *The Emotionally Intelligent Manager: How to Develop and Use the Four Key Emotional Skills of Leadership.* Hoboken, NJ: John Wiley & Sons, Inc., 2004.

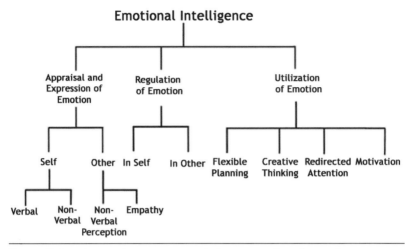

Figure 5-2: Salovey and Mayer Framework for Emotional Intelligence.[2]

Goleman's use of empathy is consistent with that of Salovey and Mayer. However, service orientation and organizational awareness were new with the Goleman framework.[3]

Service orientation and organizational awareness are both relevant to PMs. Service orientation means understanding the unstated emotional needs of a customer. Organizational awareness is the ability to interpret the emotions and politics of groups. Think of organizational awareness as the expansion of social awareness from individuals to groups. It is about the ability to accurately understand situations in spite of our own distortions.

A good question right now is what does all this mean to you as a PM? That is exactly the question we are going to address by looking at the specific aspects of social awareness that are most important to PMs. This includes a few social awareness competencies that are not part of Goleman's framework. For project management purposes, I extended the basic framework to include seeing others clearly and emotional boundaries.

■ Empathy

Empathy is one of the most important parts of social awareness and, perhaps, one of the most critical people skills for PMs and other leaders. Empathy is

[2] Peter Salovey and John D. Mayer. Emotional Intelligence. *Imagination Cognition, and Personality*, 9(3).

[3] Daniel Goleman, Richard Boyatzis, and Annie McKee. *Primal Leadership*. Boston: Harvard Business School Press, 2002, p. 39.

the ability to understand and relate to the emotions of others. It helps us walk in the shoes of another person or to see things from another's point of view. This section introduces the following facets of empathy and how they play out in the project environment:

1. Ability to read the spoken and unspoken thoughts and feelings of others
2. Ability to appreciate the thoughts and feelings of others and why they have them
3. Capacity to respect and value people from diverse backgrounds and cultures

Empathy is not a new concept by any stretch of the imagination. Most people have probably heard the following quotation:

> "Don't criticize someone until you have walked a mile in their shoes."
> —Unknown

Or, perhaps you have heard the twisted adaptation of that idea as reflected in this quotation:

> "Before you criticize someone, you should walk a mile in their shoes.
> That way, when you criticize them, you're a mile away
> and you have their shoes."
> —Unknown

That second quotation is funny only because it highlights one of the biggest challenges to empathy; our own self-centeredness. The truth is that we are all primarily selfish, self-absorbed, self-obsessed, and self-interested. We will take a closer look at that in a moment.

The importance of empathy was explained perceptively in Stephen Covey's book *The Seven Habits of Highly Effective People*. Covey's fifth habit was empathy: Seek first to understand, then to be understood.

Embedded in that phrase is the simple wisdom of orienting first to the other person. A great deal of conflict that we experience on projects could be reduced or eliminated if we simply tried to understand the other person's point of view before we tried to convince them of our own message. We need to listen with the intention of understanding what others are trying to say.[4]

---

[4]Stephen R. Covey. *The Seven Habits of Highly Effective People: Powerful Lessons in Personal Change.* Salt Lake City, UT: Franklin Covey, 1989.

Seeking first to understand is a simple premise that is often difficult to execute. Granted, many PMs excel at empathy. But for the rest of us, empathy can be difficult. Why do we find empathy difficult as PMs? Here are some possible reasons:

1. Self-Orientation

As noted, humans are selfish and self-oriented. It is unnatural to think of others first. Further, we are anxious to impose our worldview on other people. We expect them to think and act like us. After all, ours is the correct way. Covey called this our own "rightness" and putting our "autobiography" on others.

A good example is when parents say things to their children that start with "When I was a kid. . . ." Don't think this only applies to child rearing; we do the same thing to our teams. Our feedback and coaching is often based on what worked for us in similar projects or situations.

2. Results First

As PMs, we focus on results and achieving the end goals of the project. The Nike slogan, "Just Do It," was likely created by a PM. (Perhaps the PM could have enhanced it by saying "Just Do It Now!"). Spending time understanding others can be viewed as in direct conflict with the need and urgency to complete the project.

One way to overcome this thinking is to see the development of others (the project team members, our peers, and our leaders) as one of the goals of the project. People learn best by doing, and the project is a great environment for that learning.

Paradoxically, viewing the development of team members as a goal will often speed the achievement of the other project goals. Rather than taking away from the work on the project, this approach provides energy, inspires people, and builds the capacity to do more. We will explore the competency of developing others in Chapter 6.

3. Tough Stuff

Empathy requires communicating in difficult ways. For example, many of us never developed effective listening skills. We often approach conversation as simply taking turns talking. Listening for most of us is being poised, waiting for the other person to take a breath. Then, we quickly jump in, like a taxi driver waiting for enough space between the cars in the next lane so they can barge on over. We are often less invested in listening to others than we are in getting our own point across.

4. We Are Smarter Than Others

As the PM, we are smarter than everyone else—or, at least the rest of the project team, right? Otherwise, why would the project sponsor put us in charge? Because we are smarter, everyone should hear what we have to say and do things the way we want them done. Obviously, I am kidding to make a point. To the extent that we buy into that theory or act like that, we are not being empathetic.

These are probably only a few of the reasons that empathy is so hard for PMs. In the next section, we are going to explore empathy more and then discuss ways to improve our empathy toward others.

Empathetic Listening

One of the key applications of empathy is empathetic listening, listening without judgment. When we listen empathetically we: (1) focus on the words and behavior of another without judgment and (2) periodically summarize what they think, feel, and need in the moment. That seems like a pretty tall order, one that requires a little more explanation.

Empathetic listening is considerably different from just regular listening. Many of us listen half-heartedly, attempt to multitask, or view listening as a pause that allows us to gather our thoughts before we can continue with our own monologue. We might consider that pathetic listening.

Empathetic listening is when we give ourselves over to the other person and listen with his or her best interest in mind. PMs who master empathetic listening benefit by:

1. Making the speaker feel valued and important
2. Improving the depth of the communication
3. Understanding the underlying emotions, which adds richness to the conversation
4. Building trust and the relationship with the other

So how do PMs improve their empathetic listening? Consider applying the following techniques to enhance your empathetic listening skills:

1. Let Others Speak

When we listen empathetically, we simply let the other person speak. We avoid "helping" the speaker; that is, we do not provide verbal or nonverbal clues or finish sentences. When we jump in and help others with what they are trying to say, we unintentionally inject our own agenda. We may unknowingly steer the speaker toward what we want or expect them to say instead of simply letting them take the conversation where it needs to go.

2. Maintain Eye Contact

When we listen empathetically, we should maintain eye contact with the speaker. This provides the speaker with the space to say what he or she needs to say. Note that this doesn't mean we should be staring them down or boring in with our best "Dirty Harry" scowl. It does mean looking at the speaker with a neutral expression, providing minimal feedback, and breaking eye contact periodically if it becomes uncomfortable.

3. Give the Speaker Your Full Attention

As PMs, we are often trying to accomplish several things at once. In our efforts to be productive, we might try to multitask while we are listening. Empathetic listening is a single thread activity. It doesn't work if you multitask.

You probably know how it feels to have someone multitask while they are listening to you. Whether that person is reading a PC screen or looking over your shoulder to see someone else, it feels dismissive. Have you ever been speaking to someone whose cell phone rang and that person immediately turned away from you to see who was calling? This kind of behavior tells speakers that the listener does not value them.

4. Playback and Summarize

When we listen empathetically, we should periodically repeat what we heard to make sure that our understanding is accurate. This provides the speaker with an opportunity to restate or clarify anything that was misunderstood.

As an example, consider a team member who comes to you with a concern. He tells you that he is hurt by the actions of Bob, a coworker. You might say "Let me see if I have this straight. You feel dismissed by Bob when he doesn't say positive things about your contribution to the deliverable." In this way, the team member has an opportunity to either agree or clarify the concern.

5. Orient to Emotions

Empathetic listening involves interpreting the thoughts and feelings of another. In addition to playing back and summarizing what we hear, we should also add feeling words to what we say. "That sounds frustrating" or "you seem angry" might be appropriate to the team member in the previous example.

6. Try on Their Shoes

Trying on someone's shoes requires us to imagine ourselves in their situation as we listen. We need to do this in a compassionate way and not come at it from a superior, "Boy, are you screwed" point of view. We need to be thinking "What would it be like to be that person right now? What would I be feeling in that situation?" This sounds more difficult than it really is; we just need to use our imaginations or perhaps think back to a similar situation in which we were involved.

7. Suspend Our Judgment

Empathetic listening requires that we suspend our own judgments, needs, and priorities and focus on the other person. This skill requires some practice. Listening without regard for our own agenda is very generous and selfless.

What we do with what we hear during our empathetic listening is also important. I personally find it easy to jump in and problem solve or to use this opportunity to apply my own autobiography by telling them how I solved the same problem. The temptation is to simply tell them to be like me and solve it the way I did. This method is not terribly empathetic or effective. It doesn't work with my wife, and it doesn't work in the project environment.

A more effective approach is to simply say "That sounds tough," "How can I help?" or "What support do you need from me right now?" This puts the focus on the speaker, where it belongs. Often, you will find that the speaker is not asking you to solve the problem. The speaker may realize during the course of the discussion what needs to be done next; she simply needed to be heard. If we proceed to tell someone how to solve the problem when he or she simply wanted to be heard, we risk alienating that person. She will probably come away thinking that we are superior, uncaring, and unsupportive. In addition, we take on the work of that person instead of empowering individuals to solve their own problems.

One of the best and most memorable comments I received from a team member came a few years ago. This guy had worked for me for about six months when he said "You are not like other PMs I have worked with. You always ask me what you can do to support me." Frankly, I wish I were more consistent with this behavior. If you are asking a lot from people, it helps to show them that you care and are willing to help them to get it done. In the case of this particular team member, he rarely asked me for help but apparently appreciated the fact that I was willing to help if he needed it.

■ Seeing Others Clearly

We can also use our knowledge of emotions, emotional triggers, and emotional breakdowns to better understand and even predict the behaviors of others. I think of this as our ability to see others clearly. As PMs, it is important that we understand others and their emotional states. This includes our project team members, executive sponsor, and all other project stakeholders.

How do we see others clearly? How do we understand and interpret emotions in others? Actually, it is something that we already do to some extent or another. We were probably never taught a step-by-step method, but we all read people and their emotions all the time.

That said, I believe that it can be more difficult to read others in the workplace than in other settings. The workplace has become an arena in which people are not expected or allowed to show emotions. People mask, cover-up, or attempt to hide their true emotions. Many just don't believe it proper to display emotions.

Consider this example from an organization with which I recently worked. The president of the company was comfortable expressing his emotions. In fact, he was known for getting choked up and crying during presentations or heartfelt discussions. While some in the organization simply ignored it, others felt uncomfortable and thought it inappropriate. Some even believed it was contrived. Those people were uncomfortable with that level of emotional display in the workplace.

Seek the Best in Others

In the movie *Planes, Trains and Automobiles*, Steve Martin and John Candy were paired up as an odd couple stuck together in a nightmare travel scenario. The two of them had very little in common, yet they were together throughout the whole movie. Steve played a button down executive, while John played a traveling salesman.

Early on, the character played by Steve Martin establishes that he is the more sophisticated of the two, the "better" of the two. It is clear that he doesn't like John Candy's character, although he is polite enough to not say anything out loud. As the movie progresses, Candy begins to get under his skin, his irritation builds and builds, and he has a lot of trouble keeping his cool. And as their situation worsens, he starts to find more and more tiny faults in John Candy's character.

Do you do that? Do you start out polite with everyone and then, when things get tough, you begin to criticize or find fault with them? Do the little quirks and routines of others begin to grate on your nerves until you are ready to kill the other person, *just for breathing?*

I know I do. I am a natural born critic, and I tend to sell people short, although not usually when things are going well. But, when things are not going well, I tend to find every fault they have. It is almost like each little tiny quirk is magnified 100 times. Those tiny cracks and quirks cause me to grit my teeth and just want to choke someone.

The way out of this type of thinking is to make it a point to find the best in everyone. Some people are naturally good at this, while others, like me, have to work at. Everyone has strengths; we just need to pay close enough attention to determine what they are. If you haven't found someone's strengths and weaknesses, you need to try harder. The ability to size people up is an important skill.

Once you've determined someone's strengths, take it one step further by affirming them. Make it a point to call out positive points and strengths. Build the muscle of finding the best in others.

PMs may find themselves in the position of taking on new teams and new team members on a regular basis. For many years, I was taking on new projects and teams every six months or so. I learned to spend time meeting with and thinking about the key team players for those projects and to perform regular assessments of them.

This is really easy to do. I do this in a three-column format. List team member names in the first column, then list strengths in column two and weaknesses in column three. This format helps me to see if any patterns emerge—missing strengths or an abundance of one weakness. I also can see opportunities to pair people up to balance strengths and weaknesses. For completeness, I include my own name on the list.

The key to success here is not perfection—it is to raise your level of awareness of the capabilities of your team. A few weeks after I completed the analysis above, I was asked by my executive sponsor what leadership changes we needed to make. Since I was doing this assessment on a regular basis, I had a pretty good idea of the team, and I was able to make recommendations based on strengths and weaknesses. We moved one person out of a leadership position and changed the responsibilities of two others. The project team thrived as a result.

How Do We Determine What Others Are Feeling?

When someone is crying, it is easy to see they are experiencing a lot of emotion. What if some people aren't as direct about what they are feeling? Here are some techniques we can use to determine what others are feeling.

1. We can start by asking ourselves what we are feeling. Awareness of the emotions of others starts with our awareness of our own emotions. What we are feeling when we are with someone is a great clue as to what they are feeling. If we feel scared, it is likely the other person feels scared. Or, it could be that they are angry, and we are responding to that anger. If we feel happy, it is likely the other person feels happy or excited. Our emotions are a guide to the emotions of others.

2. Listen for emotion words. Another clue to what people are feeling is the words that they use. They may not always say it clearly, but if they use emotion words, we can use that as information about the underlying emotion.

When someone uses the words "disappointed," "hurt," or "ticked off," they are talking about levels of anger. If they mention "nervous," "concerned," or "worried," they are talking about being scared.

When we listen with empathy, we may want to say the emotion words back to them. For example, we might say "You sound angry" or "You sound worried." This can often prompt someone to open up and share what they are feeling.

3. Another way to determine what others are feeling is to look at their faces. Look into their eyes. As discussed, eyes are the window to the soul. It is difficult to fake the emotions on our faces. Figure 5-3 shows the 6 emotional families and how they will appear on our faces.

Look for congruence between what people say, what their faces show, and their body language. I remember an incident with a project team member who was clearly upset. When I said that she sounded angry, she sat with her arms crossed and said in a defiant tone, "I am not angry!" The inconsistency between her stated emotions and her body language was a tip off that her emotional rules said that anger was not appropriate. Even though she was very angry, she was not going to express it.

Barriers to Seeing Others Clearly

Seeing others clearly is a critical skill for a PM who is striving to be emotionally intelligent. However, it is not always easy to master. There are three main obstacles to seeing others clearly: our own filters and biases, our autobiography that we impose on others, and the shortcuts we take to categorize others.

1. Filters and Biases

We view the world through our filters. We all have a set of prejudices, biases, rules, and distortions that affect the way we see the world and the people in it. These prejudices and distortions are ingrained in us. They have been part

	SAD: Mouth corners turned down, inner brows up and together, eyes slightly closed.
	ANGRY: Teeth clenched, lips narrowed, inner corners of eyebrows down and together, eyes wide, nose flared.
	SCARED: Mouth contorted or frowning, eyes open, brows tight & raised.
	HAPPY: Smiling, rounded cheeks, crow's feet at corners of eyes.
	EXCITED: Smiling widely, eyes open, eyebrows raised, mouth open.
	TENDER: Mouth smiling lightly, eyes open & moist.

Figure 5-3: Faces of the Six Families of Emotions.

of us for so long that it is nearly impossible to be conscious of them without significant work. Like the fish in a tank, we cannot see or appreciate the water around us.

One of the biggest filters is our own family of origin or the family in which we grew up. How we see others is affected by the interactions we had with our parents and siblings. A common example is that our view of authority figures is impacted by our relationship with our fathers. Any unresolved conflicts we have with our family of origin will create conflict in other relationships throughout our lives.

Our family of origin is just one type of filter; there are others. The 2005 movie *Crash* was a big hit because it exposed the various biases and prejudices that different groups of people had toward each other. Whether the biases and prejudices are based on race, gender, appearance, social status, or ethnic background, they all have the same result. They highlight the differences between us and others and cause unnecessary separation. The net result is that we are unable to see the members of our project teams for who they are and are unable to recognize their individual strengths and weaknesses.

2. Imposing Our Own Autobiography

The second obstacle to seeing others clearly is our own autobiography. We cannot see others clearly when we impose our own story on them. We do this when we believe that others should do things the way that we did them or that ours is the right way to approach things.

I often do this when people on my teams ask me about career advancement. A frequent question is "Should I go for my PMP certification or go back to school for my MBA?" Instead of focusing on them and trying to help them think through the decision criteria, I often find myself referring to my situation and what worked for me. This doesn't serve others well.

3. We Take Shortcuts for Efficiency

The third obstacle to seeing others clearly is the shortcuts we take. PMs are generally pretty busy individuals. We take shortcuts to be as efficient as possible. One shortcut is to pigeonhole people. We do this when we try to quickly sort out what they are about so that we can put them into a category or group.

The benefit of the shortcut is that we think we understand or know all about them because of who they are, how they appear, or where they are from. We don't have to learn everything about them.

Not all shortcuts are bad, but you should be very careful when you use them. In the following section, we will look at a shortcut that will help us to identify the emotional behaviors of others.

4. We Make Others Bad

The book *Leadership and Self-Deception* is about our relationships with others and the breakdowns that occur. Specifically, it is about our ability to see and understand how our own issues prevent us from being in relationships with others at the same time that those issues perpetuate conflict. While not specifically about emotional intelligence, this book is about understanding ourselves better and improving our relationships.[5]

The interesting point the book makes is our ability to deny reality. To justify our poor behavior toward others (what the book calls betraying our-

---

[5] Arbinger Institute. *Leadership and Self-Deception: Getting out of the Box.* San Francisco: Berret Koehler Publishers Inc, 2010.

selves), we need to make others bad by highlighting their shortcomings and diminishing their good qualities. We attribute negative qualities to them (e.g., she is lazy) or use all-or-nothing thinking (e.g., he never shows up on time). At the same time, we imagine ourselves to be better than we are, and we enhance our own qualities.

The book calls this process self-deception. We deceive ourselves about what is really happening and that becomes a reinforcing cycle that is hard to break.

To overcome this habit of making others bad, we need to get honest with ourselves about our current situation. We need to see our criticism of others for what it is—a defense mechanism aimed at keeping us out of relationship. On the other hand, if we stay in denial, we simply find or produce evidence to help us stay right where we are.

Techniques to Improve on Seeing Others Clearly

For those of us who want to improve our abilities to see others clearly, here are some steps we can take.

1. Recognize Our Own Biases
We can start by recognizing that we all have biases and prejudices. Just admitting that we have them is a good first step. Then, we can start to explore what those prejudices and biases might be.

2. Practice Studying Others
We can expand our understanding of others by viewing life as a game of exploration. We can strive to learn as much as possible about each person and be empathetic toward others.

Are you taking advantage of the opportunities around you to get to know people on a one-to-one basis? The key to improving our social awareness and ability to see others clearly is to practice. Like a muscle, we need to use our social awareness, or we will lose it. Start today with the interactions you have with your project stakeholders. In your one-on-one meetings, take the time to reflect on what you think the other person is feeling. In meetings with groups, keep a tally of what people are feeling. You can use the Emotional Tally Sheet in Appendix A. Check it out with the individuals later to see if your observations were correct.

3. Practice Looking for the Best in Others
Make it a regular practice to evaluate your team and identify the strengths and weaknesses of each team member. You can use the three-column approach

described in the previous section or develop your own format. The key is to do your best to see them as accurately as possible.

4. Use the Emotional Assessment Checklist
The Assessment for Emotional Self-Awareness and Self-Control in Appendix B may be a useful framework for evaluating others. Use this checklist as a tool to understand the emotional intelligence of one of your team members, a sponsor, your manager, or some other stakeholder. The checklist includes the following sections:

- Automatic or default emotion
- Self-awareness
- Expressiveness
- Self-management
- Emotional breakdowns
- Stinking thinking
- Changes and surprises
- Stress

Try assessing yourself and others using the checklist. Be aware of the areas that you feel comfortable with, as well as those areas where you feel less secure.

■ Organizational Awareness

The third competency of social awareness is organizational awareness. What exactly is organizational awareness? In *The Emotionally Intelligent Workplace*, Cherniss and Goleman define organizational awareness as:

> "the ability to read the currents of emotions
> and political realities in groups"
> —Cary Cherniss and Daniel Goleman[6]

Hmmm . . . "read the currents" sounds a little like reading the tea leaves and that reminds me of astrology or fortune telling. I hope organizational awareness is a little more grounded than that.

Interestingly enough, organizational awareness was not even part of Goleman's original framework for emotional intelligence. Instead, he included

---

[6]Cary Cherniss and David Goleman. *The Emotionally Intelligent Workplace*. Hoboken, NJ: John Wiley & Sons, Inc., 2001.

competencies like political awareness and team capabilities. In his 2002 book, *Primal Leadership*, which he coauthored with Richard Boyatzis and Annie McKee, Goleman simplified the framework and included organizational awareness as follows:

> A leader with a keen social awareness can be politically astute, able to detect crucial social networks and read key power relationships. Such leaders can understand the political forces at work in an organization, as well as the guiding values and unspoken rules that operate among people there.
> —Daniel Goleman, Richard Boyatzis, Annie McKee[7]

That description sounds very relevant, perhaps critical, to our success as project or program managers. I believe that the more we progress as PMs, the more our success is linked to organizational awareness. As we will see, this awareness includes not just the project, but also the company, customers, and vendors related to the project.

I first heard of organizational awareness back in 1993 before emotional intelligence was popular. Back then I was a senior PM at a consulting firm. Our annual performance review was based on an instrument that measured 11 different dimensions of project management, including organizational awareness. Table 5-1 is a summary of the four levels of capability of organizational awareness. Read the description and then take a moment to see where you would place yourself on this progressive scale.

The focus of that assessment tool was to gauge a PM's understanding of the people, climate, and culture of all the players in the project environment. It was an assessment of exactly what Goleman describes as organizational awareness.

The thing I liked about that tool was that it specifically called out the PM's understanding of the entire project environment. That included the company, of course, as well as customers and vendors. I also liked that it provided me with a vision of what it meant to excel in this particular area. I strove to master all the different levels.

You can also use this as a guide to mastering organizational awareness. How aware are you of all the players or stakeholders in your project environment, including customers, clients, subcontractors, and vendors? Are you aware of whom to call to get things done? Do you know how to influence the decision makers?

---

[7]Daniel Goleman, Richard Boyatzis, and Annie McKee. *Primal Leadership*. Boston: Harvard Business School Press, 2002, p. 255.

Table 5-1: PM Assessment for Organizational Awareness

Level 1:	Understands the structure and organization of the company and the client and uses that to manage effectively.
Level 2:	Is familiar with the inner workings of the company and how to get things done informally. Is able to leverage the organizational capabilities for the client's benefit.
Level 3:	Understands and leverages not only the company but the client and vendor organizations. Recognizes key decision makers in the environment.
Level 4:	Understands the client's business as well or better than the client; consistently acts with the client's best interest in mind.

The two main aspects of organizational awareness that Goleman and Boyatzis discuss are identifying key power relationships and understanding the values and culture of the organization.

Key Power Relationships

Identifying key power relationships is about accurately recognizing the individuals who have power and political influence on our projects. How well do you think you understand the power relationships for your project and organization? Here are some questions you can ask to help you sort out the power relationships

1. Who are the real decision makers on your project and in your organization? Are there any decision makers who are outside the official project chart or organizational chart?
2. Who has influence on the decisions made? Who has the power to say yes? Who has the power to say no?
3. Who gets advice from whom?
4. Who in this organization or team worked together before at another company? Have team members always worked together, even when they moved from organization to organization?

Questions like these can remind us to be systematic in evaluating the power relationships in our environment. For many of us, this is an ad hoc or even a missing process. Recognizing the decision makers for a project or organization is a critical first step to managing stakeholders, which is part of the domain of relationship management.

Understanding the Values and Culture of the Organization

Understanding the values and culture of the organization is also important. For PMs, this analysis must be done at both the project level and the broader organization level. The values and culture may be the same at the project and organization levels, or they might be quite different.

The most straightforward way to understand the value and culture of the organization is to read the organization's description of its values. Organizations declare these values in public ways in their mission or vision statements, by their slogans, by the posters on the wall, and by other promotional material. While there could be a disconnect between what organizations say and what employees actually feel, the published version is a starting point for the analysis.

When I visited one of the many Motorola facilities in Schaumburg, Illinois, the walls of the building were plastered with posters. It would be impossible for any employee in the building not to see the posters. The Motorola posters had the theme, "My Moto," and they featured employees pictured with their various projects. Each poster showed a different facet of serving customers. The message seems to be "We're not the paternal organization we used to be; start acting like an entrepreneur."

Some organizations use symbols instead of posters. Consider the loaner bikes shown in Figure 5-4. What does this picture say to you? I saw these

Figure 5-4: Loaner Bikes at Hewlett Packard in Roseville, California.

loaner bikes at the Hewlett Packard Training Center in Roseville, California. The bikes were scattered around the grounds of the facility to allow employees to move from building to building without using a car. When I saw them I immediately felt an emotional connection. I felt tradition, a sense of family, trust, and independence, as well as stewardship. Were they intended to send an emotional message about the culture of the organization?

Take a moment to evaluate the posters and symbols in your work environment. What point is being made? What do you think is the unstated messages of those posters and symbols?

A second place to look for the values of the organization is its annual report. What does this document say about the organization? Which projects, initiatives, and successes are bragged about? Which are not mentioned?

I once led a large and long-term IT project for a big company. Each year, I scanned the annual report to see what was said about my project. When the project was prominently featured in the annual report the first year, I felt elated. The following year, when the project was not even mentioned, I felt sad. The message seemed to be that this project was no longer important.

A third way to evaluate the culture and values of the organization is to look at the recognitions and rewards. Here are some questions you can use to evaluate them in a particular organization.

1. Who gets promoted and why?
2. What behavior gets rewarded?
3. What type of behavior gets punished?
4. How does the organization react to problems or challenges?
5. What happens when mistakes are made?
6. Are there written or unwritten rules about starting early or working late?
7. Are there rules around telling the truth or not telling the truth?
8. What does it take to succeed in your organization?
9. Who gets the largest bonus and why?
10. Who has been fired and why?

I have worked for several consulting organizations where there was a practice of laying off any individuals who were not working on any specific projects and were nonbillable for any length of time. The value in those organizations was most likely "What have you done for me lately?" It is clear that this type of behavior affects project teams and the PMs who are trying to get work completed.

Consider also those organizations that reward hero-like efforts to meet deadlines. By hero-like, I don't mean people working hard. I am talking specifically about those last-minute efforts to rescue projects that are not doing well.

In one organization I know, individual hero-like behavior actually became the norm because it was rewarded. Instead of planning ahead and managing to a reasonable schedule, the teams learned to stall, delay, and set up emergency situations where it was nearly impossible to succeed. Then, the teams would work a long weekend or two (or overnight) to meet the deadline or milestone. These teams were regaled as heroes and rewarded accordingly. And, as the stories about these successes were retold, it became clear to all parties that to succeed meant to narrowly avert a crisis.

A friend of mine compared this process to a bus driver "driving the bus close to the cliff" to instill appropriate fear in the passengers. The idea is that if the bus driver doesn't make it look dangerous once in a while, the passengers will not appreciate the job he is doing. It would be equivalent to a firefighter who sets fires so that he and his fellow firefighters can rush in, put out the fire, and be heroes.

Obviously, if the organization values crises and hero-like behavior, it will not be likely to value well-planned and effectively run projects that quietly move toward completion. And, if that is the culture of the organization, it is good to recognize it up front so that you are not surprised when your well-run projects don't get much attention.

Finally, stories told by the individuals in the organization tell us about its culture and values. The stories we tell about our successes will provide a lot of information, so pay attention to the themes of those stories.

I recommend that you systematically evaluate and determine the playing field for your project and organization. Try to understand the values and culture. If you don't, you just might become a victim of it.

■ Emotional Boundaries

The next facet of social awareness for PMs is the competency of emotional boundaries. An emotional boundary is where one person's emotions leave off and another's begin. Think about the following quote for a moment:

> "Good fences make good neighbors."
> —Robert Frost, "Mending Wall"

It is pretty easy for us to understand the concept of a physical boundary, such as a fence. But, what about boundaries that are less visible? For example, how close can you comfortably stand next to another person? Three feet? Two feet? What about in an elevator? A really crowded elevator? Have you ever noticed how people in a crowded elevator will continually try to adjust their position so that they maximize their own personal space? They will automatically move closer together or farther apart as people enter and exit the elevator.

Emotional boundaries are even more difficult to discern, and that makes them harder to navigate. We discussed empathy and the need for PMs to be able to recognize and feel the emotions of others. However, empathy does not mean we should take on the emotions of others. As PMs, we need to recognize that we are separate and distinct from others. We need to be responsible for our own emotions and let others be responsible for theirs.

How do you know when there are issues with emotional boundaries? Have you ever heard anyone say "I was in a good mood until you ruined it?" Such people are implying that they are powerless to control their own moods and that you have power over how they feel. Or, consider a situation where you are in a meeting and someone gathers their stuff and walks out abruptly. As you glance around the room to gauge the responses of others, someone invariably says "Was that me or was that him?" Here are some warning signs of individuals with emotional boundary issues.

Warning Signs of Emotional Boundary Issues

Moods and Feelings of Others

Individuals with boundary issues may take on the moods and feelings of others. This is different from empathy, which is the ability to understand the moods and feelings of others. Individuals with boundary issues will become more vested in the moods and feelings of others and lose track of their own feelings. As my mentor says, they need to "take someone else's temperature to see how they are feeling." They may also become so bothered by the moods and feelings of others that they try to "fix" the other so that they can feel better.

Pleasing Others

Those with boundary issues will often sacrifice themselves to please others. This often results in forgoing their own choices or needs. As an example, consider a small group going out to lunch or making some other group choice. Some individuals will go along with a choice they do not want (and may even hate) just to fit in and please others or not rock the boat.

Victim-Like Behavior

Pleasing others can be taken such an extreme that the practitioner becomes a victim. Individuals with boundary issues often find pleasing others means never saying no. They end up feeling victimized by others. The reality is that they allow others to take advantage of them, which makes them resentful and angry. We will look more at saying no in Chapter 6.

Cannot Express Wants and Needs

Individuals with boundary issues often are unable to express their own wants and needs. They either are totally unaware of what they want or need or reluctant to share what they need. Ironically, although they cannot (or will not) express themselves, they often mistakenly believe others should anticipate their unstated wants and needs and fulfill them.

Recognizing individuals with boundary issues is necessary for PMs. Otherwise, our efforts to be more emotional in the work environment can be risky. Individuals with boundary issues will play the victim, expect you to act in certain unstated ways based on how a parent or sibling treated them, or create other problems for you. Recognizing these individuals is the first step in protecting yourself against them playing victim to your strong emotional leadership.

Respect Emotional Boundaries

A key concept of emotional boundaries is that we are responsible only for our own emotions. It is unhealthy for us to become too concerned with the emotions of others. This can be a fine line for PMs (and other leaders) looking to understand and affect the emotions of those around them. It can be difficult to discern between healthy and unhealthy concern for the emotions of others. Here are some ways that we can respect our own emotional boundaries as well as those of others.

Set Limits

Boundaries can be subtle. Sometimes, we will find others slowly crossing a boundary and feel it is not appropriate to intercept them. It is often helpful to set limits in advance, so that you establish a clear boundary with others when you start. The point is to limit their ability to impact you. This can be as simple as:

- Establishing a length of time that you will be together, whether on the phone or in person
- Establishing limits on the type of behavior you will tolerate, as, for example, you won't tolerate others yelling at you, or, you won't sit by while someone criticizes your team

Respond Appropriately

How we respond to the emotions of others is a key to our own emotional sanity. While we want to understand the feelings of others, we need to be careful not to become "hooked in" to the emotions they are experiencing. We need to exercise self-control in emotional and stressful situations. We need to choose our responses carefully. For example, if we can remain calm and steadfast when others are angry, we can help to defuse that anger. We don't need to ramp it up and get just as angry as the other person. Instead, we should remain centered and unemotional and help them deal with their own feelings.

Take Responsibility

Our response should include taking responsibility for our feelings. This means acknowledging that they are my feelings alone and that I have a choice about them. Before we can take responsibility, we have to be sufficiently self-aware to know what we are feeling.

This could be as simple as saying "I feel angry when you come late to the weekly status meeting." Do you see how this is subtly different from saying "You made me angry?" That is the difference between being responsible for our feelings and being a victim of the feelings of others. That feeling of anger is a choice that we made based on the circumstances.

Let Them Be

The flip-side of our responsibility is letting others be responsible for their feelings. We cannot control others. Often we need to simply let them react to our words or actions. If they are going to be angry or sad, so be it.

This can be tricky for PMs. We want to understand the impact of our actions, emotions, and decisions on the individuals on our teams. But we should not necessarily change just because someone is going to get angry or sad. We need to let them have their own reactions.

A few years ago, one of my team members thought he should be promoted to a team lead. I remember the angst that I felt since I knew he wasn't the best person for the job. I put off the decision because I knew he was going to be angry. Instead of simply making the announcement and letting that person have his reaction, I tiptoed around it for nearly a month. I lacked sufficient courage to simply let that person be, to let him react to the decision. I was afraid of his anger.

If you can learn to simply let others have their reaction to what you say and do, you will free yourself. Otherwise, you will be at the mercy of other people's emotions. You will be continually looking outside yourself and playing it safe. Others will quickly pick up on your lack of courage and may use it to their own advantage.

You Cannot Fix Other People

An important lesson I learned with regard to emotional boundaries is that I could not fix other people. While we want to strive to be as aware of the people on our team or in our environment as possible, this is very different from fixing them.

> Trying to fix other people is an exercise in futility.

Better Communications Around Boundaries

One way to improve our emotional communications and keep clear boundaries is to communicate with feeling words. Tell the other person what they did, how you felt about it and why, and what you want them to do differently in the future. There are four distinct parts to this communication:

"When you do . . . _____" (some behavior or action)
"I feel . . . _____" (an emotion, such as sad or angry)
"Because . . . _____" (the reason)
"I want . . . _____" (here is what I want in the future).

In the abstract, this may sound somewhat, well, formulaic. Let's look at how you might apply this strategy in the project environment. Consider a situation in which someone on your team is doing something that makes you angry. I once had a team lead named Tom who drank alcohol at lunch and then returned to work. I didn't like it and felt it was inappropriate, but I never said anything. I was scared of Tom's reaction. Here is a better way for me to have handled the situation.

"Tom, when you drink at lunch, I feel angry because I think it affects your performance and lowers the standards for our entire team. I want you to drink responsibly and not come to work under the influence of alcohol." Had I said something like that I would probably have gained agreement and buy in from Tom.

In Chapter 6 we will explore further the concept of truth telling, and we will see how important it is for our stakeholder relationships.

Seek Professional Help

If you are struggling to deal with individuals on your team who have boundary issues, you might benefit from professional help. A trained therapist, counselor, or psychiatrist might help you to prepare better for dealing with those people.

Please don't interpret this to mean that you should recommend psychiatric help for others. It is generally never wise to suggest professional help for the members of your team unless you have a high trust relationship. "You ought to see a shrink" is likely to land you in the HR department attempting to defend all your good intentions.

■ Techniques for Improving Our Social Awareness

Now that we have a solid understanding of what social awareness is all about, what can we do to improve our competency in this area? Here are thirteen techniques you can use to improve your social awareness.

1. Improve Your Empathetic Listening Skills

Improving your empathetic listening skills is one of the single most important steps you can take to improve your social awareness. Practice listening with empathy, reminding yourself of the following key aspects of empathetic listening:

- Let others speak without helping them.
- Maintain eye contact.
- Give them your full attention.
- Use playback and summarizing.
- Orient to emotions.
- Put yourselves in their shoes.
- Suspend your agenda while listening.

2. Take a Class on Listening Skills

Listening skills are important enough to warrant a class. Find a class on active or empathetic listening techniques and learn all that you can. Practice the skills at work, at home, and in every social situation that you can.

3. Track Emotions During Team Meetings

Becoming aware of the emotions of others is a skill we can learn if we practice. Use the emotional tally sheet in Appendix A to track your own feelings, as well as those with whom you interact. Try it, and see if you start to become more attuned to the thoughts and emotions of others.

If you are using this tally sheet during a meeting, don't worry that you won't be ready to talk when the time comes. Social awareness is about being aware of others and not simply waiting for your turn to talk. By the way, this technique is especially helpful to stay engaged during those interminable teleconferences where you cannot see everyone's face.

4. Identify Emotional Red Flags in Others

In Chapter 3, we discussed the importance of recognizing emotional red flags in ourselves and in others including:

- Inappropriate humor
- Use of sarcasm
- Passive–aggressive behavior
- Playing the victim
- Hostility

Watch for these emotional red flags in others. When you see them, look beyond that behavior to understand what is really going on. Beneath these red flags is most likely a great deal of sadness, fear, or anger.

5. Mirror Emotions

Mirroring is when we reflect back what we believe others are feeling. For example, when someone is describing a conflict they are having, you might sense their anger and say something like "That sounds frustrating" or "You sound angry." This helps to get the emotions out in the open, helps us to understand others, and even helps others to understand themselves.

6. Go to School

My mentor often tells me to "go to school" on people who are effective at a particular skill. He means that I should study them and learn how they do things. Are there any potential teachers in your project environment from whom you could learn empathy and social awareness? You can either study them from afar or ask them directly to help you learn or master what they do.

7. Track Your Own Emotions

Practice seeing others clearly by tracking your own emotions during conversations, listening for them to use emotion words, and watching their faces and bodies for nonverbal clues to emotions.

8. Keep a Journal

One way we can track our emotions is to keep a journal. Journaling is a great way to formalize our learning about ourselves and the individuals in our project environment. Try to approach it with discipline and write a little bit every day about what you are learning about your own emotions and those of others.

9. Explore and Learn About People

As the PM, we have the opportunity to interact with a number of stakeholders on our projects. Take the time to really explore each individual. Find the things you have in common with them, including where they grew up, went to school, and worked. What type of jobs did they have in college (if any)? What sports teams do they like? Do they have a family of their own? What is their ethnic or cultural background?

Learn about and appreciate both the differences and the things you have in common. Great PMs and leaders are always looking for areas of commonality and using them to connect with others.

10. Systematically Dissect the Organizational Culture

Treat the study of your organization as a research project. Talk to people and document the written rules, as well as what you believe to be the unwritten rules. Take an inventory of the posters, slogans, and symbols of the organization. What messages are those posters and symbols trying to convey? Determine which behaviors are recognized and rewarded and which are not.

11. Assess Your Project Team

Use the Assessment for Emotional Self-Awareness and Self-control in Appendix B to assess the team members and stakeholders in your project environment. See what you can learn about each person to enable you to see them more clearly and understand them better.

12. Practice Social Awareness During Movies

You can make a game of developing your social awareness using movies. The entire movie experience is designed to create emotional responses using images, words, and music. The next time you watch a movie, focus on one or two of the key actors and see if you can track their emotions throughout the film. You can do this informally or you can use the emotional tally sheet in Appendix A. Use your own emotions as a guide to what you believe the actor is feeling. Take a friend along and compare notes afterward. Alternatively, you can rent a movie from the list in Appendix D. You may find it easier to track emotions in the comfort of your home when you can pause and rewind if necessary.

■ Personal Action Plan: Social Awareness

Social awareness is the ability to accurately read situations and people and to understand and empathize with the emotions of others.

Key Takeaways

1.
2.
3.

My Strengths and Weaknesses in the Area of Social Awareness:

Strengths	Weaknesses
1.	1.
2.	2.

My Actions or Goals Based on What I Learned

1.
2.
3.

Relationship Management

■ An Introduction to Relationship Management

Chapter 6 is about relationship management, about using our emotional understanding of others to create relationships with them. The relationship management domain builds on the first three emotional intelligence domains. In other words, our success in relationship management is a function of our success in self-awareness, self-management, and social awareness.

What does relationship management have to do with PMs? Most people would agree that relationships are the bedrock of life, business, and, even, projects. They are especially critical to PMs for the following reasons.

Projects Are a Team Effort

Remember that project management is getting work done through others. A team of one can accomplish some things, but little of significance can be accomplished alone. Getting work done generally requires a team. The success of the team is largely a result of the strength of the relationships among its members.

PMs Often Lack Direct Authority

As compared to most functional managers and leaders, PMs often have to lead without direct authority. They have to rely on more than positional power and authority to be effective in getting others to accomplish what is needed.

This is difficult to do without a relationship between the PM and the team members.

PMs Compete for Resources

In many organizations, particularly those that use a matrix management approach, resources are shared or spread across multiple project teams. These days, however, more and more companies are trying to "do more with less." As a result, there are often severe constraints on key resources, which may be spread across three, four, or even five projects. In these environments, PMs may have to compete against each other for the resources they need at the time that they need them.

Building solid relationships is the key to success in matrix organizations and those organizations in which resource are constrained. This includes both relationships with the individual team members and relationships with the functional or resource managers responsible for allocating resources to teams.

PMs Need to Negotiate

PMs often need to negotiate to get what they need or to help parties reach agreement. PMs who use relationship management to understand the emotions and objectives of others will become more effective negotiators.

PMs Are Communicators

In the project environment, PMs are often the center of communications. They usually have the most information about the project and understand the big picture. As the center hub in a hub-and-spoke communication network (see Figure 6-1), they are often the one person who connects all of the members of the project team. Having critical information is a function of the relationships that the PM has with the team members.

That is not to say that relationship management is easy for PMs. In fact, the temporary nature of projects makes relationship building a challenge. Why should we invest in relationships on the team if the project is temporary?

This chapter considers several aspects of relationship management. We will start with what the emotional intelligence experts say on the topic. Then, we will examine the project management framework for emotional intelligence. We will explore each of these, provide examples, and discuss tools and techniques that can be applied in the project environment.

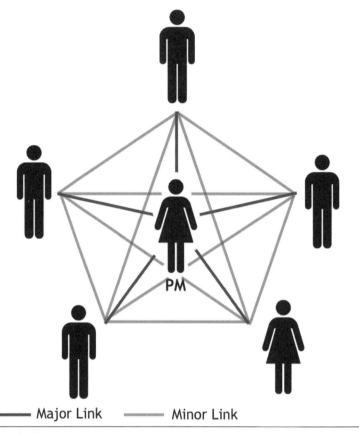

Major Link ——— Minor Link

Figure 6-1: The Project Manager as Communications Hub.

What the Experts Say About Relationship Management

As we begin to explore the emotional intelligence domain of relationship management, it might be helpful to see what the experts have to say about it. Daniel Goleman's most recent framework includes the following six competencies: inspiration, influence, developing others, change catalyst, conflict management, and teamwork and collaboration. Here is a quick summary of the each of these competencies, as outlined in *Primal Leadership*:

- Inspirational leadership—guiding and motivating with a compelling vision
- Influence—wielding a range of tactics for persuasion
- Developing others—bolstering others' abilities through feedback and guidance
- Conflict management—resolving disagreements

- Building bonds—cultivating and maintaining a web of relationships
- Teamwork and collaboration—cooperation and teambuilding[1]

The PM Framework for Emotional Intelligence

The PM Framework for emotional intelligence includes the following three competencies for the domain of relationship management: stakeholder relationships, developing others, and truth telling.

You might be wondering why the PM framework has only three competencies for relationship management in comparison to Goleman's six. For the PM framework for emotional intelligence, I chose distinguish between PMs dealing with one-on-one relationships and PMs dealing with teams. This division provides a more manageable breakdown of the concepts. In my framework, I included stakeholder relationships, developing others, and truth telling in the relationship management domain. These competencies primarily involve dealing one on one with individuals. What remains, then, are those areas where we a primarily deal with groups or project teams. These include communications, conflict management, and inspirational leadership. Although communications occurs at both the individual and the team levels, we will address it at the team level. I have included these competencies in the team leadership domain shown in Figure 6-2.

■ Stakeholder Relationships

The first competency we are going to look at under Relationship Management is stakeholder relationships. The goal of the stakeholder relationships competency is to strategically establish meaningful one-on-one relationships that are going to do the following:

- Increase our likelihood of success on the project
- Provide cushioning to weather the inevitable storms that occur on every project
- Provide an environment that is personally satisfying

Stakeholder relationship management is the process of systematically developing stakeholder relationships that help us with the project. We can break it down into the following four steps:

---

[1] Daniel Goleman, Richard Boyatzis, and Annie McKee. *Primal Leadership*. Boston: Harvard Business School Press, 2002, p. 39.

Figure 6-2: Emotional Intelligence for PMs Showing Relationship Management.

1. Identify our project stakeholders
2. Collect and analyze information about the stakeholders
3. Develop relationship strategies
4. Manage the ongoing relationships with the stakeholder

Let's tackle each of these in order.

Identify Project Stakeholders

Most PMs are familiar with project stakeholders and the importance of those stakeholders to the project. For those new to the concept of stakeholders, the simplest definition of a stakeholder is someone who is impacted by, or can make or break a project. This is an area where the PMBOK® Guide provides some guidance:

> Project stakeholders are individuals and organizations that are
> actively involved in the project, or whose interests may be affected
> as a result of project execution or project completion.

The PMBOK® Guide goes on to identify and define the following groups of stakeholders present on every project:

- Project manager
- Customer/user
- Performing organization
- Project team members
- Project management team
- Sponsor
- Influencers

It is important to cast a wide net when trying to identify stakeholders. It has been said that the stakeholder that can hurt you the most is that one you failed to identify. Don't overlook those stakeholders who are opposed to the project.

In addition to the categories above, the PMBOK® Guide also mentions other stakeholders such as owners and investors, sellers and contractors, team members and their families, government agencies and media outlets, individual citizens, lobbying organizations, and society at large.[2] Which makes me think that this exercise will quickly reach a point of diminishing returns. If you were to include society at large, pretty soon you'd have all earth dwellers as your set of stakeholders and that is a lot of people to worry about. You don't need to go to that extreme. That said, I would try to cast a very wide net initially to make sure that no significant stakeholders are overlooked. For example, here are some additional categories the PMBOK® Guide should have included:

- Senior management of the customer and performing organizations (if different)
- The program management office of the customer and performing organizations (if different)
- Functional management or resource management of the performing organization

---

[2]Project Management Institute (PMI). *A Guide to the Project Management Body of Knowledge* (PMBOK® Guide)—Third Edition, Newton Square, PA 19073-3299. Project Management Institute, Inc., 2004.

Figure 6-3: Project Stakeholders.

- Vendors (break into subcategories as appropriate)
- Suppliers
- End users of the project deliverables

Figure 6-3 shows the main categories of stakeholders and the relationship to the PM.

Using the diagram and descriptions above, think through the various stakeholders for your current or recent project. Start by listing the categories of stakeholders and then detail out the specific names for each category. It will be important to have the specific name of each stakeholder in order to effectively manage the relationships. Of course with some stakeholders, like end users, there may be too many to manage individually.

Collect and Analyze Information About the Stakeholders

Armed with an understanding of who the stakeholders are, we can begin to collect and analyze information about them. The collected data and analysis become the basis for managing the relationship effectively.

Imagine that you are a hired assassin. With each new contract you accept, you get some basic information about your target. If you are really good, you collect your own fat file of information about your target. This could include the target's likes and dislikes, hobbies, daily commuting patterns, family members, and other miscellaneous details. Knowing your target well is your key to a successful career.

As a project manager, you won't be working in life and death situations, and you needn't be so dramatic. You do need to find out what you can about each stakeholder. The more you know, the better you will be able to manage the relationship.

Much of the information is going to require an interview or conversation with the stakeholder. As a general rule, you should always meet one-on-one with key stakeholders before meeting them in a group. It is better to discuss needs and objectives individually rather than in a large group.

In fact, I recommend that you start gathering information even before you meet with each stakeholder. Ask around the organization to see what you can learn. Search the Internet or other public information sources. I have used both Google and LinkedIn to gather information about new executives. Google will turn up press releases, evidence of books authored by the stakeholder, and even information about hobbies, such as running. LinkedIn will show what companies they have worked for, which high school and college they attended, and may even reveal shared connections.

You will show a lot of initiative by gathering some information prior to meeting with the individuals. When they see your interest, they may be flattered. They may respect or trust you more. They may also be more open and less guarded about sharing information with you.

One of the techniques that I like to use early in the project life cycle is to start meetings with icebreakers. In addition to helping to build the team, icebreakers are an excellent way to begin to collect information about the project team and stakeholders. These can be used during the initial stages of the project, such as during kickoff meetings. We will explore icebreakers further in Chapter 7, Team Leadership.

Here are some suggested categories of information to collect for each stakeholder. This list starts out with easy-to-obtain or known information and ends with information that is more difficult to obtain. See Appendix C for a template that can be used to collect this information.

Stakeholder Priority

You will want to identify the relative priority of this stakeholder to the project. This should be based on the ability of the stakeholder to affect the outcome of the project. You can use a simple high, medium, and low evaluation or you can use a scale of 1 to 5. A stakeholder who can bring the project to a halt, such as a funding sponsor, should receive a high priority. On the other hand, an end user responsible for using the project deliverables might have a medium or low priority.

The value of the priority is to help us to focus our stakeholder relationship efforts. We usually have limited time, and we need to focus our efforts on the high priority stakeholders without completely ignoring lower priority stakeholders.

Role on the Project

The role on the project is somewhat self-explanatory. The stakeholder categories that we previously described may be a good starting point for role identification (e.g., vendor, end user, senior management).

Position Relative to the Project

The position relative to the project is a judgment call on how the stakeholder views the project. You could use a simple scale, such as positive, negative, and neutral. Of course, you can use a more elaborate scale that would include both direction and strength, such as strong positive or weak negative. You could also use a positive and negative numeric scale, such as −5 to +5. The idea is to understand where the stakeholder stands in relationship to the project outcomes. If you don't know what the stakeholder's position is relative to the project, that could be a problem. Make it a priority to find out.

Stakeholder Objectives

In the stakeholder objectives section, we should describe succinctly what the stakeholder wants the project to achieve. This may not be something that is readily apparent to you. If necessary, you might need to guess at first. Follow up with the stakeholders, and ask them, "What is in it for you?" Examples of stakeholder objectives include reaching personal or professional goals, getting promoted, reducing costs, increasing market share, and providing productivity tools to staffs. Each stakeholder has some objective for the project. You stand a better chance of connecting with that stakeholder when you speak his or her language, that is, when you understand that person's objectives and how the project relates to those objectives.

Facts, Passions, and Areas of Interest

This is an area where we do a somewhat subjective analysis of the person. Examples of the types of information to include in this section are background on the individual, previous jobs, conflict style, membership in clubs or professional organizations, sports teams followed, and other personal information. The idea is to get as rounded a picture of the stakeholder as possible.

A word of caution is appropriate here. Anything in this section must be factual and written as accurately as possible without being in any way offensive. Further, you should avoid documenting several categories of information, including things like drinking habits, ethnic/racial/religious background, political tendencies, and sexual orientation. For example, the fact that a major stakeholder is having an affair with one of the project team members may be important to know; I just don't recommend documenting it. This type of information has the potential to cause a lot of harm; proceed with extreme caution.

Communication Style

In the communications style section, we want to outline the preferred forms of communications for this stakeholder. Do they prefer email, voice mail or phone, or one-on-one communications? Do they want to hear from you regularly or only when there are problems?

This can sometimes be a tricky balance for a PM dealing with senior managers. There is often a tension between our need to meet and spend time with stakeholders and the stakeholders' desire to protect their time. Some stakeholders will want to minimize time spent in meetings and may ask for email or other forms of written communications. The stakeholder may also be protected by a gatekeeper who is protective of their time. Or, the stakeholder may ask that you work with a designated person in their organization.

For PMs, regular and direct communications with our key stakeholders will be to our advantage. We need to strike a balance between our need for face time and a senior manager's desire to protect their time.

Assessment for Emotional Self-Awareness and Self-Control

In Chapter 5, Social Awareness, we introduced an Assessment for Emotional Self-Awareness and Self-Control (see Appendix B). We can use that checklist on stakeholders just as we did with individuals. Going through the analysis steps for each stakeholder will provide additional insights about their level of emotional intelligence.

Emotional Connections

An emotional connection is an opportunity for us to make a heart-to-heart bond with another person. What are the topics, objectives, and common interests on which we are likely to connect with this stakeholder? These connections could be on a personal or a professional level. Examples of personal interests include having children of about the same age, sharing a passion for golf, following the same sports team, or even a love of mystery novels.

As an example, I was doing training for my first marathon during a recent project. The CEO of my client company was one of my major stakeholders. When the normally quiet gentleman learned that I was preparing to run my first marathon, he instantly perked up and became quite animated. He was anxious to share his own marathon stories and his tips for me as a new marathon runner. Over lunch with other members of the program management team, he went into gory detail on some of the hygiene issues that marathon runners suffer from. It was amazing to me that a senior manager who was normally quite shy and reserved could become so animated and excited about a topic that we shared. From that point forward, he would ask about my running whenever we saw each other and that would be the start of a friendly discussion.

In some cases, you might find it easier to connect on professional interests than on personal topics. Examples of professional interests include excelling in the profession, membership in a professional organization, advancement in the current position, and a desire to network. Once you understand a little more about the individual, it greatly expands the potential for connecting emotionally.

Information Overload?

You might be overwhelmed by the list that I have suggested. How can anyone collect all this information? The short answer is that you don't try to collect it all at once. You start with the highest priority stakeholders and gather what information you can. Then, use every meeting with a stakeholder to gather a little more information about him or her. View this as an ongoing activity throughout the life of the project. As you learn, you can apply that information to building the relationship. Pretty soon you will find that the relationship building has momentum; it will take less work to maintain the relationship.

Collecting this information requires that you learn to ask the right questions and then listen a lot, applying the empathetic listening techniques we discussed in Chapter 5. Where possible, take notes.

A mentor that I had early in my career knew the value of building relationships with a stakeholder. His strategy was to get out of the office for stakeholder meetings. He used his lunchtime, as well as his dinnertime, for opportunities to meet either one-on-one or in groups. Though he was a hard worker, he was adamant about setting personal boundaries and taking care of himself. For example, he always started his workday as early as 6:00 or

7:00 AM, and he never skipped lunch. These were sit-down meals in a restaurant; not a quick sandwich at his desk. He was also disciplined about ending his workday at 5:00 or so and then heading off for drinks and dinner.

This flew in the face of my own work style at that time, which was to get to work early, work as hard as possible all day (including through lunch), and leave when I felt I had completed all or most of my work. With coaching from my mentor, I was able to start leveraging lunch as a critical time for relationship building. Now, I consistently use lunch to build relationships. I try to ask questions and listen a lot more than I talk. I ask stakeholders about themselves as well as what they know about the other stakeholders. People are usually willing to talk about themselves and will readily open up once they feel comfortable.

I made good use of lunchtime to build stakeholder relationships with the members of a large and diverse team on a recent project. I created an award for the team player of the week. As part of winning the award, another PM and I would take the weekly winner out to lunch. This became a great time to get to know the team members in a low-threat environment. We were able to talk about the project and each individual's objectives and ideas. We were also able to go beyond the project to learn more about each person, their background, their hobbies, and even their family.

Develop Relationships Strategies

The analysis from the previous step provides the basis for us to develop strategies for the relationship. This includes identifying areas where we have emotional connections to the stakeholder, exploring relationship strategies, and then developing action steps to help us to achieve those strategies.

Given everything that we know about the stakeholder, what strategies should we pursue to build the relationship? How can we systematically develop a relationship that serves the project and the two of you? How can we show that we understand the stakeholder's interests and objectives for the project and that we will treat those objectives with importance? Here are some aspects of relationship strategy to consider:

1. The Direct Approach
Often the best strategy is the most direct one. This requires us to consider how to work closely with the stakeholder to build the relationship. We determine what types of meetings we should have and how frequently. We evaluate ways of having both formal and informal updates and reasons to stay in touch with him or her. Finally, we consider ways of directly influencing the stakeholder.

2. The Indirect Approach

Consider the indirect approach for informal or impromptu meetings with stakeholders. I was once a PM for a large IT project at the headquarters of my company. I found that even when I didn't plan to meet with my stakeholders, I would often bump into them in the hallways. The stakeholders would often ask how things were going. Unfortunately, when this first happened I was unprepared. I would blurt out something like "not good, our lead developer just left the team."

With time, I learned a better approach. I began to keep a 3″ × 5″ card in my back pocket that contained a few talking points about the project. These talking points were positive items or conversation starters. With that card in my pocket, I was prepared for these impromptu discussions. I didn't actually pull that card out of my pocket. Just going through the process of preparing my message helped me when I needed it.

3. Talk to My People

In some cases, we will have to develop strategies to reach hard-to-get stakeholders. This applies to those senior managers who have an administrator or staff member who serves as the gatekeeper to the stakeholder. The gatekeeper may have implicit or explicit instructions about your level of access. If your stakeholder is protected by one or more administrators, your strategy will need to include how to handle the gatekeeper. Otherwise, you might have good intentions for building relationships but little success in actually making them happen. Your stakeholder may simply be "too busy" to meet with you.

A related situation is when your key stakeholder has designated someone on his or her staff to work with you. The stakeholder may make it quite clear that he or she will be happy if the staff member or key manager is happy. In this situation, we need to treat this key manager or staff person with the same care we would show the stakeholder. We need to add them to our stakeholder list, collect information about them and analyze it, and develop relationship strategies as we do for the other stakeholders.

4. Keep Your Friends Close

In the movie *The Godfather*, Don Corleone advises his son to "keep your friends close and your enemies closer." This may run counter to your own intuition to distance yourself from individuals who don't like you or who oppose your project. After all, if someone doesn't like us or want our project to succeed, why would we want to be in a relationship with them? The reality is that when you have stakeholders who are neutral or negative toward the project, you cannot afford to ignore them or distance yourself from them. They are perhaps more important than those who are friendly to the project.

You need to do your best to keep them close. It is important to try to build trust and respect with them especially if they are negative toward the goals of the project. Your goal may be to earn their respect even if they don't agree with your goals and objectives.

5. Delegate Responsibility for the Relationship

Delegation is a relationship strategy that we may need to employ when there are many stakeholders and we are spread thin. There will be times when we cannot nurture stakeholder relationships personally and we need to ask for help. In those cases, we can delegate responsibility for management of specific stakeholder relationships to members of our team or even upward to our boss.

As an example, I recently led a large project with a client in another country. In addition to being far apart geographically, I was separated from the client culturally and by eight time zones. Since I was unable to get much face time with this client, I delegated responsibility for the relationship to one of the PMs who worked for me in the client's country. He had a better understanding of the culture and language than I did, and I trusted him to build the relationship and keep me informed. Though not a perfect strategy, it worked better than my efforts to directly manage the relationship remotely.

Action Steps to Nurture the Relationship

Once we have the strategy for the relationship, we can begin to document the tactics and specific steps we are going to take to build relationships with each of the stakeholders. This could be as simple as planning a series of meetings, writing a single report or set of reports, or setting up recurring lunch appointments. It could be as extensive as learning more about the policies and objectives of a particular lobbying group or attending a meeting of a professional organization. Here are some examples of action steps:

1. Regular One-on-One Meetings

As mentioned, one of my favorite techniques for managing project team members and other stakeholders is the regular one-on-one meeting. By establishing a set time on a regular basis, you can stay in touch with and be up to date on your stakeholder. Set a meeting length and frequency appropriate to the relationship. Some will require a monthly meeting of thirty minutes; others could be a weekly one-hour meeting.

2. Customized Project Briefing Reports

Consider drafting project briefings that are targeted status accounts for key stakeholders. You can present the relevant information in a way that minimizes their time investment.

I learned to do this from a mentor earlier in my career. I was having some trouble getting involvement from a key stakeholder. My mentor suggested that each week I draft a very crisp, one-page briefing report that was tailored to that stakeholder. This briefing report contained key status updates, any major issues and what was being done to manage them, and actions needed from the stakeholder. The stakeholder understood that the briefing report was written specifically for him, and he valued it. My ability to get his involvement and action on key items increased significantly after preparing the weekly briefing report.

3. After-Hours Meetings

Some stakeholders may be easier to connect after regular working hours. I once worked for a program manager who frequented a pub every night after work with his key team members. The conversation and information flowed freely. It was as if he was keeping office hours every night. No appointment was needed; I just showed up to connect with him. Whenever there was anything important to discuss, I would make it a point to go and see him at his pub. If he had an issue or wanted to talk, he would ask me to stop by for a pint.

With some relationships, it will be easier to build connections outside the workplace. This could include attendance at professional organizations, attending sporting events together, or golfing together.

4. Maintain an Action Log and Follow Up Regularly

When managing stakeholders, we should not lose sight of the basic tools used to manage other parts of the project. Simple tools, such as an action log and regular follow-ups, should be used. Even stakeholders who initially squirm under this level of accountability will often come around to appreciate it. If nothing else, the action log provides us a built-in reason for contacting our stakeholders. Be sure to include owners for each action item and follow-up dates.

5. Lunch Meetings

As mentioned, lunchtime is an excellent opportunity for relationship building. Nearly everyone eats lunch and the environment can be good for informal discussions.

I was reminded of the usefulness of lunch meetings recently by a stakeholder who was a master at effectively using lunch. Over the course of two years, I lunched with this stakeholder numerous times, and it is something I look back on fondly. He would select a very nice restaurant, sit back, and thoroughly enjoy himself. During lunch. he was entirely focused on our discussion and relationship. It was as if he had no other cares or responsibilities during that time. This was hard to imagine since he was a senior vice president of the organization. On the other hand, I had to work to relax and enjoy myself. I would be scared that somehow I wasn't working or being productive if I was spending one-on-one time with this key stakeholder.

If it helps, you can use a framework for recording all the information you collect and the strategies you've developed for the stakeholder and the relationship. As mentioned, start with the template in Appendix C, which can be tailored to your specific needs by adding or subtracting to the sections that address the areas most important to you. However you document it, I recommend that you exercise some caution with the sensitivity of the information. Don't leave the information lying around the office, don't store it on the company's shared drive, and don't leave it on the network printer.

For some people, using templates and processes for managing relationships may sound stiff, unnatural, contrived, or manipulative. It certainly is unnatural to me but then again, I am not naturally a great relationship person. If you are instinctively good at building relationships, you will succeed without templates or a rigid process. Project management is anything but a step-by-step formula. However, I don't think all PMs are naturally good at relationships, which are too important to be left to chance. An ad hoc approach to managing stakeholders just might work, but who wants to take that risk?

You might also consider tools beyond the template to help you manage information about your stakeholders. You might use a simple database program or a contact management tool, such as SalesForce.com. MS Outlook could even be used to capture much of this information. Use the tools you are most comfortable with, ones that provide the value you need.

There are a number of parallels between stakeholder relationship management and customer relationship management. An entire category of CRM tools exist today to manage customer relationships. In a project environment, each stakeholder could be thought of as a customer. Just like companies have adopted CRM applications for managing customer relationships, PMs need to treat relationships with stakeholders with the same importance.

Manage Stakeholder Relationships

We use the analysis of our collected data and our strategies to actively manage the stakeholder relationship. Based on the priorities we assigned to each relationship, we strategically and intentionally engage our project stakeholders. We don't leave it up to chance.

The collected information becomes a framework and a basis for managing the relationship on an ongoing basis. We want to be organized and thoughtful about the energy we invest in our relationships. The goal is to have deep and satisfying relationships that are going to support the project.

In addition, consider the use of this information in light of the other emotional intelligence domains we have discussed, including self-awareness, self-management, or social awareness. Knowing what we know about our stakeholders, think about the steps needed to establish more effective communications with them. By using our own emotions when interacting with them, we more easily understand what they are feeling and relate to them better. We can also consider the importance of the stakeholder's objectives, interests, and needs, and use that information to relate to them. Finally, when we are self-aware and relating to them on their level, we are more likely to be the kind of people they want to be in a relationship with.

Here are some examples of how I have used these principles to manage stakeholders on projects.

The Division Vice President

Some time ago I was in charge of implementing a project accounting package. The executive sponsor for the project was a nice guy, but he was not engaged as much as we needed. This sponsor didn't really understand his role on the project and was more comfortable staying out of the details. I needed this sponsor's help with training and roll-out of the accounting package, but found him aloof and uninvolved, so I avoided him. I did what I could to accomplish the project objectives without him.

Fortunately, my functional manager intervened and coached me to do better. He told me that I had to get the VP involved, that it wasn't optional. He encouraged me to get on the VP's calendar with a set of regular "executive briefings." Using the executive briefing approach, I was able to get the face time I needed. As a result, I learned what I needed to know about the stakeholder, and I was able to build a personal relationship with this important executive. That relationship helped me to get the project buy-in I needed from the division, to get the resources I needed for training and roll out, and to get the VP's help resolving several thorny issues.

I learned some valuable lessons from that experience. First, executive sponsor involvement wasn't optional. Second, I was coached to call the meetings with the sponsor executive "briefings," but they were really about building the relationship. Finally, I learned the importance of ongoing meetings to continue to manage the relationship.

Consulting Firm

On another project I led, there were several outside consultants from one particular firm. These consultants played a key role on our project, and we were dependent on them for our success. These consultants were great performers, but like many high achievers, they could be challenging to manage. Since they were critical to our success, it was important to keep them focused on the project's objectives and interested in staying until their work was finished.

I recognized that in this environment, the key stakeholder relationship to be managed was with the resource manager for the consulting firm. He had direct control over the resources and a strong incentive for each team member to perform at a high level. He also had insights about each of the resources that came with knowing these people for many years. I made it a point to meet with the resource manager from that firm every two weeks. We talked about where the project was going and about how each of those key consultants was performing. He was able to share with me any problems, frustrations, or suggested improvements that he heard about from the individual consultants. He was able to do so in a frank and candid way.

In turn, I was able to provide the resource manager with feedback about his consultants. Our personal relationship helped to provide a free flow of information. It also helped the project to thrive even with the inevitable staffing turnovers and transitions.

Technology Vendor

On another project I managed, a key technology vendor was critical to the project's success. The relationship with this stakeholder had been managed by a technical lead who reported to me. When my technical lead left the project, I let the relationship atrophy. This was a near disaster. We were well into the project before I realized that some of the vendor's products were not performing well and that we were not getting the level of technical support that we needed. Because of the near lock that this vendor had on the market, the company had grown arrogant about customer support. My technical staff had become dissatisfied with the support from this vendor and stopped calling to report our problems. My initial calls to them did not address my concerns and left me feeling angry and dissatisfied.

I started by working on the relationship with the vendor's business development manager responsible for our account. I was able to set up a series of face-to-face meetings with him to build the relationship, to show him that I understood and cared about his objectives, and then to focus on our problems. He and I worked together to set up meetings between my project team and his help desk and technical support team. While the relationship was never as good as I would have liked, it did improve significantly after those meetings.

Rookie Mistake—Focusing Only on the Project Team

A common mistake made by some PMs is to focus all their energy on managing relationships with the immediate project team at the expense of managing the other project stakeholders. This was a mistake I made early in my career. I focused downward and concentrated my relationship efforts solely on the team. I did not focus outward on the other project stakeholders. This was dangerous and career limiting. While good relationships with the team members are important, it is vital for the PM to manage all the stakeholder relationships. Without the support of your stakeholders, your project will suffer and could possibly fail.

This does not mean you should ignore your project team relationships. You need to strike a balance between the relationships with your team members and the relationships with the other stakeholders.

This mistake was easy for me because I placed a high priority on the relationships with my team. I also think it was because I lacked courage. Relationships with the team were easy; they were the path of least resistance. It was significantly more difficult and scarier to reach out to the stakeholders and manage the relationship with them. PMs may also find it very obvious who the team members are and less obvious who the other stakeholders are on a project. The bottom line is that we need to identify all the stakeholders and manage the relationships with them.

■ Developing Others

The second competency in the relationship management domain is developing others. For PMs, developing others means to invest in and grow the project team. Most PMs would agree that developing their staff is an important component of the job. The PMBOK® Guide mentions development of others in section 9.3, Develop Project Team. The objectives in the PMBOK® Guide are twofold:

1. Increasing team member capabilities
2. Teambuilding

The PMBOK® Guide mentions the following 6 tools and techniques for developing others:

1. A PM's general management skills, in particular, interpersonal skills
2. Formal and informal training of the team members
3. Team-building activities

4. Ground rules
5. Co-location
6. Recognition and rewards[3]

As PMs we need to recognize that developing others means making an investment in them. As a result of this investment, we create goodwill and deepen our relationship with our team members. In *Working with Emotional Intelligence*, Daniel Goleman identified the following competencies for individuals skilled at developing others:

- Acknowledge and reward people's strengths and accomplishments
- Offer useful feedback and identify people's needs for further growth
- Mentor, give timely coaching, and offer assignments that challenge and foster a person's skills[4]

This sounds exactly like the type of investment my coaches and mentors have made in me over my career. Let's explore further this concept of developing others to understand what it means for PMs.

Acknowledge Strengths and Contributions

Acknowledging the strengths and contributions of your project team members is a powerful tool for encouraging them. We must start by being able to clearly see others and to recognize and appreciate the uniqueness of each person. We need to understand their strengths and how they are contributing to the team. Of the two, contributions to the project may be easier to see. Strengths are about potential, and contribution occurs when that potential is realized. If someone on your project team is not able to leverage or apply their strengths, those strengths may not be apparent to you. If we are unable to recognize and utilize the strengths of our team members, we are not leveraging the potential of the team.

Work by the Gallup organization highlights the importance of focusing on strengths when providing feedback. Gallup has developed an online assessment tool called StrengthsFinder (see www.strengthsfinder.com) that can be used to identify the top five strengths of an individual out of a universe of forty-five strengths that include such straightforward strengths as Focus and Strategic, as well as less clear strengths such as Woo and Learner.

---

[3]Project Management Institute (PMI). *A Guide to the Project Management Body of Knowledge* (PMBOK® Guide)—Third Edition, Newton Square, PA 19073-3299. Project Management Institute, Inc., 2004.

[4]Daniel Goleman, *Working with Emotional Intelligence*. NY: Random House/Bantam Books, 1998.

Table 6-1: The Author's Top Five Strengths

Focus:	People strong in the focus theme can take direction, follow through, and make the corrections necessary to stay on track. They prioritize, then act.
Significance:	People strong in the significance theme want to be very important in the eyes of others. They are independent and want to be recognized.
Strategic:	People strong in the strategic theme create alternative ways to proceed. Faced with any given scenario, they can quickly spot the relevant patterns and issues.
Self-Assurance:	People strong in the self-assurance theme feel confident in their ability to manage their own lives. They possess an inner compass that gives them confidence that their decisions are right.
Learner:	People strong in the learner theme have a great desire to learn and want to continuously improve. In particular, the process of learning, rather than the outcome, excites them.

I have used the StrengthsFinder tool and found the results helpful and fascinating. My top five strengths are shown in Table 6-1.

Understanding my strengths was an important part of my accurate self-assessment. I am better able to appreciate why I am successful in certain areas and why others are difficult for me. Since taking the assessment, I have been more intentional about choosing opportunities that leverage my strengths. I am also able to focus on growing in the areas of my strengths.

As PMs we should also be aware of and recognize each individual's contribution to the project. Recognition is one of the most powerful, yet underused, tools in the PM's arsenal. It takes so little effort and cost to recognize team members, and the payoff can be huge. There are thousands of ways to recognize and acknowledge our team's contributions: in one-on-one meetings, in chance encounters in the hallway, in a team meeting, in an email to the individual or the line manager, in a status report, etc.

Try thanking each person on a regular basis for their appropriate contribution to the project. Hearing a heartfelt thank you for your hard work can be a major motivator for a team member.

> Recognition is one of the most powerful yet underused tools in the PM's arsenal.

Targeted Feedback

The competency of developing others also includes providing feedback. I like to qualify feedback by calling it "targeted feedback." Remember that feedback is the breakfast of champions. Providing feedback to others is an investment that we make in their growth.

There is certainly an art to providing effective feedback. Positive feedback is usually easy to give and does not require much risk. However, providing constructive feedback can take courage and may involve risks. If we don't take care and use the feedback as an investment, the team member can take offense and become de-motivated. Here are some keys to providing constructive feedback.

Stick to the Facts

Feedback to others should be based on facts. We should not rely on hearsay or jump to conclusions. If we are in doubt about the facts, we should ask the individual in question to clarify them.

Focus on the Positive

Positive feedback is always easier to hear; it is also motivational. Strive to provide feedback that recognizes those things that are going well as well as areas in which the employee's work has improved.

My wife is great at focusing on the positive when it comes to giving feedback to our kids. While I tend to react to the negative things they do, she often coaches me to wait until they do something well and compliment them on that.

Be As Clear As Possible

Feedback should not be ambiguous. Individuals should not walk away wondering what you were trying to tell them. Keep in mind that giving and receiving feedback can be stressful, and our minds may not be working very clearly. Our fear can cause us to have trouble saying what we want in a clear and concise way.

Recipients of feedback can also get so scared they do not clearly hear what is being said. They may also put their own filter on the message and focus in on only one part.

To get the best results, keep your message really simple and write it out in advance. Make notes, even in bullet form, of the message you are striving to get across. Be as clear and specific as possible and use words that are accurate and easy to understand. Use phrases like "here is what I need from you." Don't make it a mystery.

Make It Accurate

If we provide inaccurate or partially inaccurate feedback, the recipient may feel unseen and will dismiss our assessment. For example, if we use the words "always" or "never" in our feedback, we need to make sure that they are true and accurate. Rarely do individuals "always" do the thing that we think they always do. If someone hears "you never show up to my meetings on time," they will likely think of the one or two times that they did show up on time and use that to ignore or dismiss your feedback.

Keep It As Objective As Possible

While we all impose our own subjective voice on feedback, we should strive to be as objective as possible with each individual. Separate the behavior from the person. It is better to say "I don't like it when you don't meet your commitments" than to say "you are lazy." We should also avoid comparisons with others when we provide the feedback.

Invest, Don't Punish

The goal of our feedback should be to help the person to develop. Before you give feedback, explore the feelings and emotions you have toward that person. Determine if you are operating from another agenda or trying to repay some slight that you feel. For example, if you are angry, you should address that anger separately and not punish others. If you are not trustworthy with your feedback, you will not be successful in developing others.

We need to recognize that if we are feeling angry or scared, we may inadvertently make the feedback more negative than appropriate. Conversely, when we feel happy or excited about someone, our feedback may be more positive than appropriate and we may withhold candid feedback that could really help the other person.

Coaching, Mentoring, and Work Assignments

The third area of developing others is coaching, mentoring, and work assignments. This is one of the biggest opportunities for PMs. Whether it is formal or informal, coaching and mentoring can be used to develop the project team. What is the difference between coaching and mentoring?

> *Coach:* Someone who teaches and directs another person using encouragement and advice.
>
> *Mentor:* a trusted friend, counselor, or teacher, usually with more experience.

The key elements of these definitions include trust, encouragement, and experience. As PMs, we need to consider coaching and mentoring as a large part of our job. Remember that project management is about getting work done through others. By coaching and mentoring, we encourage others and help them to grow and develop, which gives them the potential to contribute more to the team.

I have been fortunate to have had several great coaches and mentors over my career, some of whom were managers and PMs. I recognize the value of their investment in me. In fact, it is hard for me to imagine having grown as a PM without receiving their valuable input over the years. As an independent consultant and business owner, I no longer have a formal manager. However, I continue to seek out coaches and mentors. I would not have been able to start and maintain my own company without the encouragement of my mentors. This book was the direct result of the investment of one of my mentors.

The final topic in the area of developing others is the assignment of work. The allocation of work assignments on a project is one of the most important roles of a PM. How the PM executes this will determine if people are given room to grow on the project or whether they feel their role is limited and perhaps the PM doesn't know or care about them.

Consider your own approach to making work assignments. What is your level of intention? Do you think of both the short-term and long-term needs of the project team? Or, do you find that when you have a short-term need you simply fill it and ignore the development needs and objectives of the team members?

We must also consider the longer term needs of the project and the individual. Sometimes we need to assign work not based on who can currently do it but who needs to learn it. We need to think about cross training and reducing risks and dependencies on key people on the team. We may also need to consider the savings we can incur in the long run by developing junior people to take on more responsibility within the team.

■ Telling the Truth

The third relationship management competency is telling the truth. Being honest and forthcoming with the people we interact with on our projects sounds quite simple but it is rarely a simple thing to do.

You might think that we should always tell the truth. I am not talking about owning up to "who chopped down the cherry tree" or "who took my lunch from the company refrigerator." I am talking about more than simply not lying. I am talking about telling the truth when it is difficult, when we are trying to be polite, when it makes us vulnerable, or when it could create conflict. Let's look at a couple of examples.

A subtle example of truth telling happened during a phone interview for a PM position in which I was interested. The interview was to start at 9:00 AM and sure enough, at 9:00 my phone rang. The women interviewing me said hello and then added that she didn't want to waste my time because the position had been offered to another candidate the previous day.

I was disappointed of course, and sad and angry. I thought about it throughout the day and came to realize that I was also bothered that she said she didn't want to waste my time. In other words, she believed she needed to take care of me and watch out for my time instead of letting me take care of my own needs and end the interview. The truth of the matter was, that she didn't want to waste her time! This is completely understandable and would have been a more truthful and direct communication. She stated it as if she were taking care of me, but the truth was she did not want to invest any more of her time. So, to be more honest, she could have simply said, "I don't want to spend any more time on this so let's not have an interview this morning." Or, "I don't want to waste both of our time with an interview."

A related example that happens frequently is when I am talking to a friend or family member on the phone. They will often end the conversation by saying something like, "I don't want to keep you any longer" or "I'll let you go." Those may both be true, but it is also likely that *they* want to go or don't want to spend any more time on the phone. They act as if they are taking care of me, when in fact they are taking care of themselves.

We have all heard this before, right? People say to us, "I am going to let you go now" or "I want to respect your time." or "I don't want to keep you any longer." What they are really saying is "I want to go now." That is much more direct and truthful.

There are other cases in which telling the truth may seem impolite. If you were out to dinner, and your spouse had broccoli stuck between their teeth, would you say something? Of course. We wouldn't want our spouse to look ridiculous. What if instead of your spouse it was the CEO or a key client? We still would probably want to tell the truth, right? What if we were in a big group? Would we still say something? What if the CEO or key client was making a presentation that everyone in the room found embarrassing? What if a man's fly was open or a woman had a bra strap or underwear showing?

There are other cases where we don't take care of ourselves or go for what we want. Consider this example. What if your boss needed you to work on a weekend and you already had other plans with your spouse? Would you simply swallow quietly and then call your spouse to cancel your plans? Or, would you stall or agree to it, and then try to find a way to avoid the inevitable conflict between work needs and your spouse? Or, would you speak up to your boss on the spot, saying that you have other plans for the weekend and that your boss will have to find another way to reach the objective?

Here is an even more vulnerable situation. How many of us have had someone say something to us that was dumb, inappropriate, insensitive, or simply politically incorrect? We can often be so stunned by something that another person says that we don't respond. I've had people tell off-color jokes and use racial epithets. My own reaction was often low in courage; I would pretend not to hear the comment or simply change the subject. A more courageous approach is to stop the discussion immediately and say something like "I don't like your comment" or "That was rude."

This is the subtlety of truth telling. We all strive to tell the truth all the time, but sometimes it is difficult and we are tempted to not be completely honest. We need to be willing to tell the truth with courage and not hold back.

I find that I really appreciate people who tell the truth. In the movie *Liar Liar*, Jim Carey plays an attorney. For a short period of time, he cannot tell a lie. As a result, he finds that both his personal and professional lives becomes untenable. My favorite part is when he is asked to say something about each of his coworkers gathered together in a conference room. Since he must tell the truth, he says things that people have not been willing to say about each other, even though they know it is the truth. Everyone finds it hilarious as he goes around the large conference table saying what everyone has thought about but never said out loud.

Unless you are ready to make a job change, I suggest that you think twice before you go into work and try to do the same. But I would contend that people who tell the truth in a direct and responsible way are valued. Think about your close friends and coworkers. Do you value the ones who "Tell it like it is" or always let you know where they stand? I know I do. Truth is critical to effective relationships.

The challenge for many of us is that we have been taught that telling the truth is not a good idea when it comes to others. Each of us were taught some rules about what is okay to say and what is not. Take a look at the following common family rules about truth telling and see if you identify with any of them.

1. If you can't say something nice, don't say anything at all.
2. Children should be seen and not heard.
3. Respect your elders
4. We don't talk about things outside of our family.

If you look at each of these rules from a "truthfulness" point of view, do you think that these rules would tend to shape children into truth tellers?

If I want to be a strong leader and PM, I need to be able to tell the truth as directly and responsibly as possible. Telling the truth makes me trustworthy, it attracts followers, and helps me to build strong relationships with others. I know all that but I still find it challenging sometimes due to my early childhood training.

Leaving out the truth can be the equivalent of not telling the truth. Some time ago, I was responsible for a critical IT program, and I reported directly to the executive sponsor. One day prior to a large program review, I received an email from my sponsor's manager "Gary," who was also a critical stakeholder. Gary said he wanted a program update directly from me. He said he wanted the unfiltered truth about the state of the program.

I was flattered and excited. He wants to hear from me! Wow, I must be important. We spoke on a Friday morning before a broader program review with my sponsor and other key stakeholders. I was pretty blunt and straightforward when I shared my thoughts and recommendations with Gary. I think I may even have quietly congratulated myself on what a good truth teller I had become. I did not, however, tell my sponsor about the call.

Later that day, in the middle of the broader program review, Gary dropped a bomb. Out of nowhere he said something like "This was one of the things that I asked Anthony about when we spoke this morning." Ouch! I did not see that coming. My sponsor didn't say anything (out loud), but his body language spoke volumes! In fact, he did not say another word to me that day.

It was clear that he didn't like being blindsided. Duh! I should have let him know I was going to talk with his boss about the program. I went from feeling like someone important to feeling like a snitch. I felt like a total idiot for not telling the complete truth to my sponsor.

Late in the day I called my sponsor on his cell phone and apologized for not letting him in on the conversation with his boss. I told him that I would always let him know whenever I had any type of conversation with his boss. He said that it was okay, and I think that I repaired some of the damage, but I know that my actions that day cost me big time in terms of his trust.

As noted above, some of have baggage about truth telling, which will make it difficult. I was taught as a child that if I didn't have something nice to say, I shouldn't say anything at all. My mother enforced this rule at our house. It certainly helped us around my dad, who was volatile and punitive. I learned early on not to volunteer to him any more information than was necessary. Some people would consider this behavior as polite or demonstrating good manners; others would consider it withholding. Withholding the truth can have the same impact as lying or being manipulative.

One of the many topics addressed in the book *Crucial Conversations: Tools for Talking When Stakes Are High* is the ability to remain focused on what we want out of our conversations. The authors describe the importance of recognizing what is at stake in a crucial conversation. When the stakes are high, we may feel as though our choices are limited to one of two things: either saying nothing at all or venting our feelings and making a mess. When the moment of truth comes, it may seem as if these are our only two choices. *Crucial Conversations* calls these two options a sucker's choice.

You have probably experienced this type of situation in a meeting where you feel that you must choose between either blowing up or being silent and withholding. The authors of *Crucial Conversations* recommend that we ask ourselves two questions to help us see beyond those initial choices. The first question is, "What is our objective?" The second question is, "What do we not want to have happen?" Once we orient back to what we want and what we don't want, we can explore alternative approaches.[5]

Consider an example from a project I led. We had a serious system problem with our network that was affecting most of my team. I set up a meeting with the responsible infrastructure manager to discuss the issue. It was clear from the beginning that he was not interested in solving my problem. He only wanted to get me out of his office. He did not provide satisfactory answers to my questions about his action plan and, worse, he had scheduled another meeting at the same time as ours. Almost as if on cue, less than 15 minutes into our meeting, one of his staff interrupted us to say it was time for his other meeting. Deflated, my team members and I shuffled out of the room.

The problem with my approach was that I saw my choices in that moment as limited to the sucker's choice. I could either blow up and tell him that he was being an ass, or I could withhold and say nothing. Unfortunately, in that moment I did not think about what I wanted. I did not go for my own satisfaction. I was uncomfortable with the way he ushered me out of the office, yet I did not say anything.

A better approach would have been to recognize what I wanted (get the action plan to fix the problem) and what I did not want (to blow up and act like a jerk) and try to come up with a third alternative. That could have involved negotiating a follow-up meeting later in the day, a brief meeting just between him and me, or some other action. To develop good relationships, we need to be willing to tell the truth. We need to share what we feel, what

[5] Kerry Patterson, Joseph Grenny, Ron McMillan, and Al Switzler. *Crucial Conversations: Tools for Talking When Stakes Are High.* NY: McGraw-Hill, 2002.

we like and dislike, and what we need in a particular situation. We also need to be willing to risk upsetting others.

Techniques for Truth Telling

Fortunately there is help for those of us who have a hard time telling the truth with diplomacy. Here are some tools and techniques to provide a framework for telling the truth in the project environment. I have listed them in order from the lowest risk to the highest risk.

Providing Your Reaction

What others do and say affects all of us. It is entirely appropriate to provide your reaction, especially if you are asked. For example, if your boss goes overboard with criticism of a team member, you might say "you probably didn't need to be so harsh to get your point across."

Saying No

Many of us struggle with saying no. When we are asked to do something, most of us like to oblige by saying yes. For some of us, we say yes to show that we are helpful and competent. For others, we say yes to be liked or valued. As a result, we may agree to things that we really should say no to. How many of us have ended up taking home extra work and even disrupting personal plans because we were unwilling to say no? How many of us, when asked, find it impossible to say no even when we are being asked to do something beyond the limits of reasonableness? When we are asked about it later, we are likely to say something like, "I couldn't say no."

Improving our ability to say no is the subject of a publication by Dr. Susan Newman, *The Book of No: 250 Ways to Say It—and Mean It—and Stop People-Pleasing Forever*. Dr. Newman gives us the following reasons for why we say yes when we should say no:

1. Most people have been programmed to think saying no is negative
2. Inability to think clearly about what is being asked due to fear or guilt[6]

For some of us, saying no is a muscle we simply have not practiced using. We tend to say yes first without thinking about it and then later we regret having responded that way. We try not to offend or disappoint without

---

[6]Susan Newman. *The Book of No: 250 Ways to Say It—and Mean It and Stop People-Pleasing Forever*. NY: McGraw-Hill, 2005.

realizing that by saying no in the first place, we are less likely to disappoint others.

When we cannot say no, we set ourselves up in a couple of ways. First, we cannot honestly say yes to anything. If we never say no, we always say yes. Our yes might actually be a "yes for now but I am going turn it into a no later." We may say yes but in reality never intend to follow through and deliver whatever it was we agreed to in that moment. We will somehow sabotage that yes and ultimately make it a no.

The second way we set ourselves up is by feeling like a victim. We may say yes now only to be able to resent others and make them pay later. Think about situations where you or someone you know volunteered to do something and then complained and showed resentment afterward. This may be a recurrent pattern in your life or their life. Some people volunteer and then find themselves stewing about others who did not volunteer.

As a PM, saying yes too much can damage our careers. We cannot always say yes to additional work, client requests for freebies, vacation requests, changes in responsibilities, or requests for individuals to be promoted or take on larger roles on the project. We need to know when to say no. If we don't protect ourselves and our team by saying no, we will alienate our team and perhaps even cause them to leave the project. We need to be able to say no and to say yes with honesty and integrity. We need to remember that we have a choice and that we should exercise that choice. Saying yes when we don't mean it can be far more damaging than saying no when we need to.

Using "I Like / I Dislike" Statements

A very helpful technique for relationship building is to state what you like or dislike. You might say, "I like when you get your deliverables done on time" as a way to encourage your team members. A higher risk version is to say, "I didn't like when you made that disparaging comment about Bob." That type of communication is clear and to the point.

Another example occurs when you have a group trying to make a decision. Let's say a group of six are trying to decide where to go for lunch. If someone suggests a Chinese restaurant, and you really do not like Chinese food, it would be responsible to say something like, "I don't care for Chinese food. How about (fill in your choice here)?" That is stating what you like or dislike.

It beomes difficult when we don't want to appear selfish or don't want to offend others. In that case, we don't say how we feel, and we wind up eating at the Chinese restaurant. We feel miserable, angry, and resentful of the others in the group. The reality is that we could have avoided that resentment by speaking up about how we felt.

Using "I Need" and "I Want" Statements

Closely related to the concept of likes and dislikes is the concept of stating our wants and needs. When we state in a clear and direct way what we want or need, we greatly increase our chances of getting it. This simple-sounding technique may often prove difficult in practice.

Many of us have developed erroneous beliefs about expressing our wants and needs. Some common misbeliefs include:

- We won't get what we want by asking for it directly.
- Asking directly for something is vulnerable and puts us at risk.
- If someone really cared about us, then they would know what we wanted without us having to tell them.

Many of us learned to manipulate instead of asking for things directly. We might say something like "I knew you liked Chinese food so that is what I ordered," instead of the more truthful, "I wanted Chinese food for lunch so that is what I ordered."

One of the most powerful phrases I learned to say in the context of a project was "I need you to do a favor for me." Early in my career, I would have felt very vulnerable saying that. As I grew as a PM and learned more about emotional intelligence, I found that asking others directly for what I needed was liberating. I could be clear and clean in my communications by just stating what it was that I wanted or needed from others.

Stating Your Beliefs or Judgments

A belief or a judgment is something we feel about others based on our own values. It is the rough equivalent of saying "If I were you in this situation, I would be feeling angry." It sounds like "my judgment is that you are angry."

As an example, consider when you have a team member who habitually arrives late and leaves early. While that person may have been productive for you and for the team in the past, lately she seem to have other priorities. You might say "My judgment is that you aren't giving the team your best effort." That clear communication can start a healthy discussion about expectations. You might follow it up with "I want you to arrive by 8:00 every day" or some other request that indicates the specific behavior you expect from them.

Getting Clear

Getting clear with someone means that you are addressing any anger or conflict in the relationship. It is the emotional intelligence of cleaning your windshield of bugs and dirt. Getting clear requires that you voice any issues you have with another person. You might say something like "That hurt when you didn't show up prepared for the staff meeting the other day. What was going on?"

It helps when we include our own emotions in the process of getting clear. A useful technique is to state the words or actions that the other person does and the emotional impact that this has on you. This technique was introduced in Chapter 5, Social Awareness.

> "When you do . . . _____" (some behavior or action),
> "I feel . . . _____" (an emotion, such as sad or angry)
> "Because . . . _____" (the reason)
> "I want . . . _____" (here is what I want in the future).

We might say something like the following: "I felt sad and angry when you made that joke at the staff meeting yesterday during my presentation. I had worked hard on that presentation, and I wanted to make the point that everyone could do a better job on quality. In the future, I want you to refrain from making comments that take the team off track."

The point of getting clear is that it frees us to move on and focus on other things. Like having a clean windshield, we no longer have issues that bog us down. We don't have to carry any of the emotional baggage of issues or conflict; we can voice them and forget them.

I once worked for a manager who was great about getting clear and then forgetting about it. On one memorable occasion, he sharply criticized me for an email that I had sent to a wide distribution list. My email was poorly written and sounded critical of him. He told me that he didn't like the email, and he wanted me to limit the distribution list on emails that were critical of him. Later, when I called to apologize, he was completely over it. He had made his point and then had moved on and let it go. He felt "clear" and he let me know that the issue wasn't going to affect our relationship.

Keep Short Accounts

A concept closely related to getting clear is the idea of keeping short accounts. When we keep short accounts, we prevent small issues from building into large ones. This is a trap many of us fall into.

How do you respond in situations where there are small hurts or issues? Do you address each one? We might feel it is better to simply let them go or ignore them. We may also feel that we are being gracious if we overlook small hurts or issues. The problem is that the issues tend to build into larger issues. We need to get clear on those small issues on a regular basis to avoid overwhelming resentment or anger.

The benefit of keeping short accounts is that we get a more accurate view of our relationship challenges. When we clear up small issues on a regular basis, we avoid getting too far off track. Others may actually be unaware of the issues we are experiencing. Or, we were in some way responsible for the problem. Rarely have I experienced these small hurts as being intentional on the part of the other person. Instead of having a justified complaint about someone else, we might actually be part of the problem. By clearing up these small issues when they occur, we provide an opportunity to better understand exactly what is happening.

What about being on the receiving end of someone who has not kept short accounts? Have you ever had a project team member or other stakeholder blow up and tell you about everything you have done wrong in the last year? Have you been surprised with the level of anger expressed over seemingly small issues or perceived slights? This is the case of holding in those hurts and resentments.

Keeping short accounts as a PM means that we don't let resentments, wounds, or anger build over time. If we have an issue, we address it quickly. PMs need to lead in relationships and encourage others to keep short accounts with us.

The Importance of Courage

A common theme through all the truth-telling techniques is the willingness to take risk and face our fears. It is not always easy or pleasant to address sensitive topics in a straightforward way. It can be scary for some of us to take risks and tell the truth. Facing that fear requires courage. Courage is not the absence of fear; it is the willingness to act in the face of our fear. Telling the truth requires taking a risk and being vulnerable in order to develop the relationship.

■ Additional Principles of Relationship Building

There are some additional principles that are important to relationship building. These include trustworthiness, co-creation, and the idea that some people are simply difficult to deal with.

Trustworthiness

Trustworthiness is an important component of honest relationships. Trustworthiness is when you can be counted on, when you are reliable, and when you do what you say you will do. It is when you have earned the trust of others.

Without a doubt, trustworthiness is important for PMs. Trustworthy PMs will find it easier to build stakeholder relationships, tell the truth (and hear the truth from others), and attract good resources to their teams. PMs who are not trustworthy will find it difficult to do any of the above.

Trust is earned over time but it can be lost very quickly. It may take only one event or action to cause others to lose trust in you. I encourage you to do what it takes to be consistent, reliable, and trustworthy in all your relationships.

Co-Creation—Results We Create Together

The principle of co-creation is an important one for relationships. It says that a relationship is created by both of the individuals involved. The quality of the relationship and the results from that relationship are a co-creation of the two individuals. This means that both parties in the relationship are responsible for the outcome; neither is solely responsible.

Co-creation is an important principle because it places responsibility and accountability for relationship outcomes on both people. It means that I share the responsibility for any outcomes from our relationship. I cannot distance myself or blame you for what we create together.

Looking at relationships this way is both sobering and empowering. It means that I cannot sit back and claim to be the victim in the relationship or claim that I didn't play a part in the outcome. If I am not getting what I want or need from the relationship, it is my job to work with the other party to change that.

On the flip side, it means that we have the power to affect relationship outcomes as needed. As PMs, we want to make things happen rather than have things happen to us. We are drivers, and we work with others to achieve the results and outcomes we want.

If we do not get the results we want, we need to first examine our own behavior. What was our part in creating the outcome? How did we contribute? This is where it can be tempting to lay the blame completely on the other person for any undesired outcomes. That is extremely unproductive. We must examine our own part.

Instead of making a list of the ways the other person created the negative outcome, make a list of the things you could have done to ensure the outcome you wanted. What could you have done differently? In what ways did your actions (or lack of actions) contribute to the result? Remember that you are not a victim. You have the power to create the outcome you want. Make a decision now to do things differently in the future.

The attraction to victimhood can be a strong one. At its heart is blaming others for our problems. If you view all outcomes as co-creations, you can no longer be a victim and blame others. You must acknowledge the part that you played in creating the outcome. There is power in this acknowledgment; you admit that you can change those outcomes. If we perceive the world as a place where things happen to us, we lack power and the ability to impact our outcomes. If, on the other hand, we view the world as a place where we have a hand in everything that happens to us, we have power, the power to make different outcomes possible.

It is not easy to own, or co-own, the results and outcomes from our relationships. We may be more comfortable blaming those around us for the things that happen.

Co-Creation Corollary—I Think I've Been Here Before

A corollary to the principle of co-creation is the idea that we will begin to see patterns in our relationships that result from the part that we contribute. This can be especially apparent when we look back over all of our relationships. We may see recurring patterns of behavior. We experience *déjà vu*, the feeling that we have been here before.

If a pattern does occur, remember that you are the common denominator. If you have unresolved issues in one relationship, those or similar ones will repeat themselves in future relationships.

Consider this example of co-creation that is so painful it is almost humorous. My father worked nearly forty-five years as a laborer in different manufacturing companies. Though an early starter and a hard worker, he had a history of moving from job to job and probably worked for over twenty different companies in his working life. As a child, I can remember him telling story after story of the different ignorant bosses he had at each job. He always found that he knew so much more than his bosses, who were all unbelievably stupid. Over time, the issues with the ignorant boss would fester and grow and eventually cause my father to quit the job. He would pack up his toolbox and move on to the next job. "Who needed that kind of BS?" he would ask. That certainly sounds like an unfortunate string of bad luck to have all those stupid bosses.

Let's look a little closer to see if bad luck was the only factor or if there was some way that my father was contributing to the situation. If we look across my father's entire work history, a clear pattern emerges. Any thinking person would have been able to predict this after just knowing my father a short while. As he took a job at a new company, he would pretty much start over at or near the bottom or entry-level position in the company. This was primarily a result of his not going for a more senior position and partly because his previous experience and attitude didn't warrant it. Even as my father grew in experience, he was rarely put in charge of more than a few people. When he started in the bottom-rung position, my father's boss would often be someone who was barely above entry level. These bosses were often younger and less experienced than my father.

My father was perhaps correct in his assessment that he was smarter than his bosses. After all, the boss was often younger and less experienced. But then my father would criticize the boss and make a point to show how much smarter he was. My father came into each relationship with a chip on his shoulder. He was angry and critical though he was street smart enough to cloak his anger in humor. He was sarcastic and used humor inappropriately. Eventually, my father would find some way to drive a wedge between himself and his boss or "the management." The outcome was usually that my dad would walk out. Sometimes he would be fired. The way my dad told the story was that a string of ignorant bosses forced him to quit good jobs.

Take a moment to consider your own history and see if you have any repetitive relationship patterns. While it may not be as obvious as a string of ignorant bosses, there are likely other situations where your behavior patterns have been consistent over time. For me it was the use of inappropriate humor and how many problems that created for me. Think about your part in any repeating patterns of conflict or issues. What specific steps do you need to take now to prevent those conflicts from happening again?

This may be the type of thing that is hard for us to see on our own. It may be helpful to ask a spouse or close friend to help you assess patterns. Find people who have known you for a long time and ask them if they see patterns of issues.

As a general rule, relationship outcomes are the co-creation of the two individuals involved. Neither individual is solely responsible; both are jointly responsible. But there may be some times when this is not the case. Let's take a look at situations where we experience relationship breakdowns that are directly related to the other person.

Working with Problem People

At some point in our careers as PMs, we are going to work with individuals who are challenging, difficult, or what I would call problem people. Even PMs who are adept at relationship building need to recognize that some people are so difficult that any unilateral relationship-building efforts will fail. We may even find that the relationship is causing unhealthy stress or putting us in danger. These relationships require strategies far different than we already described.

Rather than blame the other person, we should always orient first to ourselves. If we are having a problem with someone else, we should explore the possibility that we are causing that problem and do our best to make the relationship work. Avoid throwing in the towel too quickly and assuming the problem is with the other person.

As PMs, we need the ability to effectively deal with lots of different types of people to be successful. Whether we'll find them difficult or not is a function of two factors. The first is our skill level in dealing with challenging personalities. The second is the style, personality, and manageability of the other person. We are at greatest risk when our skill level is low and we are dealing with very difficult people. The lowest risk is when we are skilled and the other person is not very difficult. By looking at and improving our own skill level, we empower ourselves to deal with others effectively. If we ignore our own power and focus only on the other person, we will sound like a victim who is entirely at the mercy of others.

We need to continually build our skills at influencing and leading people. We will also strive to understand the various ways that people may be difficult so that we can be prepared to recognize and deal with them. It is quite similar to managing risks; we need to be aware of what can happen to our projects and prepare plans to deal with them.

Of course we aren't responsible for all the problems we encounter with others. There will be some cases where we have exhausted all efforts to build a relationship with another person or we recognize that the other person is broken in some fundamental way. The reality is that if we work in projects long enough, there will be individuals who are more than just difficult to work with. There are some people who are hurt, broken, mean, manipulative, psychotic, and flawed. These individuals will be hard to have on your project team or to manage.

We need to recognize that our own relationship-building efforts will be pointless when dealing with certain types of personalities. At the extreme, some people can even be dangerous to you. To ignore that and assume we are so good at leading that it doesn't matter would be both a denial of reality and a confidence bordering on narcissism. Here are some general categories of problem people who go beyond the definition of difficult and will thwart our efforts at relationship building.

Micromanagers and Critics
Micromanagers and critics are people who want to control or criticize everything you do. They often have difficulty with trust, control, and delegation.

They may be perfectionists who find fault with all your actions. Their underlying emotion is fear.

As your boss, micromanagers can be impossible to work with. They check in on you too often, dictate how to do things, and always seem to know the one best way to complete a task. They may be also perfectionists and constantly pick apart your work or ask you to revise your deliverables. As a team member or peer, micromanagers or critics may focus their energy on telling others what to do. They may get frustrated with others and bring issues to you that relate to how others work or to their inability to control others.

Bullies

A bully is someone who is moody and often full of rage, inconsistent, manipulative, aggressive, insensitive, and generally difficult to deal with. Each of us probably had to deal with a bully at some point in our childhood and how we responded to the bully was coded into our memory. For those of us who have to deal with bullies as adults, we tend to respond in the same way we learned as children.

Bullies keep their subordinates off balance, and they thrive on the upset that they are able to cause in others. So it is helpful to expect the unexpected when dealing with bullies. I once had a bully PM who strove to come in earlier than I did and discover any problems that occurred overnight so he could berate me for them. Once I learned to expect his surprise morning attacks, he stopped doing them. They were no longer effective in upsetting me.

That bully PM I had was brutal. He thrived on teasing and belittling others. He loved to go on the attack during meetings and usually singled out those who appeared weak. I survived by being compliant, by keeping my distance, and by using humor to deflect his attacks. It wasn't easy though, and his constant barrage of attacks took a toll on me. I was relieved to finally be able to leave his organization when the chance came.

Though my situation was on the extreme end of bullying, that doesn't mean that you won't run into bullies. What can you do to overcome a bully? First, you can keep your distance. Bullies hurt the ones they love the most and those closest to them. So, don't get close to them. If the bully in your life is your boss, it may be a good time to start working from home. Second, you can power up and meet the bully eye to eye. Often, the reason bullies feel comfortable acting as they do is that they know that they can get away with it. Obviously this can be a risky strategy especially if your particular bully is in a position of power over you. You can discuss your options with HR to reduce the risks to yourself. Third, you can build alliances and get support from others so that you are not single-handedly trying to overcome a brute. Fourth, you can calmly speak up about the process that is happening, when it happens. If you said, "It feels like you are trying to punish me because we lost the bid," you might bring out in the open the truth of the situation.

Whatever approach you use, exercise caution. Bullies place a premium on loyalty and severely punish anyone they perceive as disloyal. So try to strike a balance between being loyal without getting too close. Stay out of the kill zone.

The Narcissist—It's All About Me!

Narcissists are people who are obsessed with themselves. Their three top priorities are me, myself, and I. While perhaps not as dangerous as bullies, they can be incapable of thinking outside the box (that is, outside of themselves). They may think nothing of asking you to do difficult, uncomfortable, or unacceptable things.

Donald Trump is a good example of a narcissist. He consistently focuses on himself. If you study the media coverage for Mr. Trump, you would find that many of the stories about him were simply cries for attention. During the 2012 Presidential election, Mr. Trump offered to pay $5M to charity if President Obama would release his college records and other personal information. Was this really about President Obama, or was this about Mr. Trump?

When dealing with the narcissist, remember that they think only about themselves. They are the most important star in the universe. In fact, it has been said that the only difference between a narcissist and God is that God doesn't think he is a narcissist.

Dishonest Employees

Dishonest employees range from those who occasionally tell white lies to those who lie compulsively and may even cheat or steal. This category also includes those who act unethically or ask you to act in unethical ways. The underlying emotions for dishonest employees could be anger or fear.

Dishonest bosses can misrepresent the truth about you and your efforts. They may take credit for your work or blame you for their own mistakes. They may project dishonesty on to you and discount or discredit what you say and do. It is especially dangerous to have a boss who asks you to act in unethical ways.

Dishonest team members and peers can cause conflict by blaming others for problems. They will often assume others operate as they do and attribute malicious intent to otherwise innocuous members of your team.

Cavemen

The category of cavemen includes power freaks, racists, and sexists. They are like primitive examples of bullies, and they are easier to spot since they are less polished. They tell off-color jokes or single out individuals and pick on them. They may think they are just having fun with others by teasing when they are simply trying to cloak their aggression in humor. They are usually men but women may also fall into this category.

As bosses, cavemen may make it a point to show you who is boss or get off on treating you like dirt. They may try to make themselves feel more powerful by singling out you or one of your peers for humiliation in front of a group. Or, they may make unwanted sexual overtures or discriminate against members of the opposite sex. They may label groups of people and use derogatory language toward people who are different from themselves.

As a team member or peer, cavemen may be less threatening than if they were your manager since they are generally too scared to go after powerful individuals. However, you need to monitor the cavemen on your team closely as they can cause conflict with individuals reporting to them or working closely with them. For example, if an individual reporting to you were to tell an off-color or inappropriate joke and you either laughed or failed to take appropriate action, you could be viewed as part of the problem and be disciplined.

Addicts and the Mentally Impaired

Addicts include those who abuse alcohol or other substances. Individuals who are mentally impaired range from those with minor problems to the extreme cases of schizophrenia or manic depression. These individuals are rare in the project environment, but that is not to say you won't run into them.

Problems with addicts and the mentally impaired will have more to do with them than you despite how those individuals will want it to appear. It may be obvious to you that they have a problem if they repeatedly show up to work hungover or return from lunch slightly drunk. I once saw a team member spend the lunch break in the parking lot drinking beer in his car. Unfortunately, denial and defensiveness may make any type of communication unproductive. In the most extreme cases, a confrontation about the behavior could be dangerous to you.

If you find yourself dealing with an individual in one of these categories, proceed with caution. These people are usually not interested in your relationship-building efforts. In fact, you may find that efforts to be vulnerable, tell the truth, or identify your part of co-creation can actually backfire, or worse, create fuel for the other individual to attack you. Here are some general guidelines to apply if you find yourself working with one of these types of at-risk individuals.

1. Stick to Business and Avoid Direct Confrontations

Unlike normal relationships in which we want to express our feelings, tell the truth, and get clear, with at-risk individuals we want to avoid situations that would make us more vulnerable. Telling the truth or expressing your feelings may add fuel to the fire or spark an attack. It would be unwise in particular to try to fix them, teach them a lesson, suggest that they have problems, or diagnose them in any way. The best approach is to stick to the business at hand and to try to avoid any direct confrontations with the individual.

2. Document Everything

If you believe you are working with an at-risk manager or individual, get everything in writing. Document your understandings, instructions, responsibilities, and obligations. The documentation may help you to defend yourself against attack or to support your case if it comes down to your word versus theirs.

3. Seek Help

This would be a great time to seek help from your manager, other managers, or the Human Resources (HR) Department. If your manager is the problem person, you will need to proceed with a little extra caution. Some people are able to turn the charm on and off and conceal their true identities when necessary. This can make it hard for other managers or HR to recognize these personalities. For example, cavemen types will often power-up around those who are weaker or those who report to them. They may actually play small around those who are more powerful than they.

4. Refocus Your Energies

If you find yourself reaching a dead end in trying to build relationships with an at-risk individual, shift your focus. Unhealthy relationships can be taxing and draining and provide no payback. Choose to invest in those relationships that are healthy. You will get more support and have more energy that way.

5. Consider a Move

Getting away from an at-risk person may sound drastic but can often be the best way to save yourself from further pain. If the problem is with your manager, you may want to move to a different opportunity with the same company. You may even consider leaving the organization. Your mental health is far more important than your current job.

6. Most Important, Don't Take It Personally

Some people are broken in ways that have nothing to do with you. Try to keep that in mind and do not take on responsibility for relationship breakdowns that you did not create.

■ Techniques for Managing Relationships on Projects

Before we close this chapter on relationship management, let's discuss various techniques to help manage relationships on projects.

1. Apply the Emotional Intelligence Basics

To improve our ability to manage relationships, we may have to go back to some of the earlier concepts of emotional intelligence. Start with self-awareness, self-management, and social awareness. In relationships with others, we need to be aware of our feelings and manage our emotions. For example, use the feelings tally sheet provided in Appendix A to track how you feel. Practice sharing your feelings with others in appropriate situations. Or use the Assessment for Emotional Self-Awareness and Self-Control in Appendix B to analyze a stakeholder and assess their feelings.

2. Stakeholder Management Tool

I recommend that every PM complete the stakeholder management tool (see Appendix C) for the most important stakeholders on your project. This is an excellent first step toward systematically identifying and managing stakeholder relationships. Adapt the template to your specific project or environment as needed. While collecting the information and managing the relationship may seem artificial or mechanical at first, continue to use the tool to create team relationships that provide value for both parties.

3. Regular One-on-One Meetings

I cannot emphasize enough the importance of regular one-on-one meetings with key stakeholders and members of your project team. By meeting regularly, you will be able to stay current and keep short accounts with your project team members. You will also be able to stay on top of managing the expectations of your stakeholders.

4. Out to Lunch!

If you are the type who eats a quick lunch at your desk to save time, you are missing a great opportunity for relationship building. Try to slowly change your existing habit by designating one day a week to go out to lunch with someone. Alternatively, set a goal to have lunch out with all your key stakeholders or project team members within the next month or two.

If going to lunch with just one other person seems too intimate, invite a couple of people to dine with you. Or, invite a key stakeholder and a junior member of your team and use the same time for building relationships with the stakeholder and developing the team member.

An alternative approach is to have an informal lunch for the entire team. If your project budget supports it, have lunch brought in for the whole group.

5. Use Icebreakers and Teambuilding Exercises

Everyone tends to laugh nervously when I suggest them, but I think icebreakers provide a great way to learn more about project stakeholders in a low threat way. Are you using icebreakers and teambuilding exercises effectively? Consider the following ways in which you can break the ice for team meetings, kickoffs, and other occasions:

- At the start of a meeting, ask each person to name a favorite movie or reality TV show, musician, or book. You can also ask about the worst summer job or worst permanent job. I like to ask people to share something that others generally don't know about them. You can ask virtually anything that reveals something about each person and provides a forum for discussion. Don't be surprised if some of the quietest individuals go on and on or share something you don't expect.
- More complex team-building exercises can also be used, including activities that involve team competitions, survival type exercises, or other scenario-based exercises. One of my favorite team-building exercises was a competition to build specific items out of Legos. Teams were graded based on speed and quality, the two factors that were most relevant for that particular project.
- There are a number of team-building activities directly related to improving emotional intelligence. As an example, Adele Lynn has a workbook of 50 EQ activities called *The Emotional Intelligence Activity Book* (see Appendix E: Books on Emotional Intelligence).

In addition to these, a number of other resources are available on the Web that can be easily found with a search tool.

6. Develop Others by Becoming a Coach and Mentor

Make a shift in your approach to managing others by becoming a coach or mentor. Think about ways to become systematic in your efforts to invest in others. Set up regular meetings focused on the development of those who work for you. Consider the work assignments that you could give individuals to help them grow in their areas of strengths.

If you are not sure how you are doing, ask for feedback from the people who work for you. Find out what you can do to improve in this area. You can also get a coach or mentor for yourself and learn how to coach from them.

7. Recognize Others

Evaluate your current performance in terms of recognizing others. Remind yourself that every person craves recognition and affirmation. Are you leveraging recognition as an opportunity to build the relationship?

Consider implementing systems to become more consistent at recognition. You could make a list of the project team members or key stakeholders and use that as a tally sheet to keep track of when you recognize them for their work. Alternatively, you could use weekly or biweekly meetings as the forum for recognition. Make it a habit to start every one-on-one meeting by recognizing the contributions the other person has made to the project and why you appreciate having them on the team.

8. Assessment Instruments

The use of assessment instruments can provide information for development of your team members as well as for general team building. Many assessment tools can be used for this purpose, including general assessments, strengths assessments, and emotional intelligence assessments.

One of the most popular general assessment tools is the Myers Briggs Type Indicator (MBTI). Find a local facilitator and have the instrument administered to your project team. The four different type indicators used in the Myers Briggs assessment provide for sixteen different individual combinations. Map your team against those sixteen combinations and discuss it as a team-building exercise.

You can also administer the StrengthsFinder assessment to help an individual determine their strengths. Once you know the individual's top five strengths, this can provide a basis for your development efforts.

9. Practice Truth-Telling Techniques

Take the time to assess your ability to tell the truth with others. Are there situations where you have difficulty telling the truth? Which of the truth-telling techniques pose the biggest challenge for you?

A starting point might be to review the following list and rank your responses in terms of what you do best and what you do least well:

_____ Do you say yes when you really should say no?

_____ Do you have trouble stating what you like and simply go along with what others want?

_____ Do you have judgments or beliefs of others that you withhold to avoid conflict?

_____ Do you let hurts and resentments build up instead of quickly clearing them up with others?

_____ Do you avoid providing truthful feedback for others for fear of their reaction?

_____ Are there individuals in your environment who make you feel you need to walk on eggshells when they are around?

Select one area that you want to work on. Set a daily goal to try and improve in that area. Start slow and build up, just as if you were exercising. For example, if your challenge is saying no, you might make it a goal to say no to at least one unnecessary thing every day for a week. Start with relatively low-risk people or situations and build up to those that present higher stakes for you.

If getting clear is your challenge area, determine which individuals pose the biggest struggle for you. If there is a current issue that you have not been clear about, make it a point to meet with the individual to clear it up as soon as possible. If the person you struggle with the most is your spouse or a co-worker, set a goal to get keep short accounts with them. Try to clear up all hurts or resentments on a daily basis. Keep track of how you are doing and celebrate yourself.

10. Evaluate How You Are Co-Creating Your Outcomes

Take a look at your project and relationship outcomes and evaluate how you are contributing to any issues or problems. Do you tend to play the victim? Do you think that things primarily happen to you instead of your making things happen? Evaluate how you are co-creating the relationship outcomes you are getting. Rank your level of satisfaction with your relationship outcomes.

11. What Are Your Relationship Patterns?

Think about your recent experience on projects or in the work environment in general. Can you identify any patterns of relationship breakdowns? In other words, what would be your equivalent of a string of ignorant bosses? Do you have any recurring themes that prevent you from performing at your best?

Determine if you have any relationship patterns or are in some way re-creating the same problems with different people over time. This is an area where it might help to get some feedback from a significant other, mentor, friend, or anyone else who has known you for a while.

Once you see the pattern, the next step is to determine your contribution to the situation. Own the part that you played and then think about what you could do differently in the future to get different results. Try to identify at least two or three things that you could do.

Now think about your current relationships. Which relationships are at risk for this same pattern of breakdown? What steps can you take right now to break the pattern?

12. Enroll an Accountability Partner

Some of the techniques described above are more challenging than others. If you find yourself struggling with these despite your good intentions, you might need to enroll the help of a friend or accountability partner. An accountability partner can help you to make changes or breakthroughs that you would not otherwise make on your own.

Who would be a good accountability partner for you? See if you can identify someone who will hold the bar high for you. Share your challenges and goals with them and set up checkpoints where you can let them know how you are doing. Keep it fun and encourage them to have high expectations for you.

■ Personal Action Plan: Relationship Management

Relationships are important to life, business, and especially to project management.

Key Takeaways

1.	
2.	
3.	

My Strengths and Weaknesses in the Area of Relationship Management

Strengths	Weaknesses
1.	1.
2.	2.

My Actions or Goals Based on What I Learned

1.	
2.	
3.	

PART 4

Using EQ to Lead Project Teams

By now, you should have a solid understanding of the first four domains of emotional intelligence and their associated competencies. The following four chapters discuss the fifth domain of emotional intelligence and provide additional insights into how we can apply our knowledge to be more successful as PMs.

In Chapter 7, Project Team Leadership, we explore what it means to lead projects and how that differs from managing. We also discuss how to communicate with high emotional intelligence and the best way to develop a team, including selecting and retaining team members. We will also analyze conflict management and then close with a series of techniques to improve our project team leadership. Chapter 8, Creating a Positive Team Environment, looks at the difference between projects with and without positive team environments and discusses the PM's role in setting the tone and direction for the project. We also discuss how the team environment is affected by the culture of the organization and what the PM can do to impact that larger environment. Chapter 9, Leveraging Emotional Intelligence on Large and Complex Projects, deals with excelling with emotional intelligence on large and complex projects. Chapter 10, Success with Agile Projects, includes information on leading and coaching Agile teams, particularly for software development projects.

It is my hope that you will be able to leverage these chapters on Team Leadership to take on more complex and challenging projects.

7

Project Team Leadership

■ An Introduction to Project Team Leadership

Project team leadership is the overarching aspect of the emotional intelligence framework for PMs. It is about getting the right people on your team, successfully communicating with and motivating them, and then clearing conflicts and other roadblocks so that they perform and achieve the project objectives. This domain includes the project management competencies of communications, conflict management, and inspirational leadership, as shown in Figure 7-1.

Like the relationship management domain that we explored in Chapter 6, project team leadership builds on the previous emotional intelligence domains.

What the Experts Say About Team Leadership

Though leading teams is critical to PMs, emotional intelligence researchers have only indirectly tackled the subject. Daniel Goleman and his *Primal Leadership* coauthors looked at the various emotional intelligence competencies and how they impact leaders. (*Primal Leadership* also discusses six leadership styles that we explore in Chapter 8). Otherwise, little information is available to relate emotional intelligence to the leadership of project teams.

As noted in Chapter 7, I chose to designate several of the competencies that Goleman included under relationship management as team leadership competencies. Communications is a core competency for both project man-

Figure 7-1: EQ Model Showing Team Leadership.

agement and emotional intelligence. This includes not only empathetic listening, as discussed in Chapter 4, but also consistent and effective communicating with project stakeholders.

Conflict management is the second competency that we will explore. This is another subject that should be very familiar to PMs. Goleman views conflict management as negotiating and resolving disagreements; it includes the following competencies:

- Handling difficult people and tense situations with diplomacy and tact
- Spotting potential conflicts, bringing disagreements into the open, and helping to de-escalate
- Encouraging debate and open discussion
- Orchestrating win–win solutions[1]

[1] Daniel Goleman. *Working with Emotional Intelligence.* NY: Random House/Bantam, 1998.

Finally, we will look at what Goleman alternatively calls leadership or inspirational leadership. In *Working with Emotional Intelligence*, Goleman defines leadership as inspiring and guiding individuals and groups and includes the following aspects of leadership:

- Articulating and arousing enthusiasm for a shared vision and mission
- Stepping forward to lead as needed; regardless of position
- Guiding the performance of others while holding them accountable
- Leading by example[2]

■ Communications

Undoubtedly PMs need to be great communicators. This is one of the most important skills that a PM should possess. It is hard to imagine a successful PM who is not a good communicator.

> Project managers need to be great communicators.

Not everyone appreciates the need for PMs to be great communicators. It is entertaining to hear the criticism of PMs by team members who are new to projects. I have heard quite frequently that "All you project managers do is walk around and talk to people." I wholeheartedly agree with that statement. Walking around and talking to people is one of the important ways that PMs communicate. Unfortunately, the individuals who make those types of statements haven't yet seen the value in good communications.

I am also entertained when I hear the following from a new team lead or PM: "I didn't get anything done today; all I did was sit in meetings." This is typical of new PMs who were accustomed to being individual contributors. Frequently, they will feel frustrated with their apparent lack of contribution and the fact they were in so many meetings. To them I say, "Welcome to project management."

The reality is that for most PMs, a big part of the job is communications. That may take the form of walking around and talking with team members or stakeholders. It may also mean sitting in lots of meetings. That is communications. Communications can also include talking on the telephone, writing emails and instant messages, preparing for meetings, creating and delivering briefings, and generating status reports.

---

[2] *Ibid.*

This section focuses on how to apply emotional intelligence to improve project communications. Project communications are a rather broad topic and some level of familiarity with the topic is assumed. For PMs who are not familiar with project communications, I recommend that you start with Chapter 10 of the PMBOK® Guide, which is dedicated to this topic.

Of course, the PMBOK® Guide does not address the application of emotional intelligence to communications. For best results, we need to consider our own emotions, the emotional content of our messages, and the emotions of the recipients of our communications. In the next section, we look at how PMs can leverage emotional intelligence to improve communications with team members and other stakeholders. Then we look at specific types of communications methods, the advantages and disadvantages of each, and ways to improve them with emotional intelligence.

Communicating with Emotional Intelligence

No matter what form they take, communications contain and evoke emotions. Well-planned communications, therefore, help the PM set the emotional tone for the team. Poorly executed communications can trigger negative emotions in the team.

Communicating with emotional intelligence involves applying the domains of self-awareness, self-management, social awareness, and relationship management. PMs who are competent in each of those domains will do a better job of communicating with emotional intelligence.

If you want to be intentional about your project communications, consider the following steps:

- Determine your objective.
- Understand your own emotions.
- Choose an appropriate time, place, and mode.
- Approach others with empathy.
- Listen and respond to the emotions of others, and not only to the content of what they say.
- Share your own emotions when appropriate, being as open and honest as possible.
- Check for understanding and reactions.

Determine Your Objective

Determine your objective means to understand the point of the communications. Some examples of communication objectives include:

- Recognizing the work of others.
- Encouraging or motivating team members to work harder.
- Providing constructive feedback to encourage someone to change their behavior.

The key is to be clear about our objectives up front. If we don't set realistic objectives before we communicate, we are not likely to be clear, concise, and consistent and probably won't achieve much.

I have found it helpful to jot down a few bullet points before important meetings. These bullet points might be in addition to an agenda or any other preparation I would do for the meeting. I would typically choose my words carefully since I understand that word choices can affect the emotions evoked.

Understand Your Own Emotions

Understanding our own emotions means we are aware of our emotions or self-aware, as we learned in Chapter 3. This is a necessary first step for good communications. If we are unaware, we won't be able to accurately communicate with others on an emotional level. Our own emotional state will leak out in undesired ways, or we will misrepresent how we feel to others. We should start by using the SASHET model introduced earlier to be clear about our own emotions.

Choose an Appropriate Time, Place, and Mode

It is critical that we choose an appropriate time and place for our communications with others. Delivering bad news at the end of the day when your team is heading out the door is poor timing. Even worse timing would be to deliver bad news when you are leaving the office early and won't be around the rest of the day. You need to be careful, though, that you don't stall on delivering news because "the time isn't right." While timing is important, we should not let our own fear cause us to delay the delivery of bad news.

It is also imperative that you choose an appropriate place for the communications. Privacy is critical when discussing personal issues.

I once had a situation with a team member who had failed to meet an important deadline. I made the mistake of addressing the issue with the team member in his cubicle, which was part of the open landscaping in the office. Needless to say, it was inappropriate to discuss this person's shortcomings when others could hear the conversation.

Finally, we need to consider the modes of communications that are appropriate in any given situation. It would not be appropriate to use a fax message to fire someone. Nor would it be appropriate to use instant messaging for a tough discussion. Both of these situations would be well served by a face-to-face discussion.

There are also times when we need to use multiple modes of communication. Often, our verbal discussions will need to be supported by a written communication or some other form of documentation to keep in our permanent records.

Approach Others with Empathy

Where possible we must approach others with empathy. We should attempt to think through how they will feel before and after our communications with them. For example, consider if the other party or parties will be scared in anticipation of bad news. Think about how we expect them to feel after we deliver our message. Do we expect them to be happy after we recognize their performance? What will we need to do in order to assure that they take this in the most positive light?

Listen and Respond to the Emotions of Others

As project leaders, we need to distinguish between the content of what people say and the emotions underneath that content. In many situations, it is more appropriate to respond to the emotions than to the actual words that the individual is saying. As an example, we may say something like "you sound disappointed." We may need to lead others to appreciate what they are feeling and help them to articulate that. This includes listening with empathy and using paraphrasing or other playback methods to replay what we hear from others, as we discussed in Chapter 4.

Share Your Own Emotions When Appropriate

We also need to be able to share our own emotions when appropriate. We should strive to be as open and honest as possible. Of course, this doesn't mean that we bare our souls and share everything.

We may also want to practice the truth-telling techniques that we learned in Chapter 6. This may not be appropriate in all situations. Use your emotions to guide you in determining how much to share. Consider your objective for the communication and evaluate whether sharing additional information will bring you closer to that objective.

Check for Understanding and Reactions

Just because we delivered a message in a meeting doesn't mean that the recipient understood or retained the message. We need to follow-up with receivers to make sure that they understand what was communicated. We might also ask for their reaction to the message.

I like to leverage key project team members to check for understanding and reactions. In nearly every project team that I was on, there were a couple of team members who could be trusted to be open and candid about their reactions. I would seek them out after important meetings to see what they heard, what they took away, and any reaction they might have had to the message.

■ Methods of Project Communications

Table 7-1 provides a summary of some popular modes of communications that a PM may use, the emotional intelligence advantages and disadvantages of each, and some tips for applying emotional intelligence to each mode.

Use Email and IM Carefully

A word of caution about the use of email and instant messaging (IM) as communication tools. Each of these has its place on project teams. Email has been used for several years to support project communications. In recent years, IM has rapidly become accepted as a valuable project communications tool. It is the power of these two modes of communication that can make them risky if not used properly.

With email, you can reach a very wide audience in a hurry. This is great if there are important and urgent communications that need to go to that wide audience. It is not so great if you have lost control of your emotions and you want to vent to everyone about how angry you are.

You may not even do this intentionally. I have inadvertently sent email messages to the wrong recipients on multiple occasions. This is especially embarrassing if the message is poorly written, unprofessional, or has a critical tone. More important than proper addressing of emails is to think before you even create the message. Go back to the steps we mentioned in this section and think about your objectives and your feelings. Before creating an email, make sure that you need to send one. If you are responding emotionally, email is unlikely to be the best mode of communication.

Instant messaging has similar shortcomings though it doesn't necessarily have the power to communicate the same message to multiple people at the same time. Many people use IM to keep ongoing informal chats going throughout their day as they work on different tasks. These individuals may have three or four different conversations going on at the same time. (I find myself challenged to have one meaningful conversation at a time.) Those who have several conversations going run the risk of sending the message to the wrong recipient.

Table 7-1

Method of Communication	Emotional Intelligence Advantages	Emotional Intelligence Disadvantages	Tips for Maximizing Effectiveness
Face-to-Face Meetings	• Face-to-face meetings include visual and audio clues that supply the emotional context for the message. • Allows speaker to check for understanding and provide clarification as needed.	• You may only get one chance to say things correctly.	1. Use in conjunction with written communications. For example, hand out agendas and talking points in advance, or follow-up meetings with meeting notes or frequently asked questions.
Phone Calls and Teleconferences	• Opportunity to speak to each other when not in the same place. • Better at conveying emotions than email or other written forms of communications.	• Since we cannot see each other, we miss out on important visual clues. Puts the burden on the communicator to probe for understanding and emotions. • Forces speaker to articulate emotional content better than if the parties were together or could see each other. • Different accents and language proficiencies may create challenges simply to understand the words of another let alone the emotional content or intent of those words.	1. Use in conjunction with written communications. For example, hand out agendas and talking points in advance, or follow-up meetings with meeting notes or frequently asked questions.

	Advantages	Disadvantages	Tips
Written Reports	• We can choose our words and emotional content carefully. • Written reports provide a permanent record of the communication.	• Written reports lack the ability to clarify or answer questions, or to provide additional detail. • Written communications lack the emotional context provided by visual cues, body language, and tone of voice. This can lead to misinterpretation, de-motivation, or conflict.	1. Be consistent in style and approach with your messages. 2. Get a friend to read over anything written before it goes out. 3. If in doubt about the message, call or stop by the person to provide clarification if needed.
Email	• With emails, we can choose our words and emotional content carefully. • Provides the ability to reach many people in different locations quickly. • Widely used and accepted as the norm for many team communications. • Emails provide a somewhat permanent record of the communication.	• Emails lack the ability to clarify or answer questions, or to provide additional detail. • Email lacks the emotional context provided by visual cues, body language, and tone of voice. This can lead to misinterpretation, de-motivation, or conflict. • Email as a medium tends to be overused and people may miss important information if there is a deluge to sift through.	1. Make an investment in writing clear email messages. 2. Be consistent in style and approach with your messages. 3. When in doubt, let an email sit over night or get a friend to read. 4. Check for understanding by stopping by in person, calling or asking for a return email. 5. Try not to overuse email so that the messages you send are read and acted on.
Instant Messaging (IM)	• IM can be a fast and informal way to reach an individual immediately. • Similar to other written forms, it has the advantage of being permanent.	• Most people do not spend much time crafting instant messages. • Like email, instant messages lack the emotional context provided by visual cues, body language, and tone of voice. This can lead to misinterpretation, de-motivation, or conflict. • Reaches only one person at a time.	1. Treat IM as one more communication tool. Don't use I.M. in unprofessional or inappropriate ways. 2. Do not use for formal project communications. 3. Take care to provide the emotional context for the message.

Another risk with instant messaging is the apparent informality. The ability to chat back and forth can cause people to become less professional, or even flirtatious, or to act in otherwise inappropriate ways. It seems that every year there are scandals involving public officials and celebrities whose inappropriate texts and photos were made public.

Both email and IM suffer from a lack of context. The same message can be interpreted multiple ways. Without visual clues it might be hard to tell if someone is joking around or if they are angry and serious. Two people may read the same message and come away with a different interpretation of the message.

Improving Your Meetings

Most project team members seem to dislike the deluge of meetings that come with the job. Here are some ways to improve your meetings to make them both worth attending and enjoyable.

* Start with meeting objectives and an agenda.
* Monitor the group for emotions and aliveness. If everyone seems angry or bored, it may be appropriate to state that you've noticed this and ask why.
* Always show respect for others, in particular those not present.
* Monitor and address sarcasm and other inappropriate expressions of emotions.
* Address conflict.
* Lead with your own emotions.

Nonverbal Communications

The focus of the previous section has been on verbal communications. It is important to recognize that we communicate all the time without using words. Nonverbal communications can include body language, touch, the artifacts and items found in your office, your own physical appearance and dress, the actions you take, and even the car you drive. Each of these things sends a message about you even before you open your mouth or write something.

The most important nonverbal communication is actions. It has been said that actions speak louder than words. The actions you take, or the ones you do not take, send messages more clearly than if you had spoken the words. If your words do not match your actions, people will be more likely to pay attention to your actions than your words. As the next section describes, we need to be consistent in all of our communications.

Congruence in Communications

Congruence is a principle that applies to all of the ways in which we communicate. We need to be consistent in the message that we send with our words and our actions. We cannot tell someone they are important to us and to the team and then act in ways that send a different message.

Today's reality TV shows provide plenty of examples of nonverbal communications. Look for examples of people who are saying positive things, yet glaring at others, avoiding eye contact, or even rolling their eyes. Look for those who smile when they say they are angry, or who are clearly acting angry yet pretending not to be.

Congruence in our communications also means that we are consistent with our actions and words with different groups of people, both inside and outside the company.

■ Conflict Management

Conflict Is Inevitable

Conflict seems to be inevitable on projects. From the start, projects are built on a foundation of the conflicting constraints of time, cost, and scope. Further, projects are often created to satisfy the needs of one set of stakeholders, which may be at odds with needs of other stakeholders. During the execution of projects, conflict frequently surfaces over contention for resources, rewards and recognition, roles and responsibilities, team member diversity, technical decisions, reporting structures, and, even, individual personalities.

Lack of emotional intelligence in project team members and stakeholders can also cause conflict. Team members and stakeholders who experience emotional breakdowns or lack emotional self-control are like ticking time bombs. When these bombs detonate, they will frequently take healthy members of the team with them, which could include you as the PM. Even team members and stakeholders with high emotional intelligence may create conflict with others when they are under stress and pressure.

Project conflict can be disruptive. If not properly channeled, conflict can stifle communication, kill creativity, and squash productivity. Unmanaged conflict will create unnecessary distractions and may encourage otherwise good resources to leave the team. Project teams that are not able to manage conflict may ultimately fail to reach their objectives.

Conflict May Be Healthy

In some cases, conflict is healthy. Properly managed project conflict can galvanize teams, spark creativity, and cause healthy competition. Project conflict is an opportunity for the PM to demonstrate leadership with emotional intelligence competencies, such as empathy, self-control, and relationship management.

Conflict Management Is the PM's Job

Conflict management is an essential part of the PM's job. The PM is the one who will make the difference between leveraging conflict and having conflict wreak havoc on the team. Successfully recognizing and addressing conflict is part of the PM's role.

Recognizing That We Have a Conflict

The first step in the process is to recognize that there is conflict. In many cases, it won't be difficult to see. Consider the case where a team member said to me, "I won't work for him anymore," and then proceeded to tell me about all the shortcomings of this team leader and how hurt she felt.

In another example, two subteams were involved in a decision over two possible technical directions. One team lead calmly described the two approaches, their relative merits, and the shortcomings of each. The other team lead simply said, "Any idiot can see that this is the only valid approach."

It is not hard to see the conflict in these examples. It would not be hard if we saw or heard two individuals arguing with each other. However, the signals may not always be this clear. We need to be attuned to our environment to pick up on subtle signs that something is wrong. These signs include lack of communications, missed deadlines, poor quality deliverables, or deliverables behind schedule. Team members may reflect the conflict in their communications through sarcasm or the silent treatment. They may also do everything possible to make life difficult for other members, or avoid all meetings.

Traditional Approaches to Conflict Management

Assuming that we do recognize project conflict, how do we go about managing it? We can start with the five traditional ways managers have addressed conflicts. These modes, outlined in *Project Management: A Systems Approach to Planning, Scheduling, and Controlling,* are:

- Compromising
- Smoothing (or accommodating)
- Forcing
- Avoiding (or withdrawing)
- Confronting (or collaborating)[3]

Let's look at each of these classic modes of conflict resolution from an emotionally intelligent PM perspective.

Compromising

Compromising is when we search for a solution to the conflict that splits the difference and brings some degree of satisfaction to each party. Compromising is characterized by give-and-take from each of the affected parties. PMs who compromise are not necessarily looking for the best solution; they are simply looking for a middle ground that will be acceptable to both parties.

Compromising takes more emotional intelligence than withdrawing or smoothing because the issue is brought out into the open and discussed. However, compromising doesn't allow for the possibility of a win–win solution. It requires each of the parties in the conflict to give up something. It may encourage tentativeness in team members rather than going all out.

Compromising may be useful when the stakes are not very high and when both parties want to maintain the relationship.

Smoothing or Accommodating

Smoothing is when we minimize or avoid areas of difference. Smoothing managers tend to talk others out of being upset or try to gloss over it by emphasizing areas of agreement. They may establish a subteam to tackle a tough issue to reduce polarization of the team and avoid win–lose thinking.

A classic example of smoothing would be the plea, "Can we get along here? Can we all get along?" That comment was made by police assault victim Rodney King after the 1992 Los Angeles riots. King was trying to smooth over the areas of upset and disagreement and urge people to just get along.

As a technique for resolving project conflict, smoothing is relatively low in terms of emotional intelligence. Like withdrawal, when we use smoothing we are not dealing with the underlying issue that is causing the conflict. Instead, we are avoiding the issue.

Smoothing can often cause problems to fester and reappear in other ways. PMs who smooth over conflict force team members to take their issues

---

[3] Harold Kerzner. *Project Management: A Systems Approach to Planning, Scheduling, and Controlling.* Hoboken, NJ: John Wiley & Sons, Inc., 2006.

underground. They will often vent their concerns to others and thereby sow dissention. Team members who are encouraged to smooth over conflict may begin to downplay or withhold bad news. The message they receive from the PM is, do not rock the boat.

We can use smoothing when the stakes are not very high or when we want to maintain good working relationships. Otherwise, it should be avoided.

Forcing

Forcing or suppression is used by managers who see conflict as disruptive to team productivity and try to squelch that conflict. The manager makes it clear that disagreement is not tolerated and will work quickly to deal with any conflict. Any challenge to the manager is viewed as subordination. It is often characterized by a win–lose feeling in the team.

Forcing does not examine and address the underlying cause of the conflict and so is likely to lead to a recurrence of the problem in another form. The PM's intolerance stifles any real discussion of the conflict and extinguishes the possibility for learning and change.

As you might imagine, forcing takes very little emotional intelligence. The parties involved may see a particular conflict as one in a series of conflicts. Each may feel that if they lose this one conflict, they can even things up later. After a conflict is resolved, the two parties may simply be regrouping and preparing for the next battle.

Forcing is a shortsighted approach to conflict resolution. It should be used only when time is limited, when the long-term relationship is not important, or when no other solution will resolve the situation.

Avoiding or Withdrawing

PMs who use withdrawal will retreat from an actual or potential disagreement. They avoid disagreeing with others. They may go so far as to physically separate themselves from conflict by leaving the room or even taking a vacation. They may also distance themselves from unpopular management decisions saying, "Hey, I am just following orders."

In relation to the other approaches, withdrawal is very low in terms of emotional intelligence. In fact, withdrawal was identified as one of the emotional breakdowns described in Chapter 4. When we use withdrawal to deal with a conflict, we are disengaging from the relationship. We don't tell the truth about our feelings or our wants and needs.

As you might expect, withdrawal does not solve anything. In fact, with withdrawal we don't even acknowledge that there is a conflict. When we use withdrawal, we aren't really interested in solving the problem. We don't provide the other party the opportunity to work with us to resolve the conflict.

Withdrawal can be successful as a short-term strategy. By separating parties in a dispute, we allow the air to clear and cooler heads to prevail. Withdrawal would be very appropriate in situations where you believe that there is a risk of physical danger to anyone. Withdrawal could also be useful in situations where there is no long-term relationship. If you experience conflict in the last few weeks of a project, you may decide it is not worth working to resolve that particular issue. In all other cases, withdrawal should be avoided.

Confronting or Collaborating

Confrontation is facing the conflict directly and using problem-solving techniques to work through the disagreement. When we use confrontation, we bring the conflict out into the open so that we can deal with it. Confrontation is what is often described as seeking a win–win solution. Confrontation is the one technique that addresses the underlying cause of the conflict, making it the most economical solutions in terms of personal investment and return.

As you might guess, confrontation is the highest in emotional intelligence of all the conflict resolution approaches. It takes a PM with emotional intelligence (and courage) to confront conflict directly and work to resolve it. PMs may feel scared or inadequate to deal with the conflict.

I was taught an important but embarrassing lesson about using confrontation to resolve conflict. Several years ago, I was a co-test manager partnering with another manager to complete testing for a large systems integration project. I found working with the other manager difficult. I was organized and had experience with test planning and execution. My fellow manager was experienced with the technology we were using but lacked the skills to organize and execute the testing. I became frustrated. After some half-hearted attempts to talk to my coworker, I told the project director that I had an issue with my co-test manager. His response was to invite me to meet him for lunch that very day.

When I arrived at the restaurant, I was surprised to see the project director sitting in a cozy round booth with my co-test manager. I sat down with the two of them and immediately the project director asked me what it was about my co-test manager that I needed to discuss with him. I was embarrassed, to say the least.

The confrontation with the project director taught me a few things. I learned that I should have spent more time working on the issue with my co-test manager before bringing it to the project director. I learned that the reason the project director paired us up was exactly the issue I wanted to complain about—we had different strengths and skills sets. Most important,

I learned that the most direct way to resolve an issue was to confront it directly.

I try to remember these lessons when individuals come to me with issues or conflicts on a project. I try to tell them that the shortest distance between two people is a straight line and that is the most direct way to resolve a conflict.

One final note about confrontation. It is important for PMs to send the message to their team that they are open to confrontation themselves. You want your team to be comfortable bringing issues with you out in the open without fearing reprisal.

Applying Emotional Intelligence to Conflict Resolution

Beyond looking at the levels of emotional intelligence in each of the conflict resolution approaches, we can also use the emotional intelligence competencies to better manage conflicts. We begin with a focus on what each party is feeling.

Conflicts involve both facts and feelings. It is usually easy to get the facts. That is the "he said, she said" part of the transaction. The facts are helpful as a starting point, but they are only part of the story. We need to get beyond the facts to understand why those facts matter so much to the parties involved. That requires an understanding of the underlying feelings as well as the unstated wants and needs of each of the parties.

It is important to probe to find out what the parties in a conflict are feeling. We need to listen emphatically and pay attention to feeling words and body language. We may even need to ask questions. Recall the example described in Chapter 5 where a team member sat with her arms crossed, fiercely insisting "I am not angry." People in conflict usually feel scared, angry, sad, or some combination of all of these things. They may be angry about critical remarks from a coworker. At the same time, they may be sad because their feelings are hurt and they want to be friends with the coworker who made the remarks. Finally, they may be scared of a confrontation or scared that they need to leave the project because of that person.

It would be unlikely that a team member involved in a conflict would have the emotional intelligence to openly discuss the full range of emotions that they are feeling. More often, individuals will not be aware of the various mix of feelings they are experiencing. The PM can lead or coax team members to appreciate the different feelings they are experiencing.

Understanding the feeling is the first step. The second step is to identify the underlying want or need. Some common wants and needs of project stakeholders are shown below:

- Want to be recognized
- Want to be important
- Want to be productive
- Want to be promoted
- Want to feel part of the community
- Need to make more money
- Need to express themselves
- Need to be liked or loved

When we understand the underlying wants and needs of the affected parties, we better understand their motivation. Then we can work together to address the issue or conflict that is caused by the underlying want and need. We can help each party to the conflict understand the wants and needs of the other party and to achieve their own wants and needs.

You Might Just Be the Cause

Our approach may vary a little if we are a part of the conflict or the cause of the conflict. If we are part of the conflict, we need to first orient to ourselves. The questions that we need to ask remain the same. We need to understand what it is that we are feeling. We will typically be sad, angry, or scared. We go further by asking what it is that we are sad, angry or scared about. What is our underlying want or need in this situation? How does this conflict move us closer to or further from our wants and needs?

Once we understand where we are coming from, we can evaluate the other person. We start by trying to understand what they are feeling. Then we explore what they want and need in this situation. Then we explore ways to work with them through the conflict. We may want to think it through on our own and then discuss it with the other party. If it is tense or uncomfortable with just the two of you, ask for a peer manager or for a neutral third party to join the discussion.

Calmly leading others through conflict can help strengthen our relationships and build the team. It is also a way for PMs to demonstrate leadership.

■ Inspirational Leadership

The third and final competency of team leadership is inspirational leadership. This is the ability to inspire others by casting a vision for the individual and the team. PMs who are inspirational leaders make work attractive and interesting to the team, create high team morale, and attract and retain good resources.

In the movie, *As Good as it Gets*, Jack Nicholson plays a gifted writer named Melvin Udall who has a lot of emotional issues. He is a good example of someone with low emotional intelligence. One of my favorite moments is when Melvin Udall dines with Carol Connelly, played by Helen Hunt. After Melvin makes one of his typical harsh and narcissistic comments, Carol demands that he give her a compliment right now. It takes a few moments for Melvin to respond, but the words he says have become one of the best known movie lines of all time. Melvin says, "You make me want to be a better man."

The lesson here is that as much as we might try, we cannot force anyone to do anything. Very few PMs have the ability to hire and fire. So to get things done, we need to make people want to do them. We need to inspire them, so much so that we "make them want to be better team members."

Vision Casting

Vision casting is the process of stating a future, positive picture of the goals or objectives for the team, assisting the team to understand why they are important, and helping the team to connect with those goals and objectives. Vision casting for projects is the responsibility of the PM.

One way to cast a vision is through the use of the mission, vision, and values statement for the project or team. The mission is a short statement about the overall objective for the team or what is going to be accomplished. The vision is a statement on how that mission will be accomplished. And the team values are the framework for pursuing the mission.

Consider the following example from a recent project that I managed. I created the picture shown in Figure 7-2 to represent the mission, vision, and values for the team.

The articulation of the team mission had a galvanizing effect on the team and on me as the leader. When I began to leverage this statement, it anchored my decisions and helped me show others how their work fit into the larger picture. Each part of the mission, vision, and values statement was applicable. For example, I used the mission to help communicate the priorities for everyone on the team. Up to that point, each subteam had focused only on its own part of the project and its own work. The diagrams and words reminded them of the goals of the larger team. The vision was also important, as it showed the balance I was striving to achieve between reaching the stated project objectives as well as investing and growing the people.

Finally, the values were important since they served as ground rules or the code of conduct for the team. We developed the values list by team vote.

Team Mission

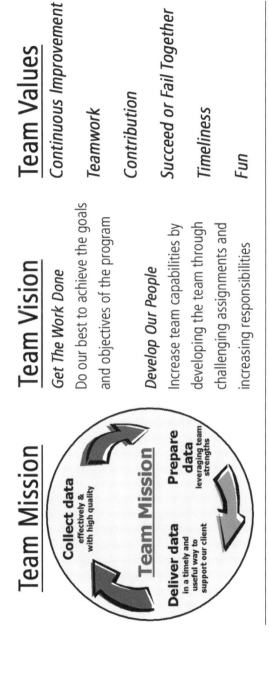

Collect data
effectively &
with high quality

Prepare data
leveraging team
strengths

Team Mission

Deliver data
in a timely and
useful way to
support our client

Team Vision

Get The Work Done

Do our best to achieve the goals
and objectives of the program

Develop Our People

Increase team capabilities by
developing the team through
challenging assignments and
increasing responsibilities

Team Values

Continuous Improvement

Teamwork

Contribution

Succeed or Fail Together

Timeliness

Fun

Figure 7-2: Example of Mission, Vision, and Values Statement.

Once we agreed to certain values, we used them to set a framework for how we would operate.

The biggest impact of the mission, vision, and values statement was that the entire team could understand what we were doing and how their particular part fit into that mission. They also began to appreciate my goals for how we would get the work done and how that would benefit them individually.

■ Additional Considerations for Team Leaders

Building the Project Team

One of the important roles of the project team leader is to build the project team. This includes selecting the best team members, taking steps to retain them, and removing resources from the team when necessary. As stated in Chapter 1, as a PM, you live or die by your resources. The skills, experience, and motivation of the resources will determine what can be accomplished by the team. It is essential that you get the right team and that you are able to retain them until the project is over.

Selecting Project Team Members

Of course we don't always have the luxury of selecting our team members. But, usually, we have some latitude when it comes to choosing who will be on the team. We need to exercise all the power we do have to maximize our chances of success.

Selecting the right team members from the beginning is very important. Many PMs act as if they have little or no say over their resources or that their choices don't matter much. Both of these attitudes stand in the way of getting the best resources for your teams. Resources are unique; they are not generic or interchangeable. Consider the fact that on IT projects, the best developers outperform the worst developers by a factor of 10 to 1.

Professional sports teams are in the business of trying to win. They take recruiting talent very seriously. Look at how professional sports teams address the draft. They understand the importance of identifying the strengths and weaknesses of their current teams and finding new players who will fill the gaps and round out the teams. A professional football team doesn't just think linebacker, kicker, or center. Each looks deeper to get just the right skills to complete the entire team. PMs could take a page out of the NFL playbook when it comes to recruiting resources for the teams.

What kinds of factors go into the decision to hire resources? Most people would consider the candidates' technical capabilities, skills, and experience as the key factors. Here are some additional factors that I think need to be considered:

- The strengths and weaknesses of the candidate versus the strengths and weaknesses of the team
- The candidate's experience with similar projects (size, technology, client)
- The candidate's attitude toward the project and team
- The candidate's personality and fit with the rest of the team
- The candidate's level of emotional intelligence

Of course it will be difficult to assess several of these factors in an interview, including the candidate's level of emotional intelligence. The point is to think beyond the basic questions of skill or experience and begin to look at the dynamics of the team and how each person will fit.

This list even mentions attitude. A good attitude is just as important as having the correct skill sets for the project. I have heard leaders say they hire for attitude and train for particular skills.

Different projects will require different approaches. I once managed a very large project that required hiring a lot of resources. I noticed that we had problems with those resources who up to that point had worked only on relatively small projects. Those resources had a difficult time dealing with certain big project issues, such as bureaucracy, recognition, and collaboration. Over time I learned to ask an additional question during interviews and that was, "What was the largest project team you've worked on?" I began to exclude those people who had worked on teams of only five or six people because they often did not perform well on a team of thirty or fifty members.

The goal of the PM when selecting resources is to add to the overall team capabilities. We want to select the individuals who will fill gaps, add to the team strengths, and generally bolster the team.

Better Decisions Through Emotional Intelligence

One of the ways in which project leaders can leverage emotional intelligence is making decisions. We talked in Chapter 1 about emotions being information and how that information is like personal radar. This section discusses how to leverage that emotional information to make better decisions.

Negative emotions should be monitored closely during decision making. In Chapter 3, we talked about how our emotions can lead us to make poor decisions or to react without thinking, resulting in emotional breakdowns. We can make terrible decisions if we let ourselves be swayed by fear, sadness, or anger without looking at the cause of those negative emotions. When we recognize those emotions, however, we can look beyond the feeling to the underlying cause. This will allow us to take in the emotion and any other issues and reframe the decision to include a full view of the situation.

In fact, David Caruso and Peter Salovey argue that each of the emotions serve us differently for different types of decisions. Their research shows that people in a sad mood can often develop more persuasive messages and better-quality arguments than people in a happy mood. Conversely, people in a happy mood may have more creative arguments than those who are sad.[4]

Which makes sense, because when we are sad or scared, we tend to be overly pessimistic. We have a hard time seeing that something is working, and we pick apart a plan and find all its faults. We are more likely to say no even when it might serve us better to say yes.

Ironically, individuals who are in positive moods can also make some very poor decisions. They will tend to underestimate the risk of negative events. When we feel happy, we may overlook key information, neglect to plan for contingencies, or gloss over negative data. We may be overly optimistic about project outcomes and fail to consider relevant risks. We may say yes to additional work or deliverables when we should say no.

Anger is a powerful emotion that helps motivate us to act. Anger can give us the power we need to make important changes or to simply get us moving when we are scared.

The starting point, then, for using emotions as input to decisions is to understand what we are feeling and, as noted in Chapter 3, to understand as much as possible why we are feeling that way. That understanding should lead to using our underlying emotions to balance our decisions. We need to understand what our gut feeling is telling us. If we feel uneasy about the interview with the candidate for the open developer position, what is behind that feeling? Armed with that information, we can approach a decision differently.

The second part of decision making with emotional intelligence is to understand and incorporate the feelings of those around us. What do others feel about this decision or the underlying issues? What is their position and why? This is where we use our social awareness skills to understand others. We can use our empathy to put ourselves in their shoes and identify what they are likely to feel. For individuals we know well, we can use our under-

---

[4]David R Caruso and Peter Salovey. *The Emotionally Intelligent Manager: How to Develop and Use the Four Key Emotional Skills of Leadership.* Hoboken, NJ: John Wiley & Sons, Inc., 2004

standing of their typical emotional state. If others tend to be overly happy or sad, that might influence the way they evaluate a particular situation.

Once we understand the emotional landscape, we can look past the emotions to the principles involved. We orient to principles when we make a decision that is grounded in the values of the team and the organization. We may be scared about a decision to bring on a new resource or try a new technology on the project but we need to see past the fear and look at the benefits we are trying to obtain. We need to make the best decision at the time in spite of how we might feel.

Getting Support

My mentor Rich has often said that big goals require big support. If we are going to live big as PMs and leaders, we need a lot of support. A good metaphor for support is the great pyramids. Think of the pyramids and the size of the base relative to the height of the peak. The higher the pyramid, the larger the base needs to be, as shown in Figure 7-3.

"Big goals require big support"
—Rich Blue

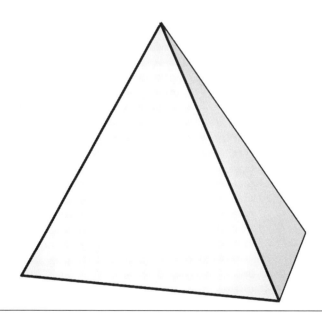

Figure 7-3: Support Base for a Pyramid.

So what is support? In this context, it means the emotional support and help of others. It could be help in the form of encouragement, accountability, listening, feedback, or coaching and mentoring.

Getting support is a relatively new concept for me, as it may be for many PMs. I used to be the type who got it all done on my own. I was independent. I rarely asked others for help and saw it as a weakness if I did.

I've come a long way in this area. I have participated in men's groups that provide emotional support for husbands, fathers, and business leaders. I've participated in several running groups that helped me qualify for the Boston Marathon. I've attended personal growth retreats at least once a year—and sometimes more—every year since 2001. This book actually sprang from my work with three different mentors, and I am honored to have different people involved in reviewing my writing and providing feedback. I have a team who holds me accountable to my weekly writing goals. Finally, my wife Norma has been an inspiration and source of support through all my work.

I feel like an evangelist when it comes to getting support and including others. In many different areas in my life, I am like a race car driver with a pit crew who is supporting me. They watch my back for me. When I need something, I ask them for help. I don't see how it is possible to be successful without enrolling others in supporting us and allowing them to participate in our goals and objectives and, ultimately, our success.

One of the reasons many people do not ask others for help is that they don't want to burden others. This fallacy is easily debunked. Consider for a moment when others have asked for your support. This could be to participate in an informational interview, to come into your office and vent, to get advice, or to provide coaching and feedback. Most people feel flattered when asked and are happy to help. I know I do. Unfortunately, I sometimes forget to apply that to others. So I hesitate to ask when it could really help.

There is another irony in asking for help. When you ask someone to help, they become invested in you and want you to succeed. They are no longer separate from your success because your success or failure reflects their input and help. By extension, they succeed or fail along with you. So, those who invest in you want to see you succeed. Instead of being bothered by your request, they become part of your team and take an interest in your success. And, the opposite is also true. If you exclude people from helping you, you deny them the opportunity to be part of your success.

A good friend of mine was recently responsible for organizing a fundraising event for a high school coach who had non-Hodgkin lymphoma. He almost hesitated to invite me to the event because it cost $100 per person, and I did not even know the coach. Fortunately, my friend did ask, and I went to the event. I was so affected by the kind words spoken by the friends and family of this coach that I walked away inspired and thinking about my own life. Later, I thanked my friend for including me. I personally benefited because I was impacted by the event. And I was happy to be able to help him. Far from feeling obligated to participate, I felt honored to be a part of this celebration of the coach.

Take a moment and think about your own support team. How would you rate yourself on getting other people involved in your success? Are there areas of your life where you are good at getting support? What are the areas where you tend to fly solo and go it alone? What stops you from involving others in your support?

■ Techniques for Improving Project Team Leadership

1. Techniques to Improve Team Communications

Plan your communications in advance whenever possible. Think through the emotional content, your own feelings, and the emotions of the recipients.

Practice your communications. You can do this alone, with your spouse or children, with a peer or trusted coworker, or with your boss. This is especially important for PMs who get nervous in front of groups.

Speak from the heart by sharing your emotions. Be honest, though, and don't try to be manipulative or to cover up your emotions; it doesn't work.

2. Techniques for Conflict Management

Expect conflict and lead by example when it comes to resolving it. Let people know that your style is to be open and take on conflict directly. Refrain from shooting the messenger so that people are willing to bring conflict to you.

One technique that I used successfully involved the opportunity for team members to vent. When I sensed there was pressure on people or that conflict was brewing, I would add a block of time to my weekly team meeting and call it "Open Rant." Each person would get sixty seconds or so in the meeting to rant about anything they wanted. They did not have to fear reprisal; the team simply held the space for each person to get something off their chest if needed. Not everyone used the time, but the ones that did were able to blow off some steam.

3. Create a Mission, Vision, and Values Statement for Your Project Team

Many people think of a mission, vision, and values statement as something done only at the company's strategic level. It is also possible to create a mission, vision, and values statement for your project team. Keep it as short and focused as possible. Include your team in the process and the outcome.

4. Cast a Vision for the Team

Whether you use a mission, vision, and values statement or simply talk about your vision for the team, be an evangelist about it. Continue over the life of the project to talk to the team about your vision, why you are excited about it, and how their work fits into that vision. Describe for them the outcomes you see for each team member and the overall team, and encourage them to embrace the goals and objectives for the team.

5. Become a Talent Scout

Getting the best resources is important to the success of the project. The PM should view themselves as a talent maven. They should be constantly on the lookout for new talent to add to the team or to keep in the back of their mind for some future project. When you are impressed by another professional in your field, you should be thinking about how to get them on your team. Add people to your team who are so good they scare you. I've actually created a category for my contacts in Outlook that is called "A-Team." I use that to flag people whom I meet and would like to work with so that I don't forget them.

6. Become Systematic About Screening and Hiring Resources

PMs who want to lead better will work to develop systematic ways of interviewing and selecting new resources. This is not something that can be left to chance. Develop systems and processes that allow for repeatability and that serve the needs of the project. This might include a checklist for hiring, a skill set template, a two-on-one interview process, or anything else that leads to better selection and hiring.

7. Tools to Address Team Strengths and Weaknesses

Try using the StrengthsFinder assessments for your entire team. The results can be plotted and used as a basis for discussion. This makes for a great offsite team-building exercise early in the life of a project.

In a creative use of the StrengthsFinder, I know of one company that conducted assessments of its top seventy-five managers. During an offsite retreat, the company posted the StrengthsFinder results anonymously and let the management participants use the results to select the leaders for the retreat. The results were interesting and not what they would have been if they had simply used the organization chart to organize the retreat.

8. Expand Your Support Base

Try expanding your support base by getting more people involved in your success. The following list includes many ways to engage people in what you are doing. You will notice that many of these start with "ask." We need to view an "ask" as an invitation for someone to participate and share in our journey.

1. Enroll your spouse or significant other in your success. Ask them to participate by giving you feedback and emotional support. Or, invite them into the planning of a large goal and then request that they hold you accountable to work toward that goal.
2. Brainstorm about who would be the best person or people to coach or mentor you to reach your particular goals without regard for whether you know them personally or think they would help. Then, reach out to them and ask for their help.
3. Ask someone to be a coach or mentor. If you don't currently have any mentors, identify someone you respect and ask them if they would be willing to mentor you. If you can afford it, hire a professional coach with expertise in your domain. As an example, I recently hired a personal trainer to help me achieve my goal of qualifying for the Boston Marathon.
4. Ask someone on your current team for feedback on the job you are doing. Be open and receptive.
5. Develop an open relationship with a peer who will serve as a sounding board for your ideas, challenges, and conflicts.
6. Join some type of support team. This could be a weekend running group, a church group, a 12-step program, a professional organization, or whatever else meets your needs.

■ Personal Action Plan: Project Team Leadership

Project team leadership means communicating with high emotional intelligence and finding the best ways to develop and nurture a team, including selecting and retaining team members.

Key Takeaways

1.	
2.	
3.	

My Strengths and Weaknesses in the Area of Project Team Leadership

Strengths	Weaknesses
1.	1.
2.	2.

My Actions or Goals Based on What I Learned

1.	
2.	
3.	

8

Creating a Positive Team Environment

In previous chapters, we explored the various aspects of emotional intelligence and project management. We started by looking at emotional intelligence for the PM, then we broadened our view to include interactions with members of the team and other stakeholders.

This chapter looks at how PMs can leverage emotional intelligence to create an environment that is positive and productive for the project team. There is a direct correlation between the team environment and the productivity and satisfaction levels of the team members. Whether intentional or not, the PM sets the overall tone and mood of the project. Through their actions and communications, PMs can create either resonance or dissonance in the project environment. We will look at ways that PMs can carry out their responsibilities and contribute to a positive team environment. Finally, we will finish with a list of techniques that PMs can put to work immediately to improve the environment of their projects.

■ What Makes a Great Project Team?

A World of Difference

If you have been involved in enough projects, you will have experienced some project teams that were good, or even great, as well as some that were perhaps not so great. Take a moment and think about a project team that was really terrific. If you are like most people, you can recall a project that was fun to work on; you even willingly worked extra hours. You likely felt happy and excited to be part of the team and sad when the project ended or when you left.

With the memory of that project in mind, think about the things that made that project so enjoyable. What was it about that project team that made you willing to work extra hours or go the extra mile to help others? What was it that made you sad when your time on the project ended? To the point, what were the characteristics of that project that made it so great?

I often ask my students about the projects they felt were great and what characteristics made those projects great. Most students respond that the best projects had the following characteristics:

- Interdependence among team members
- Diversity of team members
- Mutual respect
- The work was challenging
- They shared common goals
- Commitment of everyone
- High performance of all members
- Synergy among members

While not a scientific study, I have found the results consistent across classes. These characteristics are the context of the project. If they are not part of the values of the project or if the values conflict with these, the project environment is going to suffer.

Think about projects you have been on that were not so great. Can you recall a project you did not enjoy and could not wait to leave? Most people have at least one of these on their resume. Let's hope you were not the PM. What was it like to be in the middle of that not-so-great project? What made you want to leave? How did the project fall short of your hopes and expectations? How would you characterize the environment of that project?

It is amazing how two projects can vary so widely in terms of team morale, productivity, satisfaction levels, and motivation. There is a world of difference between project teams with a positive environment and those without it. Given the two choices, it seems clear that most people would prefer to be part of a project team that has a productive and positive environment.

> There is a world of difference between project teams with
> a positive environment and those without it.

As PMs, we want to create the best possible team environment to attract and retain great team members and help them to be productive. If we want to get the best from our teams, we need to create an environment that will support our team members and encourage them to perform at their best. The PM is responsible for creating that team environment and setting the stage so that team members can do their best work.

Resonance and Dissonance in Project Leaders

Another factor in establishing a positive environment is the level of emotional resonance or dissonance created by the project leader. In *Primal Leadership*, Daniel Goleman and his coauthors discuss the concepts of resonance and dissonance as they apply to leadership. Resonant leaders are those who can manage and direct feelings to help a group meet its goals. They leaders form strong bonds with people and create a sense of oneness across a team. Those leaders are in harmony with the team.

Dissonant leaders do the opposite. They create discord and emotional disconnects. Their messages sound off-key because they lack empathy or are unable to understand others. They transmit negative emotional messages that fall flat or, worse, disturb others and create conflict. The caveman manager that discussed in Chapter 4 would be a dissonant leader, as would the difficult and at-risk individuals discussed in Chapter 6.

While there is no 12-step program to cure dissonant leaders, PMs can take the following steps to become more resonant: (1) become more proficient at the emotional intelligent competencies introduced in previous chapters; (2) develop their self-awareness and social awareness to better understand themselves and others; (3) show empathy toward others and place themselves in the shoes of the members of their teams; (4) work to create messages that connect to the emotions and wants and needs of others; (5) show how each team member's personal goals and objectives relate to the team's goals and objectives; and (6) emphasize the common purpose of the team and focus on getting people pulling in the same direction.

PMs can evaluate their own leadership style and even learn new styles of leadership. Goleman and his *Primal Leadership* coauthors discuss four resonant leadership styles and two dissonant leadership styles. We are going to explore these leadership styles in detail in Chapter 9 and will provide some tips and techniques for leveraging these styles.

■ How PMs Set the Tone and Direction for the Project

The PM is responsible for the tone and direction of the project. Like the captain of a ship, the PM's leadership is an invisible force that guides the team.

PMs who are intentional about setting the tone and direction for the project create safety in the project environment. By this I do not mean physical safety, although that is also important. Rather, a safe environment is one where expectations and standards for behavior and performance are clear. PMs create such environments by setting standards, enforcing rules, addressing conflict, holding others accountable, and recognizing others. This safe environment encourages team members to take risks, flourish, and perform at their best.

Have you ever been in an unsafe environment? Unsafe environments are characterized by a lack of team norms, values, and rules. There may appear to be no one in charge, there is an undercurrent of dissatisfaction, and everyone complains about everyone else. Priorities are often not stated and conflict goes unmanaged.

The next sections look at how PMs set the project tone and direction by their handling of the following key PM leadership responsibilities:

- Lead by example.
- Be optimistic.
- Establish team values.
- Enforce the rules.
- Stand up to management.
- Hold others accountable.
- Keep it fun.
- Recognize individuals.

Lead by Example

I was on a large international program several years ago with upward of 100 people on the team. Many were from the United States and Canada, but others were from Europe, India, and the Philippines. My own boss lived in London.

We were moving quickly and scheduled some training in Chicago. Initially, my boss wasn't going to attend the Chicago meeting because he had been traveling for the past three weeks, and it was taking its toll on him. So, I was a little surprised on the first day of the training class to find that he turned up in person.

This was my boss's way of leading by personal example. This leader sacrificed to be with the team in the training because it was the right thing to do. Not only was he leading by making the sacrifice, he was also leading by showing that he was not above getting in and getting his hands dirty. He expected the rest of the leadership team to do likewise. Because he had done it, they were more likely to follow his example. And that made me want to do the same.

Does one instance of leading by example create a positive team environment? I don't know. I do know that a consistent policy of leading by personal example creates predictability and trust, a sense that we are all in it together.

As project leaders, we would do well to lead by example, and to not ask others to do what we are not willing to do ourselves. This might involve staying late or working through a weekend occasionally.

Be Optimistic

One key aspect of setting a positive environment is being optimistic. Optimism in this context means setting positive expectations for how your team will perform and the likely outcomes of your project. Here are some reasons that project leaders should be optimistic:

1. Our optimism is attractive and it attracts followers. As project leaders, we rely on our team to deliver the project. Optimism is a factor in attracting and retaining those high-performing team members we need.
2. Creativity comes from optimism, not pessimism. If you don't believe this, try to be pessimistic and creative at the same time. Perhaps you will creatively imagine many ways of failing, but you will be unlikely to be creative about positive things.
3. Optimism affects our ability to succeed. More often than not, we get exactly what we expect. So why not expect positive things? Whether we know it or not, what we project is often what we achieve. Conversely, if we are pessimistic, this may easily become a self-fulfilling prophecy. We often make happen what we say we most want to avoid. Or, we want so much to be right that we create failure just so that we can say—"see, I told you so."

It's not easy to be optimistic. There are plenty of negative messages bombarding us all day from the media or even within our organizations. As project leaders, we need to manage ourselves to be as optimistic as possible.

Establish Team Values

We talked about team values as part of the mission, vision, and values statement in Chapter 7. As PMs, we need to create team values and ensure that they become more than just words on a page. The team values are the norms of the project team; they are an agreement on how the team will act and treat each other. As PMs, we need to model the team values, communicate them to the project team, and hold the team to those values.

PMs should establish team values early in the life of the project either as part of the mission, vision, and values statement or as identified separately. It is usually best to create the values with the help of the project team, although there may be times when it is better for the PM to set the team values independently.

Once the values are established, we need to make sure that the team lives up to them. We do this by acknowledging team members who demonstrate the values. Several years ago I was one of eight PMs on a large program team. Our core team of PMs, together with the program manager and sponsor, created the team's value statement during an offsite meeting. Rather than simply writing the values down and forgetting them, the project sponsor had the values printed on memo pads that were freely distributed to all 100 members of the program team. The project sponsor also set up a simple recognition system based on those team values. The recognition system made it easy for any member of the program team to acknowledge and reward any other team member for demonstrating one of the team values. In this way, the program sponsor provided a mechanism for reinforcing the values of the team.

We can also reinforce the values by calling out behavior that is not in line with the values. If a team member is not playing by the rules or is demonstrating bad behavior, we can take them aside and discuss their behavior. We should not tolerate behavior that is contrary to the team values.

Enforce the Rules

In a similar way, the PM needs to be willing to enforce the team rules. Rules, the way that the PM expects others to behave, can include everything from being on time for meetings to requesting vacation time. An example of an expectations list is shown in Table 8-1. This list identified the expectations I placed on the team leads reporting to me on a particular project. The format provided a means for the team leads to do a self-check that also served as a basis for discussion between me and the team lead.

Once the rules or expectations are made clear, it is up to the PM to enforce those rules. When someone on the team is out of line, the other team members will look to the leader to see if he or she is going to address the issue. Inaction sends a clear message that the rules are not important or that they do not apply to everyone.

For a PM, enforcing the rules may feel like being the heavy, or being a bad guy. PMs may be afraid that they will not be liked or that others will get

Table 8-1: Expectations List

Expectations for Team Leads	Never	Rarely	Often Times	Very Often	Always
Show up on time for meetings	1	2	3	4	5
Review deliverables from an end users perspective	1	2	3	4	5
Lead by example	1	2	3	4	5
Conduct ongoing reviews of performance	1	2	3	4	5
Attend the weekly status meeting prepared to discuss status and issues	1	2	3	4	5
Log and work the team issues; escalate as appropriate	1	2	3	4	5
Conduct regular one-on-one meetings with each team member	1	2	3	4	5
Conduct regular status meetings with your team	1	2	3	4	5
Provide input to or prepare weekly status reports	1	2	3	4	5
Follow the program reporting structure	1	2	3	4	5
Invest in people	1	2	3	4	5
Get coverage when you will not be at work & notify stakeholders	1	2	3	4	5
Follow through on commitments	1	2	3	4	5
Tell the Truth	1	2	3	4	5
Create a fun and professional environment	1	2	3	4	5

angry with them. They may want to avoid conflict because that is easier in the short run. This can be a defining moment for a leader.

Enforcing the rules has a major impact on the environment of the project. Even a seemingly little thing like making sure that people are on time for team meetings can make a difference to the project team. In *The Tipping Point*, Malcolm Gladwell discusses the Broken Windows theory, which links the existence of broken windows in an area to a rise in crime. Essentially it says that crime results from an environment where crime is permitted. The existence of broken windows or graffiti acts as a sort of environmental indicator that crime is tolerated. Individuals who normally would not commit crimes might be tempted to do so if they saw those environmental indicators or if they saw crimes going unpunished. However, if the police crackdown on the broken windows and the graffiti and other petty crimes, the overall crime rates would drop significantly.

In the project environment, the PM is the rough equivalent of the chief of police. The PM needs to enforce the rules. When we enforce the rules, we risk upsetting people, being disliked, or creating conflict. This can be very uncomfortable and scary. We need to push through our fear and address the issue as quickly and directly as possible.

Some project team members will actually get a kick out of breaking the rules. They will test the PM to see if he or she is serious about enforcing the rules. I have seen this manifested in people who fail to ask approval before spending project funds, those who are chronically late to meetings, and those who disappear on vacation without letting anyone know. As noted previously, this could be a sign of passive–aggressive behavior. It could also be a team member testing the limits, like a small child tests its parent's limits. Like good parents, a PM needs to address the issue as directly as possible, including enforcing consequences.

There must be consequences for those individuals who break the rules. It is preferable to use positive consequences instead of negative ones. PMs may also want to have ready some lighthearted consequences for first-time offenders or for minor offenses. I have heard of teams that build up a small slush fund by requiring anyone who is late to a meeting to contribute one dollar. Some teams have progressive consequences that start out fun and quickly become less fun if the offense is repeated. This could escalate into the offender being removed from the project team at some point. In most cases, however, the best consequence is simply to talk to the offender about changing the behavior.

Here is one final note about enforcing the rules. The best approach is to create an environment where everybody is part of enforcing the rules. In this way, the PM doesn't always have to be the only enforcer. The team can often exert peer pressure to get compliance. To encourage everyone to play a part, the PM needs to send a clear message about the expected behavior and let it be known that they expect everyone on the team to enforce the rules.

Standing Up to Management

There are times when the PM will need to stand up to management on some issue. Examples include when PMs disagree with a decision or when they need to push back on a proposed change in scope, budget, resources, or timeline.

In this context, management means the PM's boss, major stakeholders, or the client.

The project team members wants to see the PM stand up to management, major stakeholders, or even the client once in a while. They want to know that their leader has the backbone to go to bat for them when needed. They want to feel like the PM has their best interest in mind.

PMs who are unwilling to stand up to management may be viewed as weak or as a pushover. Team members will feel sold out and resent the downstream impacts of PMs who are unwilling to push back. "It all rolls downhill" is a common refrain from frustrated team members. But it is not just team members you need to be concerned with. Managers, major stakeholders, and clients will become wary of PMs who never push back; they will see the PM as weak and ineffective.

That doesn't mean the PM should fight every decision that goes against the team. PMs need to choose their battles. Bob was one of my PMs who fought every decision and change. He opposed every idea that was not his own. He resisted organizational changes, fought a physical move of his team to bring them into proximity with the rest of the program, challenged budget cuts, and resisted attempts to meet the aggressive delivery schedules our client requested.

Bob was a pain for me to manage. He cooperated only when he was getting his way. Otherwise, he was stubborn, argumentative, and often ineffective.

The problem with Bob was not his unwillingness to fight for his team. It was his inability to know when to fight. He didn't know how to choose his battles and his approach of always standing up to management did more damage than good. His approach did not serve him or the overall team well. As his manager, I often thought about replacing him with someone who was more cooperative.

We also need to consider the long-term consequences of pushing back. We don't want to create ill will or enemies. In particular, we should be careful to follow the chain of command when we disagree with a decision or an issue. In most environments, it is acceptable to disagree with your boss. It is usually not a good idea to argue in public with your boss, nor is it good form to go over your boss's head or around them without trying to resolve the issue with them first. In fact, we should always strive to resolve issues at the lowest possible management level before escalating the discussion. We should exercise extreme caution any time we are about to go over someone's head, particularly our boss. Going over your manager's head or skipping levels makes sense only as a last resort. The potential for creating long-lasting conflict is high, and every attempt should be made to work things out first with the manager.

Hold Others Accountable

The effective use of accountability is a powerful lever for the PM. PMs don't perform the work of the project; they direct and make sure that others do that work. Holding others accountable is crucial when we don't have direct authority over team resources.

One way that PMs hold others accountable is by gaining agreement on goals and deliverables, stating our expectations for each person, and publicizing team roles and responsibilities. We make the commitments public and then we support others to complete the work as appropriate.

There are three key parts to accountability. The first is to get agreement on the work to be performed. Accountability is not possible without buy-in from the person performing the work. The second is to make that agreement public. PMs publicize commitments through action item lists, status reports, responsibility assignment matrixes, and project schedules. The third is to follow up. As PMs, we need to be proactive to make sure the team members are performing the activities and following through on their commitments.

Some individuals need to be held accountable to perform at their best. When we remind others of their commitments, they will usually work to meet those commitments.

PMs should be prepared for individuals who are unwilling to be held accountable. I once worked with an individual whom we nicknamed "Teflon Don" based on his ability to avoid being accountable. Don was good at avoiding responsibility for tasks. I realized that it was difficult for me to assign work to Don, and it made me uncomfortable to hold him accountable. I wanted to downplay what I needed from him, and when. However, that did not serve me very well since Don rarely delivered anything on that project.

Like Don, some people wriggle out of responsibilities or ignore them completely. PMs who avoid conflict may be scared and find it difficult to bring up the item. It takes courage to pursue individuals and hold them accountable, especially if they are senior to the PM. For example, I used to find it very difficult to hold certain people accountable, including my boss, major stakeholders, clients, and anyone I considered senior to me. Once I recognized this tendency to be scared and play small, I pushed myself to change. I made sure that I recorded the required actions, got agreement on those actions, publicized them, and followed up with the responsible party to remind them of their commitment.

PMs don't just sit by and watch if others fail in their commitments. PMs support others by reminding them of their commitments, clarifying expectations, and requesting periodic updates. If needed, the PM should also offer support or suggest creative ways to accomplish goals. However, the PM should not take the responsibility back from the owner or let people off the hook.

I once taught a class where the importance of accountability became crystal clear. It was a two-day course. Early in the first day, a number of students requested a thirty-minute lunch instead of the planned sixty-minute lunch. This would allow them to end the day sooner and avoid some of the rush hour traffic. We discussed the proposal as a group, and everyone agreed to the change. What happened next was not surprising. Only about half of the students were back in their seats and ready to start after thirty minutes; the others were missing. Students continued to arrive back from lunch over the next thirty minutes right up until the original commitment time.

It would have been easy to let this go. After all, the students paid for the class, and it was up to them to get the most out of it. However, this course was about emotional intelligence for PMs, who need to appreciate deadlines and the importance of sticking to their commitments. So after everyone returned, we spent some time talking about the incident. We recognized that everyone had agreed to the change, yet some individuals did not live up to their end of the bargain. That behavior penalized the entire class. We also talked about the message that tolerating this type of behavior would send to the team and how other behavior would deteriorate. The message I sent was that people would be held accountable. It was not surprising then that everyone returned from lunch and breaks on time from that point forward.

This unplanned incident turned out to be one of the most talked-about parts of the course and perhaps one of the most important lessons in leadership that those students received from the course. It was a great reminder to me of the importance of holding others accountable.

Keep it Fun

It may seem odd to talk about fun right on the heels of a discussion on holding others accountable, but I think keeping things fun is an important part of creating a positive environment.

Previously, we discussed the importance of appropriate humor as a way to manage our emotions. It is a great way to reduce your stress levels which is a key to emotional self-management. It is also helpful for building relationships with others when you show that you don't take yourself too seriously and are able to laugh along with others. Therefore, it helps with relationship management as well.

Do you encourage humor on your projects? Have you someone on your project team who is responsible for humor? Do you have someone in charge of making other laugh? Have you made it part of their job description?

Perhaps you should think about it. Don't get me wrong—I need people who are dead serious about their work and the success of the project or program. But, they also need to have fun, laugh at themselves, and not take themselves too seriously.

Let's face it, the ability to make others laugh is a rare and valuable commodity. I have had several bosses and many team members in my career whom I appreciated because they made me laugh. Someone who can see humor in the situation or create fun when others are getting tense provides sustaining value and a welcome relief.

I had someone on a project team who could not lighten up and have some fun. This particular individual's fear and anger prevented him from being able to laugh and, in the process, he impacted the entire team. The experience made me realize just how poisonous one individual could be to the entire team. Lack of a sense of humor is not something you can fire someone for, at least as far as I know. Perhaps you can find ways to get that person on board someone else's team to prevent them from killing the spirit of fun and enjoyment of everyone else on your team.

Recognize Individuals

When my son was seven, he walked into my home office and said, "Dad, you're pretty smart." I thought to myself, this kid is a genius and a great judge of character!

It turns out that he was doing an assignment for school. He was supposed to give a compliment and then draw a picture of the recipient's face immediately afterward. The idea was for him to draw a connection between how people feel when they are recognized. (This is part of the PATHs Curriculum I mentioned earlier).

His assignment was a great idea, and it really got me thinking about the scarcity of compliments and recognition at home and at work. I also think that would be a great assignment for all of us to take on today. Go out and compliment or recognize at least three people, then draw the faces of the recipients immediately after the compliment.

What is so relevant about this seven-year-old's assignment is that we should all be doing it all the time. As leaders, we all need to do a great job of recognizing the strengths and contributions of others. Recognition is one of the easiest yet most underutilized tools that PMs and leaders have. I've said it before, but it bears repeating. No one ever quit a job because of too much recognition! Could you imagine if someone actually gave that as a reason for leaving? It would be unheard of.

"My supervisor was always coming in and telling me what a great job I was doing. It was annoying really because I was just doing my job. Eventually I just got fed up with it and decided to go elsewhere."
—Anonymous Disgruntled Employee

In fact, Marcus Buckingham contends that regular recognition is one of the twelve measures of the strength of a workplace. In *First Break All the Rules*, he uses recognition received in the last week as a key indicator of the health of the workplace.[1]

In Chapter 6, I referred to recognition as one of the most powerful and underused tools in the PM's arsenal. In addition to building relationships with others, it is one of the ways that the PM sets the tone of the project environment.

In their book, *The One Minute Manager*, Kenneth Blanchard and Spencer Johnson introduced the phrase "Help people reach their full potential. Catch them doing something right."

"Help people reach their full potential.
Catch them doing something right."
—Ken Blanchard and Spencer Johnson[2]

There is genius in that phrase. One of the things I appreciate most about my mentor is when he says "Anthony, my vision for you is. . . ." It is as if he is holding the bar high for me; he can see me performing at a level even higher than what I believe is possible. It is closely related to the idea of positive regard discussed more in Chapter 10.

That is the model I try to follow for my team members, and I encourage you to do the same. Look for the best in people. Try to see beyond their current performance to their true potential. Hold them to that higher bar and encourage them to reach for that level of performance.

The second part of Blanchard's phrase is pure brilliance. "Catch them doing something right" encourages us to be on the lookout for ways to recognize people's goodness. We seek out the best in others and we acknowledge it.

---

[1] Marcus Buckingham and Curt Coffman. *First Break All the Rules: What the Worlds Greatest Managers Do Differently.* New York, NY: Simon and Schuster, 1999.

[2] Kenneth Blanchard and Spencer Johnson. *The One Minute Manager.* New York: HarperCollins, 1981.

The more natural tendency for me—and many others—is to focus on what people are doing wrong, so that I can criticize or discipline them. It is a habit that I acquired from my critical father. Like any other habit, it can be broken and replaced with better habits. The first step is to recognize that you have a problem. I know that I am most critical when I feel scared or angry. I try to use this awareness to make the shift to being on the lookout for the best in others.

Do you look for the best in others? Or, are you looking for the things that are wrong or need improvement? Whichever approach you are taking, it is part of the tone of the project. It becomes one of the unstated values, and it affects the behaviors of everyone on the team. We send a clear message to the team when we give recognition or when we withhold it. Team members will pay more attention to what is rewarded than to what is said. The recognition informs the team on what is important to the project team leader.

There are many opportunities to catch people doing something right. We can recognize and reward individuals for their contributions to the team, for specific results and outcomes, to reinforce the values and expected behaviors of the team, to build morale, and to motivate people.

Once we catch someone doing something right, we need to recognize that behavior. How do we do it? There are nearly infinite ways to recognize people. I have used public awards, certificates, thank you notes, lunches, and other approaches. One of the best and easiest ways is to simply stop by and thank them. You can also thank them in public, such as a department meeting. Either way, thanking people doesn't take a long time or cost anything. Tie your thank you as closely as possible to something that the individual did well. It is better not to wait to recognize others.

As PMs, we want to create a healthy and productive environment. We can use the rewards to create an environment of gratitude and recognition.

■ The Team Within the Team

Up to this point, the discussion about the project team environment has largely ignored the broader organizational environment, that is, the department, division, or company environment that surrounds the project. This could also be a client organization, if that is where the project team is performing.

The reality is that project teams don't operate in isolation. They are affected by the organizations around them. PMs cannot afford to ignore the broader organizational environment or context, which will impact efforts to create a positive project environment. If the organization environment is positive, the PM will have an easier time creating a positive project environment.

Negative Environments

PMs need to be concerned about the organizations that are not so positive. For example, I once worked for a small company whose CEO was trying to change the culture from a friendly and collegiate environment to one that was professional and client focused. I was inadvertently caught in the crossfire of this organizational culture change, as I led a large project team with a priority on meeting client needs and expectations. In several cases, my style of delivering what the client needed collided with the longstanding culture of scholarly debate. In one memorable incident, the CEO told me to keep doing what I was doing. He said that he would "deal with any ruffled feathers." I felt happy and supported in my work and that helped to reinforce the client-focused team environment.

What if the larger environment you are working in is not positive? Can you create a positive project environment? Absolutely! I believe this is something the best PMs do naturally. They don't let a negative organizational environment corrupt a positive project environment. They send the message to their team that the project is different. They communicate the values and rules of the project team, reward those team members who are in alignment, and enforce the rules.

In my classes, I often hear people say "that won't work at my company," or "they won't let me do that." I don't know if the statements are true or not. I do believe that the students who make these statements believe them to be true. Either way it is clear that the students don't feel empowered. In most cases, what is lacking is not permission for PMs to create their own environment, but the courage that PMs need to take risks and be different. PMs have the responsibility to do what is best for the project and the company. This takes courage. PMs often have more power than they think when it comes to choosing their own destiny. There are probably very few rules imposed on PMs, in particular when it comes to setting the mood, tone, and direction for the project.

If you find yourself in a negative environment that stymies any opportunity to create a positive project environment, consider leaving. Why waste your talent on an organization that is not positioned to leverage it? Don't go home at night thinking that you could be something if only management would let you. Don't be a victim to a negative workplace.

At a minimum, if you cannot leave the negative organization, at least don't let yourself be contaminated by the environment. Don't compromise your own standards for behavior. Be as positive as possible and maybe through a merger, management change, or reorganization, the organization will catch up to you.

■ Techniques for Creating a Positive Team Environment

1. Assess How Team Members View the Team Environment

I have found it helpful to poll my team to see how they feel about the environment. Most members will be flattered if you ask how they think you are doing in this area. Consider a mini-assessment that will evaluate how you are doing in terms of creating safety, establishing and communicating values, and resolving conflict.

One of my favorite mini-assessments was one I created and used frequently on different project teams to gauge overall team morale. This team health check mini-assessment, shown in Table 8-2, was used to track the health of a large project team on a quarterly basis over the course of a three-year program. I plotted the quarterly scores and used them to see trends and spot potential issues. You can use this tool as it is or tailor it to meet your specific needs.

2. Put It in Writing

PMs may choose to document their expectations for their team members to make sure those expectations are clear. Consider working with the team

Table 8-2: Team Healthcheck Mini-Assessment

Team Healthcheck				
	Strongly Disagree	Disagree	Neutral	Agree	Strongly Agree
1. I know what I need to do my job effectively	1	2	3	4	5
2. I know what is expected from me on this project	1	2	3	4	5
3. The work I am doing is satisfying and rewarding	1	2	3	4	5
4. Communications on this project are effective	1	2	3	4	5
5. This project is fun	1	2	3	4	5

Comments: _____

_____

members to create a set of values, rules, or expectations for team behaviors. Use the example expectations list provided in Table 8-1 as a starting point for your own list of expectations. Here are some additional standards to consider:

1. Deadlines for intermediate and final deliverables
2. Quality standards for deliverables
3. Status reporting deadlines
4. Time reporting standards
5. Weekend work
6. Requests for time off
7. Conflict resolution

3. Establish Clear Accountability and Hold People to It

There are a number of tools for making sure that project accountability is clear. My favorite is the responsibility matrix. You can also find sample templates on the Internet or create your own.

When developing a responsibility matrix, list the major deliverables or work assignments in the left-most column. List the responsible people across the top. Use the RACI convention to indicate the role of each person for each deliverable or work assignment, where R = responsible, A = accountable, C = consulted, and I = informed. There should be just one person listed for the responsible and accountable columns.

Once you have established responsibility and accountability for deliverables, you need to hold others to it. Rate yourself on how you are doing in this area. If you are not doing as well as you would like, think about what you need to do to make it better. Are you better with some individual team members and stakeholders than with others? Try to understand what is behind the resistance you feel; it may be your desire to be liked. Determine what steps you need to take to improve in this area.

4. Hold Others to Your Highest Vision for Them

Just as my mentor has done for me, position yourself to hold others to a high vision. Dedicate a chunk of quality quiet time to think about each person on the team and his or her true potential. Try to see people at their very best. Envision what their future could look like and how you see them succeeding.

Then, set up a time to talk about that vision with the individual and encourage them to live up to your vision for them. On an ongoing basis, remind them of how you see them at their best. Continue to adjust your vision to the reality of their growth.

5. Catch People Doing Something Right

Develop the habit of catching people doing something right, and make it part of your leadership style. Make it a point to track your efforts for each individual. Give more to those people who are junior or new to the team to help them integrate.

Establish systems so that you are able to follow through on your good intention of seeing the best in others. One simple way is to use your team roster to create a tally sheet. Track the times you were successful in catching each team member in the act of doing something right.

You might want to create more sophisticated measures for yourself if you are having trouble breaking the habit of catching people doing something wrong. Set a target and track your rate of positive versus negative comments. Reward yourself for achieving your goals when you do. When you don't, make it a point to up the ante in the next week.

You can also enroll others to support you in this area. Ask your boss, a coach or mentor, or a peer for support and accountability. Or, if you fall short on follow through, ask someone to help you to set a standard or goal for yourself and to hold you accountable to that goal.

You can also spread the wealth by getting everyone involved in identifying positive behavior. Let team members know that you are on the lookout for people doing something right. Encourage them to identify and bring forward examples of people performing well. This will go a long way toward creating an environment of acknowledgement. While you are at it, try to catch stakeholders doing things right also.

6. 1001 Ways to Recognize People

Some time ago I stumbled across a book entitled *The 1001 Rewards & Recognition Fieldbook*. The title helped me to appreciate that the ways to recognize and reward the individuals on our teams are nearly unlimited.

Do a self-check to see how you are doing in this area. Make a list of the people on your team and track how many times you recognize their work over the course of a week. See how creative you can be in recognizing the work of others. No one ever complained about too much recognition. Let people know that you are serious about recognizing and appreciating the efforts and results of the team.

7. Fix Your Broken Windows

You can apply the broken windows theory to your project environment. Take a moment to conduct an honest assessment to see if there are any rules or standards that people don't adhere to in your environment. Develop an inventory of the rules and standards, and if there are lapses, develop action plans to address any regulations that are not being followed.

You can get the team or key members of your team involved. Use their input in those areas where you may have blind spots.

■ Personal Action Plan: Creating a Positive Team Environment

Creating a positive team environment is necessary for a positive and productive team.

Key Takeaways

1.
2.
3.

My Strengths and Weaknesses in the Area of Creating a Positive Team Environment

Strengths	Weaknesses
1.	1.
2.	2.

My Actions or Goals Based on What I Learned

1.
2.
3.

9

Leveraging Emotional Intelligence on Large and Complex Projects

■ Are You Ready to Lead Large and Complex Projects?

Many PMs see career progression as taking on larger and more complex projects. PMs who want to succeed with these projects must have high emotional intelligence. It is possible to get by on small or even medium-sized projects with low emotional intelligence, but there is very little room for error on a large and complex project. There are too many stakeholders and too many opportunities for breakdowns.

I personally prefer large projects to smaller ones. Larger projects have a higher risk than small projects, but they also have a much greater reward. Often the increase in risk is less than the increase in reward. This is because large projects usually get a high priority within the organization, which makes it easier to attract good resources. Small projects are often given a low priority and are frequently understaffed, which can make them even more risky than bigger projects. For a small increase in risk, larger projects provide more visibility, recognition, and personal satisfaction. I generally recommend that people step up, take on the risk, and go for the large and complex projects.

If the thought of managing a large project intimidates you, this chapter should be of interest. We look at the characteristics of large and complex projects and how emotional intelligence plays a role in our success with those projects. In addition, Daniel Goleman's six different leadership styles of inspirational leadership are presented, along with a discussion of how good leaders need to select the style appropriate to the situation, the characteristics of each of the inspirational leadership styles, when to use each, and the emotional intelligence competencies that underpin those leadership styles. The chapter also explores the world of virtual teams and ways to bring emotional intelligence into those virtual teams. We close with a set of techniques intended to help you succeed when you manage large and complex projects.

■ Characteristics of Large and Complex Projects

While all projects are different, large and complex projects tend to have similar characteristics that differentiate them from small projects.

Stakeholder Conflict

All projects come with conflict. On large projects, various stakeholders will often disagree about the goals and objectives of the project. Some groups will receive benefits, and others will experience greater costs or penalties. This leads to built-in conflict that may be in the open or that may be underground.

Layers of Staff

Large projects tend to have large project teams. The larger the team, the less direct contact the PM has with each team member. The largest projects will have subteams headed up by team leaders or PMs. This affects the PM's communication plan and approach as well as choice of leadership style.

Vendors and Subcontractors

Large projects are more likely to include vendors or subcontractors than small projects. When dealing with vendors and subcontractors, the PM needs the ability to negotiate with, direct, and lead those third parties in order to achieve the goals of the project.

Importance to the Organization

Large projects are usually more important to the organization than smaller ones. There is a larger investment in resources, greater expectation for returns, and a higher priority placed on success. While it is usually desirable to lead those critical projects, the priority, importance, and visibility can place pressure on the PM and key stakeholders to succeed. A lack of strong self-management skills can lead to emotional breakdowns that disrupt the team and undermine the PM's effectiveness.

Role of the Project Manager

With a large team, the PM role is less likely to be related to the deliverables and more likely related to leadership, stakeholder management, facilitating, coaching and mentoring, and delegation.

Virtual Teams

With the increase in team size comes an increased likelihood that there will be a virtual component of the team, that is, some of the team will be working remotely. PMs have to deal with time zone and cultural differences, and this work is frequently done over the phone. We will look specifically at tools and techniques for applying emotional intelligence to virtual teams later in this chapter.

■ Concerns for Large-Scale Project Managers

As PMs take on large and complex projects, the types of issues that they deal with will change, as these projects have some unique concerns.

It's Lonely at the Top

The bigger the team that the PM is managing, the more likely it is for the PM to feel isolated and alone. With a small team of three or four members, the PM can feel like part of the group. However, the likelihood of feeling isolated increases when a PM is managing seventy or more members, particularly if the PM has many direct reports. Team members are less likely to engage you in conversation, invite you to lunch, or include you in activities outside work. PMs can begin to feel sad, lonely, and isolated.

PMs can overcome this loneliness by investing in the relationships with team members and by reaching out to others for support. Team members who are uncomfortable initiating conversation with the "boss" may welcome invitations from the PM for conversation or for lunch. In addition, the PM should be using regular one-on-one meetings to develop and invest in the relationship with each individual.

The PM should also develop a support network of relationships to lean on when needed. The network could include the relationships with their own manager, peers, and mentors. It may also include relationships outside the work environment, such as family, spouses or significant others, support groups, fellow members of professional organizations (like PMI), and coaches.

Role of the Project Manager—Delegation

Managing large and complex projects requires us to step away from the day-to-day details, activities, and deliverables. PMs need to be focused on leadership, stakeholder management, facilitating, coaching, and mentoring. Stepping away from the day-to-day aspects of the project does not mean abandoning them. It does mean delegating the responsibility for those deliverables and activities and holding others accountable for the results.

Delegation can be challenging for PMs, especially for those with subject matter expertise or those accustomed to being involved in the details. The reason that delegation is challenging is usually rooted in fear and a lack of trust:

- PMs do not trust their subordinates to do it right (or to do it their way).
- PMs do not trust their subordinates to get it done on time.
- PMs are scared that if the subordinate does the work, the PM may not be viewed as valuable.
- PMs are scared to not to be in control over the activity and how it will reflect on them.

Delegation is a critical skill for PMs who want to grow and take on larger projects. If you are not good at delegating, try the following to improve your delegation skills:

- Use the self-awareness techniques to understand the emotions that come up for you around delegating. Are you scared, and if so, what are you afraid of?
- Be aware and mindful of your desire to control. Practice letting go of how the work gets done and focus only on the results.
- Practice delegating as a learning experience for you and for the delegatee. Start small and work your way up, developing yourself and your resources as you go. Talk about the experience with them before, during, and after.
- Develop a responsibility matrix and use it to identify responsibilities and hold others accountable.

Importance of Business Skills Versus People Skills

The application of emotional intelligence has focused on improving our interpersonal skills. This does not mean that technical and business skills are not important. In fact, to be effective and manage large and complex projects, PMs must have people skills, business skills, and some level of technical skills. The exact mix of required skills is going to vary based on the industry, project type, and organization. Those PMs with a strong set of interpersonal skills who also understand and can speak the language of the business will succeed over those without the business skills.

The reality is that running a large project is a lot like running a small business. In large-scale projects, we need to pay attention to both business matters and people matters. We need to balance the other core project management skills like contract or integration management with EI skills like empathy and self-awareness. We need to apply the correct leadership style to the project.

■ Applying Different Leadership Styles

In the large project environment more than any other place, the PM has to be flexible in approach and have the ability to vary leadership style. In *Primal Leadership*, Goleman and his coauthors described six inspirational leadership styles. Four of those styles are considered to be resonant, that is, they cause a positive effect on the team environment.

- Visionary
- Coaching
- Affiliative
- Democratic

The remaining two leadership styles are considered to be dissonant. The dissonant leadership styles are those that cause disturbance or disruption in the team environment.

- Pacesetting
- Commanding[1]

Let's look at each of these styles in detail to see how PMs can apply them and to understand the underlying emotional intelligence competencies. We will also look at some of the considerations that go into deciding which leadership style is appropriate for a given project. As you read about each of

---

[1] Daniel Goleman, Richard Boyatzis, and Annie McKee. *Primal Leadership*. Boston: Harvard Business School Press, 2002, p. 55.

the leadership styles, think about your own project history. See if you can determine your own dominant leadership style.

Visionary Leadership

Visionary leaders tell people where they are going; they provide the vision and the big picture. On a project, visionaries describe the end goals, but leave individuals plenty of latitude on how to achieve them.

The attraction of the visionary leader is the ability to connect the individual's work with the vision for the project so that team members understand how their work fits into the big picture. Team members benefit from a leader who shows them not only how what they do connects with the vision, but also why what they do is important. Visionary leaders help the team members to resonate with the project goals and objectives.

The visionary leader relies heavily on the emotional intelligence competencies of self-awareness, self-confidence, and empathy. In particular, empathy is critical, as the visionary needs to understand where people are in order to help them connect to the bigger picture. Vision casting is also an important emotional intelligence competency for visionary leadership.

Goleman's research indicates that visionary leadership is the most effective style of leadership. However, there is a caveat to the use of the visionary style. That is when there are many experts or more senior people reporting to the PM. In those cases, the vision casting by the PM may fall flat and fail to resonate with those experts or senior people. The visionary may fail to get the appropriate buy-in. Otherwise, the visionary leadership style would be appropriate to any type of project. It would be especially beneficial to projects that are in recovery mode or those that are stalled and need a fresh vision to energize the project team.

Coaching Style

The coaching style focuses on personal development rather than on the accomplishment of tasks. A PM with a coaching style sees the project as the vehicle for the development of the members of the team. The goal of accomplishing the project is almost secondary to the goal of helping people to learn and grow. The project becomes the vehicle that we can use to help people stretch and develop. The key outcome for the coaching style leaders is the growth of the team members.

I had an excellent manager named Rick for several years; he was a terrific example of the coaching style leader. We worked together on three large projects over the course of about four years. Rick showed great interest in my development, and he encouraged me to share with him my long-term goals. In return, he showed me how my current assignment would benefit me and how it connected to my long-term goals and objectives.

One hallmark of Rick's style was his use of one-page weekly objectives. He worked with me to break down my responsibilities into weekly goals that fit on one page. We sat down together each week to develop the objectives. We started by reviewing the goals from the previous week, discussing in detail the progress that was made and any hurdles or issues. Then we would jointly set the objectives for the next week. Though the document would have appeared cryptic to an outsider because of our shorthand notes, we both understood precisely what it meant. Our initials at the top of the page indicated that both of us were committed to the goals.

The one-page objectives worked for that relationship, but they are not necessary to use the coaching style. It is critical, though, that the PM be involved with the team members at a detail level. The PM coaches the team member with specific steps and provides encouragement and feedback as they perform.

Another key to the coaching style is the manager's belief in the ability of the team member. I always felt that Rick firmly believed that I could do anything. He didn't seem to think that I had any limitations and his one-page weekly objectives often included stretch goals that I would not even have attempted had he not encouraged me to believe they were possible.

Rick's belief in me encouraged me to try to accomplish the goals even when I didn't see a way to make them happen. Once I ran into some trouble meeting key project milestones. I wanted to take the easy route of pushing out the schedule. This would delay the entire project, cost my company money, and disappoint the client. Rick told me flat out to go back to the drawing board and come up with a solution that did not involve delaying the project. His confidence that I could do it encouraged me to look for that creative solution. I chose to believe that there must be a creative solution if Rick thought that there was one. As it turned out, I was able to come up with a solution that enabled us to hold the line on the dates.

It is easy for me to understand why the coaching style leads to high motivation levels for the team members. I felt motivated to meet the high expectations Rick had for me. I wanted to do what he asked me to do. In fact, I continually raised my own internal standards and expectations based on his expectations for me. If he thought I could do it, then I chose to believe that I could.

The coaching style works best when employees seek direction and feedback and are willing to partner very closely to get agreement on the work to be performed. It requires a high level of trust between the coach and the team member.

The coaching style doesn't work when trust is lacking, when team members are not interested in getting input on their performance, or when the team member feels micromanaged. On a recent project, I consciously applied the coaching style to four different junior members of the same team. With two of the members, I was very successful. Those two team members saw my involvement with them as an investment and kept requesting feedback on a regular basis. The coaching style failed with the other two team members who saw the same style as de-motivating, critical, and micromanaging. These team members did not like my close involvement and found the coaching demeaning. They wanted to have the latitude to work without checking in with the boss. The main differences in these relationships were the emotional intelligence level of the team members and the level of trust. In those cases where the team members were secure about their role and believed that I had their best interest in mind, it worked great. When the team members had low emotional intelligence or did not trust that I had their best interest in mind, the coaching styles failed.

Affiliative Style

Affiliative leaders are great relationship builders. They tend to focus less on tasks and goals and more on building relationships with their team members. Affiliative leaders create an environment of harmony and friendly interactions. They work to nurture personal relationships using empathy and conflict management.

With affiliative leaders, feelings and relationships are a clear priority. Taken to an extreme, feelings are given priority over results. Affiliative leaders may find themselves wanting to be liked, and they may make decisions that place a priority on being liked. Team members may view affiliative managers as soft or indecisive. Team members may also feel they are in the dark about the project direction and their work. They may feel left on their own to make decisions.

I once worked for an organization that emphasized the affiliative style. The company had grown quickly from a partnership between the two founders to being part of a large corporation at the time that I joined. Yet the co-operative nature of the original partnership was part of the DNA of the company and a priority was placed on everyone getting along.

My manager Tom ran the project management office, which included all the PMs. I was helping Tom with the development of the standards for project delivery, including methodology and best practices, but I was continually frustrated by his insistence on getting input from all areas of the company and involving others in the discussion. In our efforts to get cooperation from across the company, it was not possible to get consensus without watering down the methodology to the point where it was unusable.

Tom was ineffective because of the priority he placed on everyone getting along and on being liked. He was very good at relationships; unfortunately, he was not able to get the results he needed from the project management office.

The affiliative style of leadership works best when you are trying to improve morale and communications or repair broken trust. The affiliative style will not work as well when leaders fail to do the right thing in order to be liked.

Democratic Style

The democratic style is similar in some ways to the affiliative style. Democratic leaders tend to take input from many sources. This input leverages the experience of the team, provides for better decisions, and gets buy-in from the entire team.

Early in my career I worked for a democratic manager named Charley, who was responsible for a corporate-wide competency center. In his role, he supported engineers and engineering managers across the company. In turn, funding for the competency center was provided by each of those engineering managers.

What worked well for Charley was his willingness to get input from everyone. He was a good listener and would spend time with the engineers he supported to find out what they needed. As a former engineer himself, Charley was empathetic to their situation and could place himself in their shoes.

The downside to the time Charley spent working one-on-one with the engineers was the lack of overall direction for our group. Those of us who worked for Charley felt like we didn't know where the group was heading. We seemed to spend more time talking about our work than actually completing work. For example, we were always preparing presentations on the projects we were working on at the competency center and their value to the engineers. We were busy trying to sell the value of the competency center rather than completing the work required.

A big disadvantage of the democratic style, as demonstrated by Charley, is a perceived lack of decision making. Democratic leaders may seem like all talk and no action. They are often struck by delays and conflict. Further, there are times when consensus doesn't make sense and it is more important for the leaders be decisive.

Pacesetting Style

The first of the two dissonant leadership styles is the pacesetting style. Pacesetters are usually individuals with a high personal drive to achieve. The pacesetting leader expects excellence and models that to the team. They have high expectations for performance and for continuous improvement. Pacesetting leaders tend to put pressure on everyone on the team to perform at their very best.

The pacesetting leader places a high priority on results, and this can hurt their relationships with team members. Pacesetters often lack empathy; they tend to believe that everyone thinks like they do. Like perfectionists, pacesetters often feel dissatisfied with the current performance and want to continue to improve it. The pacesetters' message that they are dissatisfied with the current performance can lead to alienation of team members who feel blamed and criticized. Team members may feel that they cannot do enough to measure up.

I have seen the pacesetting style used by Mike, a friend of mine who is a leader in a private business. Mike is obsessed with competition and improvement. Whether he is at work or at play on the golf course, he is competing and pushing everyone around him to do better.

Mike and I share an interest in running. His pacesetting style comes through in his training, when he pushes himself hard to run as fast as he can. Not only that, he encourages everyone around him to push themselves. Once when we had planned to run ten sprints of 800 meters each, I mentioned that I wasn't going to run all ten. Without flinching he said that anyone who didn't run all ten sprints was a wimp. That comment made my competitive juices flow. His comment made me want to push myself, which was exactly what he intended.

A well-known pacesetter is Michael Jordan. Jordan's style of play and leadership on the basketball court sent the message "keep up with me if you can." Jordan was always pushing himself and his teammates. He played hard and expected those around him to play hard as well.

A couple of Michael Jordan quotations reflect his pacesetting style and his obsession with winning. Jordan once said that "There is no I in team, but there is in win." He also said "I play to win, whether during practice or a real game. And I will not let anything get in the way of me and my competitive enthusiasm to win."

The danger of the pacesetting style is that the team can begin to feel as if nothing is good enough. Pacesetting managers never seem to be satisfied with the current performance. They overlook the positive and tend to focus in on what is not yet working or what can still be improved.

I have unknowingly applied the pacesetting style in previous projects. While it is not my dominant style, I have found it easy to focus on continuous improvement and lose sight of the needs and feelings of my team members. I didn't take the time to acknowledge what was working and recognize people for that.

There are times when the pacesetting style is appropriate. It works best when you are leading a team of experienced and competent professionals. It also works well when paired with the visionary or affiliative styles. It doesn't work well when used exclusively or when you are dealing with inexperienced team members who need more positive encouragement and feedback. It doesn't work with team members who don't perform well under the pressure exhibited by the pacesetting leader. In any case, the pacesetting style should be used sparingly.

Commanding Style

The commanding style is one in which leaders require everyone to do it their way. PMs who use the commanding style don't want questions; they want compliance. They are reluctant to share power and authority, and they rarely take the time to explain themselves fully. Like the parents of a small child, commanding leaders may come across as saying, "Just do it because I said so."

I had a manager named Bob who used the commanding style. He was recruited to take over and turn around a large program that had failed. The program included three major projects and several hundred team members. I was part of Bob's recovery team.

Bob quickly made it clear to everyone that he was in charge and that things were to be done his way. He also made it clear that the failed policies and practices of his predecessor would not be tolerated. He was ruthless about enforcing his way and showed no compunction about removing individuals from the team even for minor issues. He would joke about firing individuals from the team and kept a running tally of the number of "drive-by firings" he had performed.

Bob was highly successful in the program recovery and earned himself an award from the chairman of the company. In this situation, the commanding style worked because it was appropriate. Bob's military background contributed to his command and control approach, which is characteristic of the commanding style. Bob needed to be clear about his expectations for people and he demanded that people change from the ways of the previous program manager. Unfortunately for Bob, it was the only style he knew and he used it in every situation.

Bob was a lot like my dad so initially I found it easy to work for him. His style was both familiar and predictable to me. Bob was extremely critical and often seemed to be personally attacking me or other team members. Eventually, however, his style of leadership took a toll on me. Like other leaders relying on the commanding style, Bob lacked the people and relationship elements of the affiliative or democratic styles or the attraction of understanding the big picture that is characteristic of the visionary style.

The commanding style should be used sparingly. It works best during emergencies or crisis situations, such as during a project turnaround, when there is no time to explain the rationale behind every decision. Otherwise, the commanding style takes a toll on the team and should be avoided.

Application of the Leadership Styles

Table 9-1 shows each of the styles, the underlying emotional intelligence competencies required for the style, project situations to apply that style, and any traps or situations not to apply the style. Most leaders have one dominant style of leadership. Based on the descriptions above, were you able to identify your dominant style?

Good leaders are able to use different leadership styles in different situations. To excel on large and complex projects, we need to be able to switch and adjust our leadership style to the needs of the situation. Daniel Goleman likens the various leadership styles to the golf clubs a player has in their bag. Each club has a different application. The more clubs that players have, the more flexibility they can bring and the greater their chance of success.[2]

Consider what steps you need to do to expand the styles available to you. In particular, if you rely predominantly on the dissonant leadership styles, a quick win for you will be to incorporate one or more of the resonant styles.

■ Applying Emotional Intelligence to Virtual Project Teams

The Challenges of Virtual Teams

Increasingly, we are working in teams that have at least some virtual component. On large-scale projects, virtual teams are almost a given. Virtual teams are composed of people who are working in different physical locations rather than side by side or face to face. It is not uncommon to have executives in

---

[2] *Ibid.,* p. 54.

Table 9-1: Leadership Styles

Leadership Style	EI Competencies	When to Apply	Traps/When not to Apply
Visionary	• Inspirational Leadership • Self-Confidence • Self-Awareness • Empathy	• Apply as often as possible, in particular when PM wants to inspire team to grow and be creative.	• When team members are more senior or have unique expertise and PMs vision-casting will sound hollow.
Coaching	• Developing Others • Self Awareness • Empathy	• When team members trust and want the leader to invest in them. • When developing people is important.	• Team may lose sight of project goals in efforts to develop people.
Affiliative	• Relationship Management • Empathy • Conflict Management	• When it is important to bring team together or when healing team divisions is necessary.	• Some affiliative leaders fall prey to being liked by others or lose sight of the project goals and objectives.
Democratic	• Teamwork and Collaboration • Conflict Management • Influence	• When the leader needs to get the input from the team to make decisions; to reach consensus.	• Leader must be open to input from the team. • Team must have valuable input to offer. • Team members may find leader indecisive or bogged down in endless meetings.
Pacesetting	• Achievement • Initiative	• Works well when used with either the visionary or affiliative styles, or when leader applies empathy and self-management to counter the pressure placed on the team. • Works to get the best performance from an experienced and competent team.	• Pacesetters often lack empathy, self-awareness, communications skills, and emotional self-management; may communicate that goals are more important than people. • Team members may feel anxious, criticized, and unappreciated.
Commanding	• Influence • Achievement • Initiative	• Emergencies, crisis, or turnaround projects. • When leader is significantly more experienced than the team.	• Use only in those situations where appropriate and balance with other styles.

one location, end users in another, and development teams in a third. Often, the team members are in different time zones, which adds further complexity. There are often cultural differences to be considered.

Emotional intelligence is more important than ever for virtual teams due to the reliance on the telephone and email for communications. Neither medium allows for seeing the face or body language of the team members and that makes communications and relationships more difficult.

I have been part of the leadership team for two very large programs with considerable virtual components. In the first case, we were implementing an enterprise-wide solution across a multinational corporation using an international team of over 120 people. In another program, we were developing and implementing solutions for a country in the Middle East. We used over 100 resources in locations from the Middle East to the West Coast of the United States. Keeping everyone on the same page with a virtual team can be a struggle for PMs. Many of the following tips and techniques were learned from these program experiences.

Emotional Intelligence Helps Virtual Teams

Applying EI techniques in the virtual environment may be more important than anywhere else. Here are some ideas for making virtual teams work for you.

Face-to-Face Meetings

To get the most out of virtual meetings, make it a point to have at least one face-to-face meeting with each team member early in the project. This will help the communications later when you cannot see the team members' faces or read their body language. If possible, I also recommend that you make it a point to meet in person over the course of the project.

When I had a virtual team working for me on the other side of the globe, I initially did not think it was necessary to travel there just to meet with them. However, I did travel there on several occasions. I learned that even if I was visiting for other reasons, I could still make time to meet with people one on one and in groups in order to connect. In fact, I made it a point to go out to lunch to get to know them personally and understand their goals and objectives. The meetings I had served me over the life of the program.

Another application of the face-to-face meeting is when part of the team is local and part is working virtual. When some team members are dialing in, the local team members may gravitate toward calling in from their desks or homes instead of coming to a central meeting location. I have been on calls where individuals in side-to-side cubicles both dialed in to the same teleconference. Their logic is that since everyone cannot be together, there is no reason for the local team to get together. This approach tends to be isolating, and it works against the PM. Team members are more likely to be multitasking than engaging with one another at these types of teleconferences. A better approach is to stress the importance of face-to-face meetings and request that individuals make it a priority to meet as a group. This may not always be possible, but it will be more likely if the PM requests it.

Leverage Technology

Use technology to improve your communications with remote team members. The ways to do this are limited only by your creativity. Technology enablers include the use of instant messaging (IM), satellite or cell phones, text messaging, bulletin and discussion boards, blogs, a project web site, voicemail distribution lists, video conferencing, teleconferencing, email, Skype, Face-Time, and collaboration tools.

The key is to make the technology work for you and the team, not against you. For example, some PMs are not familiar with IM and may view it as a tool for goofing off. Rather than fight it or outlaw it at your company, as a leader I know recently did, embrace it. Get on board with it yourself and use it to connect to the more technically savvy members of your team.

One time, we used a map as a low-tech way of staying connected. A key team member left his home in the United States and traveled between London and Shanghai. He was still a project leader and still dialed in to the project teleconferences. We used a world map and a small icon of him and his family to track where he was. In this way, we were able to better connect with him. He was more than simply a disconnected voice on the phone.

In the same way, consider including pictures of all team members available in a central location or on the project web site. Traditional teams can take a page out of the Agile team playbook. During intense periods of activity, they can use a daily coordination meeting called the standup or scrum meting to align activities across all locations.

Make Communications Work for Everyone

Good communications planning and stakeholder relationship management should help to identify and resolve communication needs. However, recognize that on virtual teams, it is easier than ever to get disconnected. PMs should constantly evaluate the regular communications and make sure that they are sufficient and that all stakeholders' needs are being met. On every project there is invariably an occasion where some stakeholder steps forward and says, "I didn't know that" or "I never heard about that."

Don't be afraid to experiment with your communications. During intense periods of activity, it may be necessary to coordinate across all the work sites with a brief "stand-up" type meeting once per day. Or, it may be appropriate for each team to hand off its work at the end of their day when you have teams spread across time zones.

As the PM, be aware of the amount of time you spend with each stakeholder and those reporting to you. With a virtual team, it is very easy to spend more time and better quality time with those who are located near you than those who are remote. You can compensate for this by investing more in those who are remote. If you spend thirty minutes every week with each direct report in a face-to-face meeting, consider spending forty-five or sixty minutes on the phone with those who are remote.

Try to be consistent across locations. If you have an all-hands meeting in one location, either have others dial in or repeat the meeting with those who are remote. Develop and share frequently asked questions with the entire team. Archive and distribute minutes from those meetings for any individuals who are not able to attend.

Use Humor

When it works, humor helps us to connect and see each other in a more positive light. It can bring levity to situations and lighten tensions so people feel more comfortable. If your virtual team spans countries and cultures, use of humor can be even more risky.

Humor can also work against us, particularly in the virtual environment where facial expressions and body language are not available to indicate that someone is "just kidding." In virtual environments, it may not be possible to hear others laughing or to get the responses of others to our own humor. Humor, when it doesn't work, can highlight the differences between people and serve to alienate us.

As a general rule, humor works best when team members know each other. When individuals do not know each other, humor can be easily misinterpreted or misconstrued. Self-deprecating humor works better than poking fun at others. In general, PMs should avoid joking about others, especially if they are not present. Joking about others can cause distrust and alienation among the team.

As a PM, I create an environment in which people know that I try not to take myself too seriously. I joke about myself and point out the things that I do that people find funny. At one point another PM pointed out that my jokes were not very funny and offered to raise his hand in meetings so that others would know I was joking.

Injecting humor into our written status reports can breathe some energy into what are often very lifeless documents. Use of humor can make the document more interesting and easier to read and may lead to more status reports actually being read.

I once had a PM who wielded humor very effectively as part of a large virtual team. His daily status report from the client location in the Middle East included a mini trivia quiz at the top. Every day he added a movie quote to his status report. Between his use of humor and the movie quotes, he created a report that was well read by the rest of the team.

Build Relationships Off the Call

Virtual teams are often characterized by a seemingly endless series of teleconferences, which tend to be formal and typically lack opportunities for developing interpersonal relationships. Individuals can be lost in the formality and structure of all of these teleconferences. Relationships with team members may be superficial, and the team members may view the PM as lacking in warmth and personality.

To improve relationships and make teleconferences more personal, use the time off the call to invest in and build relationships with virtual team members. Don't limit your investment in them to the structure of a regular meeting. Use the time off the call to let your true nature show. Be as informal as possible and encourage them to talk and to share their concerns, interests, hobbies, and objectives. PMs can leverage Skype or other low cost video conferencing tools to build these relationships off the call.

■ Emotional Intelligence Techniques for Large and Complex Projects

1. Learn to Identify Leadership Styles

You can use your experience to help you identify different leadership styles. Make a list of the PMs and other managers you have worked with over the last five or, even, ten years. For each one, identify the emotional intelligence competencies you experienced with them. See if you can identify their dominant leadership styles. Evaluate, if possible, whether they used different styles with different team members.

2. Identify Your Dominant Leadership Style

In this exercise, you will determine your own dominant leadership style. Start with the list of EI competencies. Based on what you know about those from the earlier chapters, list the ones that you feel are your strengths. Then reread the descriptions of the six leadership styles. Is one of them clearly your dominant style? Or, do you believe that you use multiple styles?

Take this exercise one step further by getting input from others. Ask those on your current team to review the list of characteristics of each of the leadership styles and see if they can determine your dominant style. You can expand the discussion to your boss, spouse or significant other, and perhaps even your own children as appropriate. Get as much input as possible to see yourself as others see you.

3. Build New Leadership Muscles

Once you determine your own dominant leadership style, select another style that would best complement it. If you don't currently use visionary leadership, that would be a great choice since research has shown it to be the most effective.

After selecting the leadership style, start with the underlying emotional intelligence competencies for that style. Once you determine which competency you need to strengthen, go back to that competency in the previous chapters. Review the various techniques provided for improving that competency.

If you need help, consider enrolling someone in this process. A mentor or even a member of your team would be in a good position to help track your progress and provide feedback as you build those new leadership skills.

4. Improve Your Delegation Skills

If you find delegation difficult due to fear or control issues or if you just want to improve, there is no time like the present. Decide today to begin to practice delegating. Start small and perhaps with the person you trust the most. Gradually increase your level of delegation while you monitor your feelings and emotions around the process. Track your progress and celebrate your successes in this area.

Alternatively, identify someone in your work environment who is good at delegating and ask them to help you to improve. Find out what works and doesn't work for them and try those techniques for yourself. Set goals and ask them to hold you accountable for the results.

5. Check the Roster for Your Virtual Team

If you are managing a virtual team, take the time to walk down through the roster of team members. Are you connecting with everyone on the team, especially those you don't see? Make a note of how much time you spent in the last few weeks with each of the team members. Is that amount appropriate for the size of the team and the role of the individual? Are there any team members who are not getting enough of your time and attention?

Consider polling your virtual team members to find out how well connected they feel to you. Put together a short survey or simply call each of them. Either approach will provide valuable feedback. Calling them may reveal information that a written survey will not. However, team members may be more forthcoming with a survey than they would with a phone call.

6. Work on Relationships "Off the Call"

If you are leading a virtual team, what steps are you taking to build relationships? If the communications are typically conducted through a series of conference calls, select a member of the team you don't know well and choose to work on that relationship. Make it a point to call them or visit them off the call and get to know them on a personal basis.

■ Personal Action Plan: Leveraging Emotional Intelligence on Large and Complex Projects

PMs who want to succeed with larger and more complex projects must have high emotional intelligence.

Key Takeaways

1.
2.
3.

My Strengths and Weaknesses in the Area of Leveraging Emotional Intelligence on Large and Complex Projects

Strengths	Weaknesses
1.	1.
2.	2.

My Actions or Goals Based on What I Learned

1.
2.
3.

10

Success with Agile Projects

The last five to ten years have seen a tremendous growth in Agile projects. Whether Scrum, Lean, XP, or some other methodology, Agile methods are quickly becoming mainstream for software development projects, and inroads are being made into other types of projects. I have seen firsthand the efficacy of Agile methods—and am a huge fan.

Anyone who has used Agile methods though will attest to the fact that leading Agile teams is not the same as leading traditional teams. Agile teams are expected to be self-organizing. This doesn't mean there are no leaders, but it requires a style of leadership that is less prescriptive and more supportive. It is often called Servant Leadership, and it requires a lot of emotional intelligence.

In this Chapter, we look at some of the key roles that PMs will play in relationship to Agile teams and provide some tips for success in each of these. We will also look at the proper functioning of other key stakeholders in the Agile ecosystem, including program managers, functional managers, and executive leaders.

■ Agile Project Managers, Scrum Masters, Coaches. and Team Leaders

PMs usually have different titles and roles when working in the Agile environment. Scrum is the most common Agile method used today; it is a project management framework for Agile teams. The Scrum Master is the facilitator for the Scrum Team and is the rough equivalent to the PM. In Extreme Programming, the team has a coach who serves a similar function. Agile teams might also have an Agile Team Leader or a PM, although both of these titles are less common.

Whatever the exact title, the roles require a similar style of leadership, one that relies heavily on emotional intelligence. The challenge for most PMs is that they are used to interacting with teams and management in different ways. They assign work to people, direct activity, hold others accountable, gather progress reports, and provide updates to management on the progress of the team. The self-organizing Agile teams do things differently; most of these activities are handled by the team, and not by the PM. In any case, the team doesn't need an individual controlling them or telling them what to do. In fact, when working with Agile teams, we must be vigilant that any form of top down, autocratic, or heavy-handed leadership is erradicated. This is often easier said than done.

It is for this very reason that a colleague of mine contends that tradtionally trained PMs make poor Agile team leaders or scrum masters. He feels that it is too hard for them to make the transition from a command-and-control style of leadership. Commanding and controlling may have been the strength that got them into project management, but it doesn't serve them with Agile teams.

How do you think you would rate in terms of your level of command and controlism? Here are some questions that you can use to evaluate yourself:

- Do you distrust people, and feel that you need to monitor them so that they don't slack off?
- Do you believe that you generally know what is best, and willingly offer solutions and advice to the team?
- Do you tend to interject yourself into problem solving, even when you are not invited to get involved?
- Do you try to make the team results conform to your preceonceived ideas of what the results should be?
- Do you try to directly or indirectly control things? Do you feel uncomfortable when others are in control, and you are not?
- Do you feel threatened by the idea that the team may operate fine without you?
- Do you feel the need to be involved in all the details and decisions to reduce the risk of the project failing or having a misstep?
- Do you feel solely and personally responsible for the success and failure of the teams you lead?

One clue as to your own level of command and control is your ability to see it in others. We discussed the concept of reactivity in Chapter 4, along with the old adage, "If you spot it, you got it." If you get bugged by command-and-control behavior in others, that is a great insight for you on the level of your own command and controlism. For me, I find it very easy to spot this less than desirable behavior. So, yes, that means I am a recovering commander and controller!

This ability to spot the behavior serves me well in my role as an Agile Coach. I've worked with lots of PMs and team leaders trying to adapt to Agile projects. A recent example was a veteran PM, who was PMP certified. She was accustomed to directing and controlling the work of the team and felt wholly responsible for the outcomes of the team. Perhaps I should say that she had the illusion of directing and controlling the work of the team, because I don't think anyone can actually do that. Just because she had a project schedule broken down to the hour didn't necessarily mean that the project was under control. She spent a lot of time trying to figure out why things were not going according to her detailed plan and then trying to bring the team performance in line with the plan.

Her command-and-control style of leadership resulted in her feeling all the deadline pressure for the team. She literally felt that the success or failure of the team was on her shoulders, instead of on the team. This is one of the main challenges with command-and-control leadership. With Agile teams, we need to share the accountability for results. We need to let the team feel the pressure of success or failure, and the thrill of figuring things out for themselves.

So how do Scrum Masters and Agile Ms recover from command and controlism? When I do this well, I let go, get out of the way, and let the team figure it out and succeed. I don't react when people chose to do things differently than I would have. I resist the temptation to share all my wonderful knowledge with the team.

Here are some other ways to succeed:

- Don't offer unsolicited advice. When asked directly for my advice, I try to stop and weigh the pros and cons of sharing it. Sometimes just saying, "What do you think you should do?" puts the focus back on the team.
- Let go of specific outcomes. Instead, focus on learning and growth. One of the things I like about the Agile framework is that it serves as a tool to run controlled experiments and learn from them.
- Be willing to let teams fail. Not as in complete catastrophe, but as in teams stumbling and learning to recover from their missteps.

- Don't jump in! Uncomfortable silence can respresent great thinking and processing time for teams. Don't spoil it by jumping in and trying to solve problems, ask questions, or offer advice.
- Focus on understanding and quieting your own internal voices. Many of us are prompted to speak up by our own internal chatter. Most of our internal chatter is just plain nonsense or fear–driven diatribes. Self-awareness is a key skill as we will talk about in the next section.
- Do the job that you are supposed to be doing! In many cases, when I am meddling with a team it is because I am avoiding more strategic or important work. I avoid this other work because I am uncomfortable doing it, or it causes me to push myself out of my comfort zone. So when I find myself getting involved in the details of self-organizing teams, I need to ask, what is it that I am avoiding right now?
- Learn and adopt servant leadership. We are going to talk about servant leadership more in the sections that follow.

Program Managers

Program Managers often are responsible for multiple teams working together toward common goals. It is common today for one or more of those teams to be Agile, while the other teams use traditional methods. This leaves program managers trying to figure out how to manage both. In doing so, program managers must be careful that they don't stifle the productivity of the Agile team.

I saw this recently in a program with five subprojects, only one of which had an Agile team. The program was delivering a key capability needed by the executive team, and the five teams were nervous and excited to deliver that capability. All the teams developed a high-level schedule and high-level requirements and then began to focus on their part of the solution.

The Agile team created a prioritized backlog and high-level release plan for its work. Unfortunately, the program manager was new to Agile and didn't understand how the Agile team was going to deliver. He insisted that team members produce a schedule from MS Project, as the other teams had. He also wanted a requirements list and weekly status reports that matched what the other teams produced. Of course, it is possible for the Agile team to produce the equivalents of each of these, but it is not always productive.

The program manager was asking for these things because he was afraid. He didn't trust that the Agile team was going to deliver, and he thought he would be more secure if the Agile team provided the same planning artifacts as the other teams. It was not at all surprising that the Agile team was the one team out of the five that delivered on time and under budget.

Functional Managers

Other leaders in the organization may also need to adjust their style to work with Agile teams. This may be a bigger change for functional managers and executive leaders than for anyone else in the organization. Many functional managers are threatened by the introduction of Agile into their environment. The ways that they have added value in the past are often not helpful to success with Agile teams. Like Agile project and program managers, they need to trust and empower their teams. Here are a couple of examples of functional managers who have struggled with overseeing Agile teams.

Stuck In The Middle

A functional manager struggled when his team moved to Agile. He was accustomed to having daily meetings with every member of his team, in addition to the normal standup meeting that was part of Scrum. During the daily meeting, each team member would update him on everything being done, and he became the central hub of all information. This behavior grew out of a desire to avoid surprises and stay on top of the team. The question is, was this behavior helpful as he transitioned from traditional development to Agile?

As you've likely guessed, the behavior was not helpful at all. While he knew everything going on, he became the only one who did. He was the only person with the complete view of the solution. His team members interfaced directly with him, and he controlled all the communications. Team members were not accustomed to thinking and acting like a team—they acted like individuals. They did not communicate to each other or coordinate their efforts as a team.

A more healthy behavior would be to get out of the middle of the process. If a functional manager needs to do a daily standup, and most don't, they should make sure that the standup meeting is focused on the team members communicating to each other. Functional managers should encourage teams to self-organize and coordinate their efforts. They should focus on removing roadblocks and encouraging people to be engaged. They should be quiet more often, and let the people on the team step forward and fill the void.

I'm in Charge Here

Another functional manager that I knew tried to be Agile, but his style just didn't lend itself to Agile leadership. I was coaching a new team in the process of transitioning to Agile. I had delivered some training and was digging in with the team on the user story backlog and iteration planning. The manager who had been too busy to show up for the training, showed up for the planning. He immediately began questioning two of his team members about what they were doing, and it created a negative mood in the room. He was so disruptive with his beratement of the two team members that the discussion ground to a halt and the team actually took a step backward.

Observing the behavior, I asked the team to return to its planning activities and invited the manager to step out of the room to discuss his concerns. He was visibly upset, and I made it a point initially to just listen to him. While he couched his concerns in terms of project risks, it was clear that this was about the impact that the Agile approach would have on him and his position in the organization. He felt threatened.

Ultimately this manager feared loss of control and relevance. He had placed himself in a position where he reviewed and approved every thought, idea, and action his resources had. It was to the point where the resources had been conditioned to let the manager think for them, rather than to think for themselves. He stifled creativity, productivity, and progress.

As if that were not enough, I learned there was more going on behind the scenes. This manager had established himself as the conduit for his resources to interface with the business and other IT resources. He limited what his resources knew about the business needs and other IT teams, so that he personally could add that value. He also requested that his resources keep him in the loop on everything. In a particularly noteworthy example of waste, his resources spent time in meetings taking incredibly detailed notes of the conversation so that they could send them to the manager. They didn't actually participate in the conversation, unless asked; they just kept typing away like court stenographers. There were other losses of productivity, as these two resources were essentially untapped. Their creative potential was not being used; it was being held back by this manager.

I Don't Trust You Guys

In another case, the first and second level functional managers in a particular organization were vocally supportive of the move to Agile. However, they were also very concerned about the team performance and their own lack of control over the Agile teams. As a result, they insisted on listening to the daily standup calls of the distributed Agile teams. This actually led to lower productivity and creativity in the teams.

Since the organization was quite hierarchical, and there was a high proportion of contract resources, the impact of the managers listening in on the calls was that the team did not really function as a team. Most team members were simply silent on the standup calls. They knew that the senior managers were listening in and chose not to take any risks. There was no "self-organization" and very little collaboration. As a result, the standups became more of an interview (or interrogation!) conducted by the Scrum Master.

■ Servant Leadership Is an Alternative to Command and Control

As noted, the key to success with Agile teams is servant leadership. As the name implies, servant leadership is about making the needs of others a priority, and then serving them. In the case of Agile, it means putting the needs of the Agile team first. The key ways that Agile leaders do this is through removing impediments and supporting the team to work better together. When leaders make the resolution of impediments a top priority, they help the team be productive and, more importantly, they send the signal to the team that the leader is there to serve and contribute.

So how does this work in practice? At a minimum, the Agile team members should voice their impediments as part of the daily standup meetings. A team member might say, "I am still waiting on my replacement laptop before I can begin coding," or, "the DBA team hasn't responded to my request for a new table." These types of impediments are easy to spot. Agile leaders would do well to hone their listening skills to pick up on more subtle impediments that are not stated directly. They don't need to interrupt the daily standup meeting to dig in, but they can circle back and probe with resources to make sure that they understand the issue and are able to work on resolving it.

Another form of servant leadership is helping the team to work better together. This can take many forms, including encouraging pairing to promote knowledge sharing, bringing in pizza for an informal lunch and learn training session, or hiring a coach for the team (or yourself!).

I recall a newly formed team that I was coaching. The team had no experience working together and included mostly contractors from different organizations. We were moving very slowly throught the team formation process when someone suggested we colocate into the same room. There were a few tentative nods, but no one on the team wanted to be the first to move their desk. So I worked with two of the developers and led by moving the three of us into the larger team room. Within two days, every member of the team had moved in to be colocated in the same room.

Servant leadership may run counter to your particular style, especially if you have relied on command and control for your success in project management. It is a change in style that many PMs find difficult to make. A recent speaker put it this way, we need Nelson Mandela, not General Patton! How do you enleash your inner Mandela? It is all about your emotional intelligence.

■ Agile Leaders Need to Be Emotionally Intelligent

All of the lessons in the previous chapters about emotional intelligence apply to Agile leaders, perhaps more so than even to traditional PMs. Here are some specific examples from the emotional intelligence framework for PMs.

Self-Awareness

Agile team leaders/scrum masters must be aware of their emotional state before engaging with the team. They need to be in the here and now, fully present and engaged. They also should be aware of any 'baggage' or negative emotions that they are bringing into the environment. For example, if you have a fight with your spouse as you head out the door in the morning, you are going to carry that negative baggage into your early morning team meeting. Similarly, if one of your close family members was just recently hospitalized, you will carry a sense of sadness or fear that will color all your interactions. You need to put your emotions to the side and focus entirely on the team.

Self-Management

Awareness is the building block to begin to do something about our emotional state. We can quietly acknowlege our emotions about an incident. Then, however, we need to put the fight or our fear gently to the side to allow us to focus on the team. If we cannot put it to the side, we may need to excuse ourselves from the meeting. Or, we may need to "put it all out there," that is, we might need to just state where we are in the moment so others will understand where we are coming from. The key is to be conscious and to deal with our emotions directly, so that we are clear when we deal with the team.

The alternative is to let our emotional state impact the team. Let's say that we just received some negative news about our finances, such as an unexpected tax bill, that causes us to feel scared and angry. If we aren't aware of and managing those emotions, we will bring that fear and anger into the team. We will say and do things or be reactive when we should not be. We need to use the self-management techniques discussed in Chapter 4 to avoid that.

■ Social Awareness and Relationship Management

When we are aware and managing ourselves, we can engage effectively with our teams. We can focus on Servant Leadership and on meeting the needs of others. It's difficult to do this if you haven't first addressed your own needs.

If you find that are not able to focus on the needs of others, it probably means that you need to revisit the basics of self-awareness and self-management. We can't focus on the needs of others if we are constantly thinking about ourselves. How many of us have been in the position where we are supposed to be listening to someone else and our own minds are going a thousand miles an hour? We appear to be listening, but the reality is that we are somewhere else. I know that I have. When that happens, we need to find ways to calm ourselves, get out of our own way, and focus on the the other person. Many of the suggestions in Chapters 2 and 3 on Self-Awareness and Self-Management are applicable to achieve this. The key is we need to make those suggestions and ideas a regular practice so that we come to each interaction with clarity and self-awareness.

■ Positive Regard

The role of progam managers and functional managers often shifts to coaching and mentoring teams. With self-organizing teams, the leader or coach's job is to support the team's efforts at self-organization so members can figure out for themselves what to do next. The leader should not solve problems for them. A self-organizing team is one whose members feel that they own their own destiny and can solve their problems better than you can. You simply need to put the onus on the team to figure it out, rather than owning it yourself.

This reminds me of something that my mentor Rich says frequently. If I said I was unsure which direction to take or if I asked him what he thought, Rich would often ask me, "What do you think you should do?" If I said I didn't know, he might say something like, "Well if you did know, what do you think the answer would be?" I often gave an answer to that second question—showing that I actually did know what to do more often than not.

This is closely related to the concept of positive regard. Positive regard is assuming that individuals are whole and complete and have the ability to figure things out for themselves. It is based on the field of humanistic psychology pioneered by Carl Rogers. Rogers believed that all people are inherently good and that they have all the internal resources required to grow as individuals.

When we hold others in positive regard, we see them as individuals who are capable of solving their own problems. We assume that they, rather than we, know best what to do. And we expect they will do what is best; that they will figure things out. We don't provide unsolicited advice, we don't criticize, and we don't second guess. We simply hold them in high regard and help them to figure things out for themselves.

A great resource for Agile PMs, coaches, program managers, and functional managers is Lyssa Adkins' 2010 book, *Coaching Agile Teams: A Companion for ScrumMasters, Agile Coaches, and Project Managers in Transition*. Lyssa provides many ideas for supporting Agile teams, overcoming command and controlism, and leading ourselves.

■ Techniques for Improving Our Success with Agile Projects

1. **Evaluate Your Level of Command and Controlism.** Take a step back and really evaluate the ways you use command and control. Are you holding back the teams you lead by trying to control them? If you are having trouble seeing it in yourself, note whether you see it in others. Or, ask those you trust to provide you accurate feedback on your behavior.
2. **Proactively Step Back and Let Others Step Up.** Try stepping back and letting others decide what to do. Spend less time trying to impose your will on others or to manipulate them to do what you think they should do. Trust that whatever they do, they will learn from their behavior.
3. **Say Less; a Lot Less.** Rather than always being the first to speak up, trying shutting up and listening more. Really tune in to what others say, rather than your own internal chatter, or simply waiting for your chance to speak. See where the leadership comes from when you don't hog all the airtime. Try the empathetic listening techniques discussed in Chapter 5.
4. **Practice Some Form of Daily Mindfulness.** This is important for all PMs, but it is especially important for leaders of Agile teams. Whether you use meditation, prayer, journaling, or some other technique, establish this as a daily practice that you do to be clear with yourself before you engage with the team. Put to use some of those self-awareness techniques discussed in Chapter 3.
5. **Get Underneath Your Fear.** Most of us who feel the need to control do so out of fear, and many of our fears are irrational or unwarranted. Look below the surface to see if you can determine what you are afraid of. I know that for me this is usually a fear of failure. I am afraid that the team will fail and that it will reflect poorly on me. Some of us also fear a loss of relevance. After all, if the team can do great work or come up with great ideas without me, what value do I have? Dig deep into what your underlying fears are, so that you can understand how those are affecting your behaviors with the team.
6. **Ask Rather Than Decide.** Put decision making back on the team members rather than jumping in and reaching the decisions for them. Try holding

back on your own opinion even when asked. Take time to pause and to ask the team, "What do you think we should do?" You might be surprised at what they say. Or you might say, "Is anyone else feeling the pressure to decide right now besides me?"

7. **That's a Great Idea!** Some of us are so hungry to be affirmed that we often find it hard to accept new ideas or perspectives from others. We're used to saying things like, "That is a good idea BUT it won't work because of...." To overcome this type of behavior, practice saying "That's a great idea!," and then look for every opportunity to say it. It may not come easy.

8. **Use Positive Regard for Everyone.** See the team members at their very best, not necessarily in their worst moments. Know that they will rise to the occasion when they need to, that they will learn from their experience, and that they will get better over time. Hold each member of the team, and the team as a whole, in high positive regard.

9. **Be a Servant Leader.** Agile team leaders, Program Managers, and Functional Managers all need to support the Agile team. They frequently need to serve as a buffer between the Agile team and the rest of the organization. Tune in to the organizational norms that run counter to Agile and run interference for the team. Help streamline mandatory documentation or other PMO requirements so that the Agile team can be empowered and self-organizing.

■ Personal Action Plan: Success with Agile Projects

Leading Agile projects requires a style of leadership that is less prescriptive and more supportive. It is often called Servant Leadership, and it requires a lot of emotional intelligence.

Key Takeaways

1.	
2.	
3.	

My Strengths and Weaknesses in the Area of Success with Agile Projects

Strengths	Weaknesses
1.	1.
2.	2.

My Actions or Goals Based on What I Learned

1.	
2.	
3.	

█ Epilogue

If you've gotten this far, you've learned the importance of applying emotional intelligence to become better PMs. The previous 10 chapters have provided the theoretical underpinnings, as well as specific and practical steps you can take to improve your emotional intelligence. We shared a variety of tools, techniques, and mini-exercises that you can use to improve your emotional intelligence and your project success.

We can always improve in the area of people skills. And, the great news is, no matter what our current level of EQ is, we all have the ability to improve our level of emotional intelligence. After ten years of studying the topic and working with a coach, I still find myself learning and growing in this area. I occasionally take a step backward and fall into old habits or make mistakes. However, when I do that, I recover faster. I try to remind myself of how far I have come and how much better I am at managing my emotions than I was in the past. And I try not to take myself (or others) too seriously.

Change and growth rarely happens without work. The personal action plan at the end of each chapter is a tool you can use to track what you learned, your own strengths and weaknesses, and your logical next steps. If you skipped over any of those action plans, or the techniques or exercises, go back to those that hold the most potential for your improvement. Try all the exercises, even those that seem silly, and see if you can improve your competency in each area.

The following appendixes contain additional tools and more information that PMs may find helpful for improving their level of emotional intelligence. Useful tools include the Emotional Tally sheet in Appendix A, and the Assessment for Emotional Self-Awareness and Self-Control in Appendix B. Though certainly not unique to emotional intelligence, the Stakeholder Management Tool in Appendix C is a valuable tool for PMs trying to improve their emotional intelligence.

Appendix D provides a list of Hollywood movies that are helpful to individuals trying to learn more about emotions. Appendix E contains a list of books related to emotional intelligence for individuals seeking more information. Finally, Appendix F provides information about some of the most popular assessment instruments available for measuring emotional intelligence.

Appendix A
Emotional Tally Sheet

One of the key skills underpinning all emotional intelligence is emotional self-awareness. Knowing what we are feeling right now in this present moment is a critical skill. What follows are a couple of tools that can help you to tune in to your emotions and those of others. The tally sheet shown in Figure A-1 is helpful for tracking and identifying patterns in your emotions over the course of a week.

The tally sheet shown in Figure A-2 is helpful for tracking multiple individuals at the same time, for example, in a meeting.

	Sad	Angry	Scared	Happy	Excited	Tender
Monday						
Tuesday						
Wednesday						
Thursday						
Friday						
Saturday						
Sunday						
Total for Week						

Figure A-1: Emotional Tally Sheet (1)

	Sad	Angry	Scared	Happy	Excited	Tender
Tim						
Dennis						
Jim						
Z						
Cortney						
Bill						
Barry						
Stephen						
Rick						
Neale						

Figure A-2: Emotional Tally Sheet (2)

Appendix B
Assessment for Emotional Self-Awareness and Self-Control

1. **Automatic or Default Emotion** *Does the individual have an overriding or default emotion? Are they predominantly happy or sad? Put a check mark beside the top 2 emotions they experience on a regular basis.*	☐ Sad	☐ Happy
	☐ Angry	☐ Excited
	☐ Scared	☐ Tender

2. **Self-Awareness** *How self-aware is this individual? Do they know what they are experiencing at any one time?*	**Self-awareness Rating**		
	Not Very Self-Aware Aware Very Self-Aware		
	1 2 3 4 5 6 7 8 9 10		

3. **Expressiveness** *How emotionally expressive is this individual? Do they express emotions in what they say, how they say it, or through their actions?*	**Expressiveness Rating**
	Not Very Expressive Expressive Very Expressive
	1 2 3 4 5 6 7 8 9 10

4. **Self-Management** *How effective is this individual in self-management? Does this individual apply self-control for both positive and negative emotions?*	**Self-Control Rating**
	Poor Some Good
	Self-Control Self-Control Self-Control
	1 2 3 4 5 6 7 8 9 10

5. **Emotional Breakdowns** *Does this person experience emotional breakdowns?*	☐ Angry Tirades ☐ Door Slamming ☐ Email Letter Bomb ☐ Withdrawal & Isolation ☐ Holding Grudges & Getting Even	☐ Criticizing ☐ Sarcasm ☐ Inappropriate Humor ☐ Playing the Victim ☐ All or Nothing Thinking

6. **Stinking Thinking** *Does this individual experience stinking thinking?*	☐ All or Nothing Thinking ☐ Using Always & Never ☐ Being Negative	☐ Filling in the Blanks ☐ Should Statements ☐ Personalization and Blame

7. **Changes and Surprises** *Look at how they react to changes or to surprises. Are they open and receptive? Or shut down, reactive, and negative about new things?*	**Handling Changes and Surprises**
	Not Very Receptive Receptive Very Receptive
	1 2 3 4 5 6 7 8 9 10

8. **Stress** *They say that stress will reveal a person's true character. How resilient is this individual under pressure? Are they graceful or, are they mean and vindictive?*	**Handling Stress**
	Not Very Resilient Resilient Very Resilient
	1 2 3 4 5 6 7 8 9 10

9. **Social Awareness** *How aware is this individual to their environment and the people around them? Consider their level of empathy toward others, their organizational awareness, and their ability to set emotional boundaries.*	**Empathy**
	Not Very Empathetic Empathetic Very Empathetic
	1 2 3 4 5 6 7 8 9 10
	Organizational Awareness
	Not Very Aware Aware Very Aware
	1 2 3 4 5 6 7 8 9 10
	Emotional Boundaries
	Poor Boundaries Some Boundaries Good Boundaries
	1 2 3 4 5 6 7 8 9 10

Figure A-3: Assessment for Emotional Self-Awareness and Self-Control

Appendix C
Stakeholder
Management Tool

The stakeholder management tool is used to identify stakeholders and organize information about them. See Figure A-4 for an example of a blank template. Figure A-5 is an example of a stakeholder management tool that has been partially completed.

Stakeholder	Priority	Position	Role on Project	Stakeholder Objectives	Facts, Passions, and areas of interest	Communication Style	Emotional Connections and Relationship Strategies	Action Steps to Maintain and Nurture this Relationship

Figure A-4: Stakeholder Management Tool, Blank

Stakeholder	Priority	Position	Role on Project	Stakeholder Objectives	Facts, Passions, and areas of interest	Communication Style	Emotional Connections and Relationship Strategies	Action Steps to Maintain and Nurture this Relationship
Debbie Brown	H	+	Executive Management	• Increase role and visibility of her organization	• Strives for excellence • Enjoys fine dining & likes to try new restaurants • Likes to work over lunch • Has 3 children	• Prefers informal communications and welcomes voicemail updates • Likes to go out and talk shop over lunch	• Stay in touch; keep Debbie informed and current	• Schedule regular lunches (1 per month) • Find ways to provide interesting updates from the "project front lines"
Bob Hague	H	N	Client	• Use project as stepping stone for better job • Look as good as possible • Maintain control over other client stakeholders	• Interested in database technology • Concerned with project's impact on career • Can be hard on his own staff • Starts early each day and leaves early	• Prefers written status reports and updates • Dislikes all meetings	• Maintain formal and informal communications • Keep very short accounts	• Submit well written and accurate status reports • Bring issues to him immediately • Make it a point to stop by for informal chats • Provide advance notice of staffing changes
Jim Smith	M	+	Subcontract Labor Manager	• Interested in putting more of his people on the team • Wants feedback on his resources so they can improve	• From Iowa and follows Big Ten college sports • Enjoys travel	• Likes to call and chat or to go out and talk shop over lunch	• Maintain informality & full disclosure	• Plan for short bi-weekly meetings before work.
Tom Donahue	M	–	Software Vendor	• Use project as reference project • Increase Sales of Produce • Wants to use project as reference	• Can come off as arrogant and uncaring; takes relationship for granted • Is defensive about product shortcomings	• Prefers face to face communications	• Regular meetings to discuss issues; have offline discussions to build relationship	• Bi-weekly status call; publish notes and action items from the calls

Figure A-5: Stakeholder Management Tool, Partially Completed

Appendix D
Emotional Intelligence Movies and Scenes

Movies are a great place to study emotions. We can observe the emotions in the performances of actors on the screen. We can also track our emotional responses to what we see on the screen.

There are nearly an infinite number of movies to help you observe or experience emotions. The list below provides some specific movies that can be used to explore emotional intelligence. The title of each movie is followed by a brief description including the emotions that you are likely to observe or experience.

Movie	Description of Emotions
As Good As It Gets	Jack Nicholson plays a social and emotional misfit extremely well in this entertaining movie. Emotions include anger, sadness, happiness, and fear.
Christmas Vacation	If you like to laugh at good plans and intentions gone awry, this movie will make you feel happy.
Crash	The entire movie is about exposing and confronting the biases and prejudices we have toward each other. Emotions include sadness and anger.
Horrible Bosses	Kevin Spacey plays one of three horrible bosses in this movie, each of whom excels at making life miserable for their employees. Look for examples of working with difficult people.
Hotel Rwanda	The genocide and nonsensical war in this movie is likely to produce feelings of sadness and anger.

Movie	Description of Emotions
The Incredibles	The scene with Mr. Incredible and his boss at the insurance company is good for showing both the toxic manager as well as a loss of self-control by Mr. Incredible. The emotions include happiness, anger, and excitement.
The Kid	The character played by Bruce Willis has several funny interactions in the first fifteen minutes of the film. His dramatic interaction with the mayor, other clients, and his fellow travelers reveals his sarcasm and unexpressed anger. The interactions may make you feel happy, angry, or, even, sad.
Liar Liar	This is a hilarious movie that shows how often we don't tell the truth and what can happen when we are forced to.
Office Space	This classic movie about life in corporate cubicle land provides many exaggerated examples of senseless policies, the inability to say no, and fear in the workplace.
One Flew Over the Cuckoo's Nest	This movie will take you on a roller coaster ride of emotions through sadness, happiness, excitement, tenderness, anger, and fear.
Steel Magnolias	This movie has several funny parts but it is an overwhelmingly sad film. Look for the emotions of the characters and observe whether you feel depressed by the drama.
Tommy Boy	David Spade's use of sarcasm in this movie is funny. It's used as a cover for his anger. Also, Tommy Boy (played by the late Chris Farley) provides comic relief in many scenes, including one with a fan where he is saying "Luke, I am your father."
Trains, Planes and Automobiles	This movie shows how resentments can build, how we can make others bad, and how differences can cause rifts. It also shows how to leverage team member diversity to overcome challenging situations.
Twelve Angry Men	Many scenes provide examples of attacking and hostile behavior, lack of self-control around anger, smoothing, and avoiding.
What About Bob?	This movie provides examples in which therapy patient Bob's normal and psychopathic behavior reveals character flaws, a lack of self-control, and eventually prompts an emotional breakdown in his psychologist. Look for examples of boundary issues, passive–aggressive behavior, anger, and denial.

Appendix E
Books on Emotional
Intelligence

The following books provide additional information about emotional intelligence.

1. *Choosing Appropriate Project Managers.* J. Rodney Turner and Ralf Mueller. Newton Square, PA: Project Management Institute Inc., 2006.
2. *Crucial Conversations: Tools for Talking When Stakes Are High.* Kerry Patterson, Joseph Grenny, Ron McMillan, and Al Switzler. New York: McGraw-Hill, 2002.
3. *Emotional Intelligence (Life Balance).* Linda Wasmer Andrews. New York: Scholastic, 2004.
4. *Emotional Intelligence and Projects.* Nicholas Clarke, PhD and Ranse Howell. Newton Square, PA: Project Management Institute Inc., 2009.
5. *Emotional Intelligence at Work.* Hendrie Weisinger. San Francisco: Jossey-Bass, 1998.
6. *Emotional Intelligence: Why It Can Matter More Than IQ.* Daniel Goleman. New York: Bantam Books, 1995.
7. *Primal Leadership.* Daniel Goleman, Richard Boyatzis, and Annie McKee. Boston: Harvard Business School Press, 2002.
8. *The Emotional Intelligence Activity Book.* Adele B. Lynn. New York: AMACOM Books, 2002.
9. *The Emotionally Intelligent Manager.* David Caruso and Peter Salovey. San Francisco: Jossey-Bass, 2004.
10. *The Emotionally Intelligent Workplace.* Cary Cherniss and Daniel Goleman. San Francisco: Jossey Bass, 2001.

11. *The EQ Difference: A Powerful Plan for Putting Emotional Intelligence to Work.* Adele B. Lynn. New York: AMACOM Books, 2005.

12. *Working with Emotional Intelligence.* Daniel Goleman. New York: Bantam Books, 1998.

Appendix F
Emotional Intelligence
Assessment Instruments

While several assessment instruments are available that measure emotional intelligence, there is a great deal of controversy over the validity of these instruments. The first three assessment instruments listed below were created by some of the leading researchers in the field of emotional intelligence.

■ Emotional Competence Inventory 360, from Daniel Goleman

The full title of this assessment is the "Emotional Competency Inventory 360: A 360 Assessment of Emotional Intelligence Competencies." This was developed by Daniel Goleman and Richard Boyatzis based on the Emotional Intelligence Competencies. The assessment is available both for individuals to self-assess and in a multirater version for 360-degree assessments. The instrument is distributed through the Hay Group, one of the members of the EIConsortium.

■ EQi, the Bar-On Emotional Quotient Inventory, from Dr. Bar-On

The EQi assessment was developed by Dr. Reuven Bar-On based on a number of years of research. It has reportedly been used on nearly 50,000 individuals. Dr. Bar-On cleverly named the competencies being measured the "Bar-On Emotional Quotient Inventory." This assessment is available in individual and multi-rater versions. It is also available in a youth version.

■ The MSCEIT, from John Mayer, Peter Salovey, and David Caruso

The MSCEIT assessment was developed by three of the original researchers of Emotional Intelligence and based on the EI model developed by Mayer and Salovey. This instrument is available in individual and multirater versions.

■ Emotional Intelligence Appraisal, Me Edition

This appraisal is from Travis Bradberry and Jean Graves, authors of *The Emotional Intelligence Quickbook*. This assessment is fast and easy to take and to score. The workbook was easy enough to use to calculate your emotional intelligence score for each of the four Goleman competencies (self-awareness, self-management, social awareness, and relationship management). You can find this assessment either by searching on line or by ordering the self-scoring paper assessment from amazon.com.

■ Index of Emotional Intelligence

This assessment is from the Adele Lynn Group. It is available in a Self-Scoring Assessment Version that consists of forty questions that take about fifteen minutes to answer. The assessment can be ordered through the Lynn Leadership store at a cost of $29.95 + shipping.

Results are provided for five major categories and ten subcategories of EQ. The five major categories are self-awareness and control, empathy, social expertness, personal influence, and mastery of purpose/vision. Results are plotted graphically on a scale of 1 to 28.

■ SEI, Six Seconds Emotional Intelligence Assessment

Focused on self-development, the SEI is based on Six Seconds' proprietary emotional intelligence model. The test measures eight fundamental skills, such as emotional literacy, navigating emotions, intrinsic motivation, and empathy. Report comes with over twenty pages of interpretation and actionable, substantive development suggestions.

Index

Accommodating, 187–188
Accountability, 212–213, 219
   partners, 171
Action log, 140
Addicts and mentally impaired people,
   165–166
Adkins, Lyssa, 251
Agile projects, 174, 242–252
   emotional intelligence and, 243–245, 249
     self-awareness, 249
     self-management, 249
     positive regard, 250–251
     social awareness, 249–250
   functional managers, 246–247
   leadership, 243, 251–252
   program managers, 245
   servant leadership, 248
   success, techniques for improving, 251–252
All or nothing thinking, 80
Always and never thinking, 81
Amygdala, 68–69
Anger, managing, 86
Angry All the Time, 51
Angry tirades, 69
Arbinger Institute, 110
Assessment for Emotional Self-Awareness and
   Self-Control, 112, 124, 135, 167,
   256, 260–261
Avoiding, withdrawing or, 188–189

Backtracking, 56–57
BarOn, Rueven, 11, 269
Blame, 46, 70, 77–79, 159–160, 164
Blanchard, Kenneth, 215
Blue, Rich, 3–4, 30, 86, 91, 197–198, 250
Body language, 99, 108, 235–236. *See also*
   Nonverbal communication
Boyatzis, Richard, 113, 269
Breathing exercises, 58, 89–90
Broken windows theory, 209–210, 221
Bullies, 163
Buy-in, 212, 229–230

Carlson, David E., 22–23
Caruso, David R., 16, 98–99, 196, 270
Catching people doing something right,
   215–216, 220
Cavemen, 62, 164–165, 166
Changing jobs, to get away from problem
   people, 166
Cherniss, Cary, 9, 112
Choosing Appropriate Project Managers
   (Turner/Mueller), 12–13
Clarke, Nicholas, 13–14
Coaches and mentors, 3–4, 30, 51, 89, 90,
   197–199, 201
   definitions for, 148–149
   developing others and, 148–149,
   168–169

*Coaching Agile Teams: A Companion for
     ScrumMasters, Agile Coaches, and
     Project Managers in Transition*
     (Adkins), 251
Co-creation, 83, 159–161, 170
Collaboration, confrontation or, 189–190
Communications, 178
     around boundaries, 121
     congruence in, 185
     effective, 16–17
     with EI, 178–181
     empathy in, 180, 205–206
     methods of, 177, 181–185, 235–238
     nonverbal, 184
     PMs and, 127, 177–178
     stakeholders' style of, 135
     team leadership and, 27, 29, 175–185
     techniques to improve, 199
     time, place and mode for, 179–180
     understanding and reactions to, 180–181
     with virtual teams, 233–238, 239–240
Compromising, 187
Conflict
     being cause of, 191
     as healthy, 186
     inevitability of, 185
     recognizing and anticipating, 15–16, 186,
          199
     stakeholder, 223
Conflict management, 15–16, 27, 29
     team leadership and, 27, 29, 175–176,
          185–191
     techniques for, 199
     traditional approaches to, 186–187
Confrontation, 165–166, 189–190
Congruence in communications, 185
Contact management tools, 140–141
Counseling and Self-Esteem (Carlson),
     22–23
Courage, for truth telling, 158
Covey, Stephen, 89, 101–102
Criticism
     backtracking, defensiveness and, 56–57
     blame and, 77–79
     emotional breakdowns and, 69, 70–71,
          76, 77–79
     as emotional trigger, 70–71, 77–79
     looking ahead for, 77–78
     micromanagers and, 162–163, 228–229
     own worst enemy and, 77

*Crucial Conversations: Tools for Talking When
     Stakes Are High* (Patterson/Grenny/
     McMillan/Switzler), 153

Decision making, 4, 26–27, 195–197, 230
Delegation, 139, 225, 239
Developing others
     acknowledging strengths/contributions and,
          145–146
     coaching/mentoring and, 148–149,
          168–169
     feedback and, 147–148
     relationship management and, 27, 29,
          128–129, 144–149
Dishonest employees, 164
Documentation, 166, 180, 218–219
Door slamming, 69
Dwelling, 71, 74

EI. *See* Emotional intelligence
Ekman, Paul, 40
E-mails, 90, 157, 181, 183, 234–235
Emotion(s), 3–5
     definitions for, 22–23
     facial expressions and, 40–43, 55, 99, 108
     families of, 21, 22–24, 35–36, 38–41, 108,
          110
     as information source, 4, 13–15, 49–50,
          98–99
     inhibiting/suppressing, 37–38, 43
     mirroring, 123
     mixture/range of, 36–38, 54–55
     negative, 22–23, 57, 62–63, 64–65,
          195–196
     as personal radar, 16, 50, 99
     positive, 23, 65–66, 196
     sharing, when appropriate, 180
     tracking, 122, 123
     words, 108, 121
Emotional boundaries, 27, 27–29, 97,
     117–122
     respecting, 119–122
     warning signs of, 118–119
Emotional breakdowns. *See also* Emotional
     triggers
     anticipating/avoiding, 15, 66–80
     causes of/triggering events for, 15, 61,
          70–92, 179–180, 224
     examples of, 69–70
Emotional hijacking, 66–68

Emotional intelligence (EI)
  applying
    to Agile projects, 243–245, 249
    to conflict resolution, 190–191
    to project management, 12–18
    to virtual teams, 233–238
  assessments of, 9–11, 24, 30, 269–270
    abilities and, 9–11
    instruments for, 9–11, 24, 51, 167–168,
      169, 255–256, 269–270
    traits and, 9, 11
    validity and, 11
  communicating with, 177–181, 182–183
  decision making and, 4, 16, 195–197
  definitions of, 8–9, 22–29
  frameworks for, 11, 21, 22–29, 128–129,
    269–270
  generic *v.* PM-focused models of, 26–29,
    128–129
  good news about, 12
  leveraging, on large and complex projects,
    222–240
  popularity of, 21–22
  resources for additional information on, 21,
    29–30, 267–268
  self-awareness as starting point for, 35–36
  tests, 4, 24
  as vital to PMs, 18–20
"Emotional Intelligence" (Mayer/Salovey), 24,
  26, 99
Emotional Intelligence Activity Book, The (Lynn),
  168
Emotional Intelligence and Projects (Clarke/
  Howell), 13–14
Emotional Intelligence Appraisal, Me Edition,
  270
Emotional Intelligence Movies and Scenes,
  124–125, 256, 265–266
Emotional Intelligence Quickbook (Bradberry/
  Graves), 270
*Emotional Intelligence: Why It Can Matter
  More Than IQ* (Goleman), 5, 8–9,
  21–22, 66
Emotionally Intelligent Manager, The (Caruso/
  Salovey), 16, 99
Emotionally Intelligent Workplace, The
  (Cherniss/Goleman), 9, 112–113,
  128–129
Emotional quotient (EQ), 11, 24
Emotional red flags, 43–49, 69–70, 82, 123

Emotional self-awareness, 3–4, 5, 36–50
  emotional red flags and, 43–50
  journals for, 43, 53–54, 124
  physical manifestations and, 39–40, 54–55
Emotional Self-Awareness and Self-Control
  Assessment, 260–261
Emotional tally sheet, 54, 122–123, 124–125,
  167, 255, 257–259
Emotional triggers, 54–55, 61
  reducing vulnerability to, 80
  types of, 70–80
Emotions, and parental modeling, 38, 39, 151
Empathetic listening, 103–105, 108, 135–136
  improving/class on, 122
  playback and summarize with, 103, 180
Empathy, 4
  in communications, 179–180, 205–206
  leadership and, 227, 228–229, 230
  social awareness and, 27, 28–29, 97, 99–105
Energies, refocusing, 166
EQ. *See* Emotional quotient
EQi (BarOn Emotional Quotient Inventory),
  269
*EQ Difference: A Powerful Plan for Putting
  Emotional Intelligence to Work, The*
  (Lynn), 71
Expectations list, for teams, 208–210, 219
Eyes, 40–43, 104, 109

Facial expressions
  body language and, 99, 108, 109, 235,
    235–236, 237–238
  emotions and, 40–43, 54–55, 99–100, 109
Failure, 76, 76–77, 80–81
Family of origin, 109
Fear
  management of, 84–87
  role of, 86
Feedback
  developing others and, 145–149
  negativity and, 81–82
  with paired sharing, 55–56
  self-assessment and, 50–51
  support and, 197–199, 201
  targeted/constructive, 147–149
  from virtual teams, 239–240
Feelings. *See also* Emotion(s)
  journal, 124
  taking responsibility for, 120
Filling in the blanks, 82

Filters and biases, 108–109
Follow-up, 140, 212
Forcing, 188
Foreshadowing, 70, 72–73
Frost, Robert, 117
Functional managers, and Agile projects, 246–247

Gardner, Howard, 24
Gates, Bill, 52–53
Getting clear, 74, 156–157, 170
Gladwell, Malcolm, 209–210
Goals, achieving, 102. *See also* Objectives
Goleman, Daniel, 8, 9, 11, 24
    books by, 5, 8–9, 21–22, 24, 50–51, 66,
        112–114, 145, 175–177, 205, 226
    on developing others, 145
    Emotional Competence Inventory 360, 269
    generic model, 21
    on frameworks for EI, 21, 24, 24, 26,
        128–129, 269–270
    on leadership, 175–177, 205, 222–223,
        226–227, 233
    on organizational awareness, 112–114
"Go to school," on people, 123
Grenny, Joseph, 153
Grudges, getting even and holding, 69
*Guide to the Project Management Body of
    Knowledge. See PMBOK® Guide*

HALT (Hungry, Angry, Lonely, Tired), 88
Help, seeking, 75, 77, 83, 121–122, 166,
    198–199
Hero-like behavior, 117
Hostility, 48, 123
Hot words/hot buttons, 71, 76–77
    going beyond, 77
    second opinions on, 76
Howell, Ranse, 13–14
Humor
    appropriate, 90–91, 213–314, 237–238
    inappropriate, 43–44, 70, 123, 162, 165

Icebreakers, for meetings, 133, 168
"I like / I dislike" statements, 155
Illness and fatigue, 79–80, 91
Index of Emotional Intelligence, 270
"I need / I want" statements, 82, 156
Instant messaging (IM), 179–180, 181, 183,
    184, 181, 183, 184, 236–237

Intelligence quotient (IQ), 21, 24
Interpersonal skills, 6, 18–19, 225–226, 255
Interviews, team member, 196
    hiring qualities and, 200
IQ. *See* Intelligence quotient
Isolation, 69, 224–225, 235–236

Johnson, Spencer, 215–216
Journals
    for emotional self-awareness, 43, 53–54, 124
    to track reactivity, 59
Judgments, 105, 156

Know thyself, 87–88

Large and complex projects, 6, 14
    characteristics of, 223–224
    importance of, 223–224
    layers of staff with, 223
    leveraging emotional intelligence on, 222–240
    PMs and, 224–226
    readiness to lead, 222–223
Lead by example, 206–207
Leadership. *See also* Project team leadership;
        Team leadership
    by example, 206–207
    Goleman on, 175–177, 205, 222–223,
        226–227, 233
    inspirational, 26, 27, 29, 175, 175, 176,
        191–194, 226–233
    optimistic, 207
    styles, 204–205, 222–223, 226–233
        affiliative, 229–230, 234
        application of, 233
        coaching, 227–228, 234
        commanding, 232–233. 234
        democratic, 230, 234
        pacesetting, 231–232. 234
        visionary, 227
Leadership and Self-Deception (Arbinger
        Institute), 110
Lincoln, Abraham, 90
Listening, 102–105. *See also* Empathetic
        listening
Logic, foreshadowing interrupted by, 73
Limbic system, 68
Lynn, Adele, 71, 168, 270

Matrix organizations, 127
Mayer, John D., 8, 11, 24, 24, 99–100, 270

McKee, Annie, 113
McMillan, Ron, 153
Meditation, 58, 90
Meetings
   face-to-face, 182, 235–236
   icebreakers for, 133, 168
   improving, 184
   lunch, 140–141, 167–168
   one-on-one, 139, 167, 224–225
   "Open Rant," 185
   tracking emotions during, 122–123
Mentally impaired people, addicts and, 165–166
Mentors. *See* Coaches and mentors
Micromanagers, criticism and, 162–163, 229
Mirroring emotions, 123
Mission, vision, and values statements,
   115–116, 191–194, 200, 207–208
Mistake quotas, setting, 78
Movies, 109–110, 125, 138, 151, 256,
   265–266
MSCEIT assessment, 270
Mueller, Ralf, 12, 13
Myers Briggs Type Indicator (MTBI), 169

Narcissist, 164
Negativity
   emotional breakdowns and, 72–73, 80–82
   emotions and, 22–23, 56–57, 62–63,
      64–65, 195–196
   positive team environment *v.,* 217
   positive thinking *v.,* 81–82
Negotiation, 127
Neocortex, 68
Nonverbal communication, 184–185
Non-verbal perception, 99–100
"No," saying, 118–119, 154–155, 170

Objectives, 178–179, 179, 227–228
   stakeholders', 134
   vision casting for shared, with project teams,
      18, 191–194, 200
Obsessing, 74
1001 Rewards & Recognition Fieldbook, The,
   220
One Minute Manager, The (Blanchard/
   Johnson), 215–216
Optimism, 207
Organizational awareness, 27, 28–29, 97,
   112–117
   assessments for, 113–114, 124

Others
   behaviors of, 48–49, 106–112
   developing, 26, 28–29, 102, 129, 130,
      144–149, 168–169
   exploring and learning about, 124
   fixing, 121
   highest vision for, 219–220
   imposing own autobiography on, 102, 105,
      108–109
   letting them speak, 103–104
   look for the best in, 111–112
   moods, attitudes, and feelings of, 71–72,
      107–108, 118, 195, 196
   orienting to emotions of, 105
   pleasing, 118
   practice studying, 111
   recognizing, 169
   responding appropriately to emotions of,
      120, 180
   seeing others clearly, 27, 28–29, 97,
      106–112
   we are smarter than, 103, 160–161

Paired sharing, 55–56
Parents, and modeling emotions, 38, 39, 151
Passive-aggressive behavior, 44–46, 123
Patterson, Kerryu, 153
Personal emotional dashboard, 91–92
Personalization, 83, 166
Physical environment, emotional triggers and,
   79, 88
Physical sensations, emotions and, 39–40,
   54–55
Plan and prepare, 92
PMBOK® Guide, 5–6, 19, 130–132, 144–145,
   178
PM Network, 12
PMPs. *See* Project Management Professionals
PMs. *See* Project managers
Poker players, 42–43
Positive environment, 213–214
Positive regard, and Agile projects, 250–251
Prayer, 58, 90
Prethinking, 71, 72–73
Primal Leadership (Goleman/Boyatzis/McKee),
   113, 128–129, 175, 205, 226
Primitive brain, 68
Problem people, 161–166
Problem-solving, 105–106, 188–189
Program managers, and Agile projects, 245

Project(s). *See also* Large and complex projects;
  Stakeholder(s)
  long, 65–66, 81
  recovering red, 62
  relationship management on, 167–171
  scheduling tools, 6
  success, stakeholder relationships and, 4–5,
    15
  as unique and temporary, 18–19, 97
Project leaders, resonance and dissonance in,
    205, 226–233
Project management
  applying EI to, 12–18
  as competitive, 6–7
  taskmaster style of, 4
*Project Management: A Systems Approach to
    Planning, Scheduling, and Controlling*
    (Kerzner), 186–190
Project Management Professionals (PMPs),
    certification of, 3, 6–7, 8
Project managers (PMs)
  and Agile, 242–245
  communications and, 127, 128, 175, 176,
    177–178
  conflict management as role of, 185
  EI as vital to, 18–20
  emotional mastery for, 5–6, 34
  large projects and, 224–226
  negotiation and, 127
  power and authority of, 18–19, 126–127,
    232–233
  qualifications, 7–8
  relationships and, 126–129
  resources of, 127, 194–196, 200
  standing up to management, 210–211
  surveys of, 5, 255–256
  tone/direction set by, 205–216
Project stakeholders
  identifying, 130–132
  objectives of, 134
  position of, 134
  role of, 134
Project team(s)
  assessing, 124
  building, 194–195
  great, 203–205
  with large and complex projects, 14
  member selection for, 194–195, 200
  negative emotions' impact on, 64–65
  relationships with, 4–5, 129

  vision casting for shared objectives with, 18,
    191–194, 200
Project team leadership, 174, 175–201
  communications and, 16–17, 177–185
  introduction to, 175–177
  techniques for improving, 199–201

Quiet time, 58

RACI (responsible, accountable, consulted,
    informed), 219
Reactivity, track with a journal, 59
Recharging, 75
Recognition, 146, 169, 208
  rewards and, 117, 124, 214–216, 220
Red flags, emotional, 43–49, 69–70, 81–82,
    123
Relationship(s), 3–5. *See also* Stakeholder
    relationships
  identifying key power, 114
  identifying patterns in, 73, 83, 160–161,
    170–171
  one-on-one, 129, 139
  with project teams, 4–5, 129
  outside workplace, 140
Relationship building
  relationship management and, 158–166
  with stakeholders, 135–136
  virtual teams and, 238, 239–240
Relationship management, 126–171
  co-creation and, 83, 159–161, 170
  developing others and, 26, 29, 111–112,
    129, 130, 144–149
  experts on, 127–129
  introduction to, 126–129
  problem people and, 161–166
  on projects, 167–171
  relationship building and, 148–166
  stakeholder relationships and, 15, 26, 27,
    29, 114, 129, 129–144
  truth telling and, 26, 27, 29, 121, 130,
    143–158, 166, 169–170
Relaxing, 75
Reports
  annual, 116
  customized project briefing, 139–140
  written, 182, 237–238
Resources
  for additional information on EI, 21, 29–30,
    267–268

organization structure impact on, 195
of PMs, 127, 194, 200
Responsibility assignment matrix (RAM), 219, 255–256
Results, getting and achieving, 102
Risk taking, 85
Roosevelt, Theodore, 79
Rules, team, 194, 208–210, 217, 221

Salovey, Peter, 8–9, 11, 24
on emotions, 16, 98–99, 195–196
Mayer and, 24, 99–100, 270
Sarcasm, 44, 70, 123, 162
SASHET (sad, angry, scared, happy, excited, and tender), 22–24, 35–36, 40–42, 108–111, 179
Scrum masters, and Agile, 242–245
Seeing others clearly, 26, 27, 28–29, 97, 106–112
obstacles to, 108–111
techniques to improve on, 111–112
SEI, Six Seconds Emotional Intelligence Assessment, 270
Self-assessment, 26, 27, 28, 36, 50–51
Self-awareness, 35–59, 74. *See also* Emotional self-awareness
accurate self-assessment and, 26, 27, 36, 49–50
Agile projects, 249
self-confidence and, 26, 36, 52–53
self-management and, 62–63, 84–87, 96
as starting point for EI, 35–36
techniques for improving, 53–59
Self-care, 89–90, 91
Self-confidence, 26, 27, 28, 36, 52–53, 73, 76–77
Self-control, 26, 27, 28, 62, 63–72, 119
additional techniques for, 87–92
for all emotions, 65–66
avoiding emotional breakdowns with, 66
negative feelings and, 64–65
Self-deception, 110–111
Self-management, 61–92. *See also* self-control
additional techniques for, 87–92
Agile projects, 249
emotional breakdowns and, 15
self-awareness and, 62–63, 84–87, 96
techniques to improve, 87–92
Self-organization, and Agile projects, 242

Self-orientation/selfishness, 101, 102
Servant leadership. *See* Agile projects
Setting limits, 119–120
Seven Habits of Highly Effective People, The (Covey), 89, 102
Short accounts, keeping, 157–158
Shortcuts, for efficiency, 110
"Should" statements, 82
Slogans, symbols and posters, of organizations, 115–116, 124
Smoothing, 187–188
Social awareness, 97–125
Agile projects, 249–250
conflict and, 15–16
emotional boundaries and, 26, 27, 28–29, 97, 117–122
empathy and, 26, 27, 28–29, 97, 100–105, 119–120
experts on, 99–100
introduction to, 97–100
organizational awareness and, 26, 28–29, 97, 112–117
seeing others clearly and, 26, 27, 28–29, 97, 106–112
setting limits, 119–120
techniques for improving, 122–125
Soft skills, 6. *See also* Interpersonal skills
Stakeholder(s). *See also* Project stakeholders
building relationships with, 135–136
collecting/analyzing information about, 132–135, 141, 167, 262–264
communication style of, 135
conflict, 223
facts, passions, and areas of interest of, 134–135
management tool, 133, 167, 255, 262–264
priority of, 133–134
Stakeholder relationships, 96
action steps to nurture, 139–141
action log/follow-up as, 140
after-hours meetings as, 140
customized project briefing reports as, 139–140
lunch meetings as, 140–141, 167–168
one-on-one meetings as, 139, 167
managing, 141–144
project success and, 4–5, 15
relationship management and, 15, 26, 29, 114–115, 129, 130, 129–144

Stakeholder relationships (*continued*)
    strategies for, 137–139
        delegation as, 139
        direct/indirect approaches as, 137–138
        keep your friends close as, 138–139
        talk to my people as, 138
Stinking thinking
    as cause of emotional breakdowns, 80–83
    identifying patterns of, 83
Stories, of organizations, 117
Strengths and weaknesses, assessing, 28, 51,
        106–108, 200–201
StrengthsFinder assessment, 145–146, 169,
        200–201
Stress, 15, 89–90
Support, 15, 38–39, 83, 197–199, 201,
        224–225. *See also* Coaches and mentors
Switzer, Al, 153

Team(s). *See also* Project team(s)
    expectations list for, 208–209, 219–220
    players, award for, 137
    rules, 194, 208–210, 217, 221
    team within, 216–217
    virtual, 223, 224, 233, 235–238
Teambuilding exercises, 168, 169, 200
Team environment
    healthcheck mini-assessment of, 218
    positive, 17–18, 18–19, 203–221
        negative *v.,* 217
        techniques for, 218–221
Team leadership, 26, 27, 29. *See also* Project
        team leadership
    additional considerations for, 194–199
    communications and, 26, 27, 29, 177–185
    conflict management and, 26, 29, 175–177,
        185–191
    experts on, 175–177
Team members. *See also* Project team(s)
    difficult, dealing with, 15–16
    interviewing, 196, 200
Teasing yourself, to avoid dwelling/obsessing,
    75
Teleconferences, 182, 233, 235–237
Thinking brain, 66–67

Time limits, thinking, 75
Time outs, 90
Tipping Point, The (Gladwell), 209–210
Tomkins, Silvan, 40
Triple constraints, 7–8
Trustworthiness, 158–159
Truth telling, 149–158
    courage for, 158
    relationship management and, 26, 27, 29,
        121–122, 129, 130, 149–158, 166,
        169–170
    techniques for, 154–158
        getting clear as, 156–157, 170
        "I like / I dislike" statements as, 155
        "I need / I want" statements as, 156
        keeping short accounts as, 158
        providing your reaction as, 154
        saying "no" as, 154–155, 170
        stating beliefs or judgments as, 156
Turner, J. Rodney, 12–13

Vacations, 75, 89, 90
Values
    culture and, 113, 115–117, 124
    statements, mission, vision and, 115–116,
        191–194, 200, 207–208
    team, 207–208, 217
Victim, playing
    blame and, 45–46, 70, 159–160
    co-creation and, 45–46, 159–160, 170
    emotional boundaries and, 118–119
    as red flag, 70, 123
    saying "No" and, 118–119, 154–155
    and work, 47–48
Virtual teams, 223, 224, 233–238, 239–240
    applying emotional intelligence to, 233–238
    challenges of, 233, 235
Vision casting, for shared objectives, with
        project teams, 18, 192–194, 200

Wants and needs, inability to express, 119
Withdrawal, 69, 188–189
Work assignments, 148–149, 170
Working with Emotional Intelligence (Goleman),
        24, 26, 50–51, 145, 177